SUE MONK KIDD

The Secret Life of Bees

CORNELSEN
SENIOR
ENGLISH
LIBRARY

W0038714

Cornelsen

Sue Monk Kidd **The Secret Life of Bees**

Herausgegeben von:
Gerhard Zimmer

Verlagsredaktion:
Ralph Williams

Technische Umsetzung:
zweiband.media, Berlin

Umschlaggestaltung:
Cornelsen Verlag Design; Bildrecherche: Josephine Wolff

Umschlagfoto:
© 2009 Trey Hill/Flickr/Getty Images

© Sue Monk Kidd, 2002

www.cornelsen.de

1. Auflage, 3. Druck 2020

Alle Drucke dieser Auflage sind inhaltlich unverändert
und können im Unterricht nebeneinander verwendet werden.

© 2012 Cornelsen Verlag, Berlin
© 2020 Cornelsen Verlag GmbH, Berlin

Druck: AZ Druck und Datentechnik GmbH, Kempten

ISBN 978-3-06-033062-1

PEFC zertifiziert
Dieses Produkt stammt aus nachhaltig
bewirtschafteten Wäldern und kontrollierten
Quellen.

www.pefc.de

PEFC/04-31-2260

Contents

For my son, Bob,
and Ann and Sandy
with all my love

Abbreviations and Annotations

adj	adjective	**infml**	informal
adv	adverb	**jdm./jdn.**	jemandem/en
AE	American English	**n**	noun
ca.	circa; about	**p., pp.**	page, pages
cf.	confer; see	**pl**	plural
derog	derogatory	**sb.**	somebody
e.g.	exempli gratia; for example	**sl**	slang
esp.	especially	**sth.**	something
fml	formal	**usu.**	usually
i.e.	id est; in other words	**v**	verb

The annotations are arranged chronologically; the first time a word is used is where you will find it explained.

The queen, for her part, is the unifying force of the community; if she is removed from the hive, the workers very quickly sense her absence. After a few hours, or even less, they show unmistakable signs of queenlessness.
Man and Insects

Chapter One

At night I would lie in bed and watch the show, how bees squeezed through the cracks of my bedroom wall and flew circles around the room, making that propeller sound, a high-pitched zzzzzz that hummed along my skin. I watched their wings shining like bits of
5   chrome in the dark and felt the longing build in my chest. The way those bees flew, not even looking for a flower, just flying for the feel of the wind, split my heart down its seam.

During the day I heard them tunneling through the walls of my bedroom, sounding like a radio tuned to static in the next room, and
10 I imagined them in there turning the walls into honeycombs, with honey seeping out for me to taste.

The bees came the summer of 1964, the summer I turned fourteen and my life went spinning off into a whole new orbit, and I mean *whole new orbit*. Looking back on it now, I want to say the bees
15 were sent to me. I want to say they showed up like the angel Gabriel appearing to the Virgin Mary, setting events in motion I could never have guessed. I know it is presumptuous to compare my small life to

hive: *Bienenstock*   **sense sth.**: become aware of sth.   3 **high-pitched**: (of a sound) very high   4 **hum**: *summen*   5 **longing** (n): strong feeling of wanting sth.   7 **seam**: *Naht*   9 **static** (n): constant disturbing noise on the radio (e.g. during a thunderstorm)   10 **honeycomb**: *Bienenwabe*   11 **seep**: flow slowly and in small quantities   13 **spin off**: happen as a new or unexpected result of sth. that already exists   **orbit**: *Umlaufbahn*   16 **set events in motion**: make things happen as a result of sth.   17 **presumptuous**: too confident, not respectful enough hers, but I have reason to believe she wouldn't mind; I will get to that. Right now it's enough to say that despite everything that happened that summer, I remain tender toward the bees.

July 1, 1964, I lay in bed, waiting for the bees to show up, thinking of what Rosaleen had said when I told her about their nightly visitations.

"Bees swarm before death," she'd said.

Rosaleen had worked for us since my mother died. My daddy – who I called T. Ray because "Daddy" never fit him – had pulled her out of the peach orchard, where she'd worked as one of his pickers. She had a big round face and a body that sloped out from her neck like a pup tent, and she was so black that night seemed to seep from her skin. She lived alone in a little house tucked back in the woods, not far from us, and came every day to cook, clean, and be my stand-in mother. Rosaleen had never had a child herself, so for the last ten years I'd been her pet guinea pig.

Bees swarm before death. She was full of crazy ideas that I ignored, but I lay there thinking about this one, wondering if the bees had come with my death in mind. Honestly, I wasn't that disturbed by the idea. Every one of those bees could have descended on me like a flock of angels and stung me till I died, and it wouldn't have been the worst thing to happen. People who think dying is the worst thing don't know a thing about life.

My mother died when I was four years old. It was a fact of life, but if I brought it up, people would suddenly get interested in their hangnails and cuticles, or else distant places in the sky, and seem not to hear me. Once in a while, though, some caring soul would say, "Just put it out of your head, Lily. It was an accident. You didn't mean to do it."

---

6 **visitation**: appearance of sth. (esp. in a religious or supernatural context)
7 **swarm**: come together in a group   10 **orchard**: place where fruit trees are grown
11 **slope out**: move out at an angle forming a slope   12 **pup tent**: small tent
16 **guinea pig**: *Versuchskaninchen*   26 **hangnail**: a piece of skin near the bottom or at the side of the fingernail that is loose and sore   **cuticle**: hard skin round a fingernail

That night I lay in bed and thought about dying and going to be with my mother in paradise. I would meet her saying, "Mother, forgive. Please forgive," and she would kiss my skin till it grew chapped and tell me I was not to blame. She would tell me this for
5 the first ten thousand years.

The next ten thousand years she would fix my hair. She would brush it into such a tower of beauty, people all over heaven would drop their harps just to admire it. You can tell which girls lack mothers by the look of their hair. My hair was constantly going off in
10 eleven wrong directions, and T. Ray, naturally, refused to buy me bristle rollers, so all year I'd had to roll it on Welch's grape juice cans, which had nearly turned me into an insomniac. I was always having to choose between decent hair and a good night's sleep.

I decided I would take four or five centuries to tell her about the
15 special misery of living with T. Ray. He had an orneriness year-round, but especially in the summer, when he worked his peach orchards daylight to dusk. Mostly I stayed out of his way. His only kindness was for Snout, his bird dog, who slept in his bed and got her stomach scratched anytime she rolled onto her wiry back. I've
20 seen Snout pee on T. Ray's boot and it not get a rise out of him.

I had asked God repeatedly to do something about T. Ray. He'd gone to church for forty years and was only getting worse. It seemed like this should tell God something.

I kicked back the sheets. The room sat in perfect stillness, not
25 one bee anywhere. Every minute I looked at the clock on my dresser and wondered what was keeping them.

Finally, sometime close to midnight, when my eyelids had nearly given up the strain of staying open, a purring noise started over in the corner, low and vibrating, a sound you could almost mistake for
30 a cat. Moments later shadows moved like spatter paint along the

---

4 **chapped**: sore, cracked   11 **bristle roller**: metal or plastic tube used to make hair curl   **Welch**: US company known for its grape fruit juice   12 **insomniac** [ɪn'sɑːmniæk]: person unable to sleep   15 **orneriness** (AE): bad-temperedness, unpleasantness   18 **bird dog**: a hunting dog that brings back birds that have been shot   19 **wiry**: (of hair) *borstig, drahtig*   20 **pee** (infml): urinate   **get a rise out of sb.**: make sb. react in an angry way   24 **sheet**: *Bettlaken*   28 **purr**: make a low continuous sound like a happy cat   30 **spatter paint**: *verspritzte Farbe*

walls, catching the light when they passed the window so I could see
the outline of wings. The sound swelled in the dark till the entire
room was pulsating, till the air itself became alive and matted with
bees. They lapped around my body, making me the perfect center of
a whirlwind cloud. I could not hear myself think for all the bee hum.   5

I dug my nails into my palms till my skin had nearly turned to
herringbone. A person could get stung half to death in a roomful of
bees.

Still, the sight *was* a true spectacle. Suddenly I couldn't stand not
showing it off to somebody, even if the only person around was   10
T. Ray. And if he happened to get stung by a couple of hundred bees,
well, I was sorry.

I slid from the covers and dashed through the bees for the door.
I woke him by touching his arm with one finger, softly at first, then
harder and harder till I was jabbing into his flesh, marveling at how   15
hard it was.

T. Ray bolted from bed, wearing nothing but his underwear.
I dragged him toward my room, him shouting how this better be
good, how the house damn well better be on fire, and Snout barking
like we were on a dove shoot.   20

"Bees!" I shouted. "There's a swarm of bees in my room!"

But when we got there, they'd vanished back into the wall like
they knew he was coming, like they didn't want to waste their flying
stunts on him.

"Goddamn it, Lily, this ain't funny."   25

I looked up and down the walls. I got down under the bed and
begged the very dust and coils of my bedsprings to produce a bee.

"They were here," I said. "Flying everywhere."

"Yeah, and there was a goddamn herd of buffalo in here, too."

"Listen," I said. "You can hear them buzzing."   30

He cocked his ear toward the wall with pretend seriousness.
"I don't hear any buzzing," he said, and twirled his finger beside his

---

3 **matted**: *verflochten*   4 **lap around sth.**: (here) touch sth. softly and regularly
7 **herringbone**: *Fischgrätmuster*   15 **jab**: push sharply   **marvel at sth.**: be surprised
by sth.   17 **bolt**: move quickly   20 **dove** [dʌv]: *Taube*   24 **stunt**: difficult action
performed to entertain the people   27 **coils of bedsprings**: *Windungen der Bettfedern*
31 **cock your ear**: listen carefully   **pretend** (adj, infml): not real, pretending

temple. "I guess they must have flown out of that cuckoo clock you call a brain. You wake me up again, Lily, and I'll get out the Martha Whites, you hear me?"

Martha Whites were a form of punishment only T. Ray could
5 have dreamed up. I shut my mouth instantly.

Still, I couldn't let the matter go entirely – T. Ray thinking I was so desperate I would invent an invasion of bees to get attention. Which is how I got the bright idea of catching a jar of these bees, presenting them to T. Ray, and saying, "Now who's making things
10 up?"

My first and only memory of my mother was the day she died. I tried for a long time to conjure up an image of her before that, just a sliver of something, like her tucking me into bed, reading the adventures of Uncle Wiggly, or hanging my underclothes near the space heater
15 on ice-cold mornings. Even her picking a switch off the forsythia bush and stinging my legs would have been welcome.

The day she died was December 3, 1954. The furnace had cooked the air so hot my mother had peeled off her sweater and stood in short sleeves, jerking at the window in her bedroom, wrestling with
20 the stuck paint.

Finally she gave up and said, "Well, fine, we'll just burn the hell up in here, I guess."

Her hair was black and generous, with thick curls circling her face, a face I could never quite coax into view, despite the sharpness
25 of everything else.

2–3 **Martha Whites**: (in USA) brand name for grits (= *Maisgrütze*), which are mostly eaten in the Southern states   12 **conjure up an image of sb./sth.**: form a picture of sb./sth. in your mind   **sliver**: small, thin piece of sth. (e.g. wood, glass)
13 **tuck sb. into bed**: cover sb. so that they are warm and comfortable   14 **Uncle Wiggly**: the main character of a series of American children's stories   **space heater** (AE): electric heater   15 **switch**: a thin stick   16 **sting sb.**: hurt sb. by making them feel a sharp pain   17 **furnace** ['fɜːrnɪs]: heater   19 **jerk at sth.**: pull violently at sth.   20 **stuck paint**: paint that sticks two things together   24 **coax sth. into view**: succeed in picturing sth.

I raised my arms to her, and she picked me up, saying I was way
too big a girl to hold like this, but holding me anyway. The moment
she lifted me, I was wrapped in her smell.

The scent got laid down in me in a permanent way and had all
the precision of cinnamon. I used to go regularly into the Sylvan   5
Mercantile and smell every perfume bottle they had, trying to
identify it. Every time I showed up, the perfume lady acted surprised,
saying, "My goodness, look who's here." Like I hadn't just been in
there the week before and gone down the entire row of bottles.
Shalimar, Chanel No. 5, White Shoulders.   10

I'd say, "You got anything new?" She never did.

So it was a shock when I came upon the scent on my fifth-grade
teacher, who said it was nothing but plain ordinary Ponds Cold
Cream.

The afternoon my mother died, there was a suitcase open on the   15
floor, sitting near the stuck window. She moved in and out of the
closet, dropping this and that into the suitcase, not bothering to fold
them.

I followed her into the closet and scooted beneath dress hems
and pant legs, into darkness and wisps of dust and little dead moths, 20
back where orchard mud and the moldy smell of peaches clung to
T. Ray's boots. I stuck my hands inside a pair of white high heels and
clapped them together.

The closet floor vibrated whenever someone climbed the stairs
below it, which is how I knew T. Ray was coming. Over my head I   25
heard my mother, pulling things from the hangers, the swish of
clothes, wire clinking together. *Hurry*, she said.

When his shoes clomped into the room, she sighed, the breath
leaving her as if her lungs had suddenly clenched. This is the last
thing I remember with perfect crispness – her breath floating down   30

4 **scent**: pleasant smell   5 **cinnamon**: *Zimt*   5–6 **Sylvan Mercantile**: store in
Sylvan   13–14 **Ponds Cold Cream**: (brandname) a face cream   17 **closet** (AE):
wardrobe   **bother to do sth.**: take the time to do sth.   19 **scoot**: move quickly
hem: *Saum*   20 **pants** (AE): women's trousers   **wisp**: small quantity   **moth**: *Motte*
21 **moldy**: *muffig, schimmelig*   26 **hanger**: *Kleiderbügel*   **swish**: soft sound of quick
movement   27 **wire**: thin piece of metal (here: of the hangers)   28 **clomp**: sound of
feet hitting the ground   29 **clench**: press tightly together   30 **crispness**: sharpness

to me like a tiny parachute, collapsing without a trace among the piles of shoes.

I don't remember what they said, only the fury of their words, how the air turned raw and full of welts. Later it would remind me
5 of birds trapped inside a closed room, flinging themselves against the windows and the walls, against each other. I inched backward, deeper into the closet, feeling my fingers in my mouth, the taste of shoes, of feet.

Dragged out, I didn't know at first whose hands pulled me, then
10 found myself in my mother's arms, breathing her smell. She smoothed my hair, said, "Don't worry," but even as she said it, I was peeled away by T. Ray. He carried me to the door and set me down in the hallway. "Go to your room," he said.

"I don't want to," I cried, trying to push past him, back into the
15 room, back where she was.

"Get in your goddamned room!" he shouted, and shoved me. I landed against the wall, then fell forward onto my hands and knees. Lifting my head, looking past him, I saw her running across the room. Running at him, yelling. "Leave. Her. Alone." I huddled on
20 the floor beside the door and watched through air that seemed all scratched up. I saw him take her by the shoulders and shake her, her head bouncing back and forth. I saw the whiteness of his lip.

And then – though everything starts to blur now in my mind – she lunged away from him into the closet, away from his grabbing
25 hands, scrambling for something high on a shelf.

When I saw the gun in her hand, I ran toward her, clumsy and falling, wanting to save her, to save us all.

Time folded in on itself then. What is left lies in clear yet disjointed pieces in my head. The gun shining like a toy in her hand,
30 how he snatched it away and waved it around. The gun on the floor. Bending to pick it up. The noise that exploded around us.

---

4 **welt**: mark on the skin after being whipped   6 **inch**: move slowly   9 **drag sb./ sth.**: pull sb./sth.   19 **yell**: shout loudly   **huddle**: lie or sit with your arms and legs pulled together   21 **scratched up**: *aufgekratzt*   23 **blur**: become less clear
24 **lunge** [lʌndʒ]: move quickly and suddenly   **grab**: take sth. suddenly
25 **scramble for sth.**: struggle to reach sth.   29 **disjointed**: that do not fit together properly

This is what I know about myself. She was all I wanted. And I took her away.

❀

T. Ray and I lived just outside Sylvan, South Carolina, population 3,100. Peach stands and Baptist churches, that sums it up.

At the entrance to the farm we had a big wooden sign with OWENS PEACH ENTERPRISES painted across it in the worst orange color you've ever seen. I hated that sign. But the sign was nothing compared with the giant peach perched atop a sixty-foot pole beside the gate. Everyone at school referred to it as the Great Fanny, and I'm cleaning up the language. Its fleshy color, not to mention the crease down the middle, gave it the unmistakable appearance of a rear end. Rosaleen said it was T. Ray's way of mooning the entire world. That was T. Ray.

He didn't believe in slumber parties or sock hops, which wasn't a big concern as I never got invited to them anyway, but he refused to drive me to town for football games, pep rallies, or Beta Club car washes, which were held on Saturdays. He did not care that I wore clothes I made for myself in home economics class, cotton print shirtwaists with crooked zippers and skirts hanging below my knees, outfits only the Pentecostal girls wore. I might as well have worn a sign on my back: I AM NOT POPULAR AND NEVER WILL BE.

I needed all the help that fashion could give me, since no one, not a single person, had ever said, "Lily, you are such a pretty child," except for Miss Jennings at church, and she was legally blind.

4 **stand** (n): *Verkaufsstand*   8 **perched** (adj): placed in a high or dangerous position
9 **fanny** (AE sl): a person's backside   10 **crease**: fold in the skin   12 **moon**: show
your bare backside to people as an insult   13 **slumber party** (AE): party for
children when they stay overnight   **sock hop** (AE): organized dance at school
15 **pep rally** (AE): meeting to encourage team spirit, often with cheerleaders
participating   **Beta Club** (AE): organization for 5th–12th graders in the USA
15–16 **car wash** (AE): students get paid for washing cars, usu. on Saturdays
17 **home economics** (AE): school subject which is concerned with doing
housework   17–18 **cotton print shirtwaist** (AE): woman's shirt made of cotton
with colourful patterns   18 **crooked**: not straight   **zipper**: *Reißverschluss*
19 **Pentecostal** (AE): belonging to a conservative Protestant church, which requires
women to dress modestly   23 **legally blind** (AE): with such bad eyesight that you
are officially a blind person

I watched my reflection not only in the mirror, but in store windows and across the television when it wasn't on, trying to get a fix on my looks. My hair was black like my mother's but basically a nest of cowlicks, and it worried me that I didn't have much of a chin.
5   I kept thinking I'd grow one the same time my breasts came in, but it didn't work out that way. I had nice eyes, though, what you would call Sophia Loren eyes, but still, even the boys who wore their hair in ducktails dripping with Vitalis and carried combs in their shirt pockets didn't seem attracted to me, and they were considered hard up.
10   Matters below my neck had shaped up, not that I could show off that part. It was fashionable to wear cashmere twinsets and plaid kilts midthigh, but T. Ray said hell would be an ice rink before I went out like that – did I want to end up pregnant like Bitsy Johnson whose skirt barely covered her ass? How he knew about Bitsy is a
15   mystery of life, but it was true about her skirts and true about the baby. An unfortunate coincidence is all it was.

Rosaleen knew less about fashion than T. Ray did, and when it was cold, God-help-me-Jesus, she made me go to school wearing long britches under my Pentecostal dresses.
20   There was nothing I hated worse than clumps of whispering girls who got quiet when I passed. I started picking scabs off my body and, when I didn't have any, gnawing the flesh around my fingernails till I was a bleeding wreck. I worried so much about how I looked and whether I was doing things right, I felt half the time I was
25   impersonating a girl instead of really being one.

I had thought my real chance would come from going to charm school at the Women's Club last spring, Friday afternoons for six weeks, but I got barred because I didn't have a mother, a grandmother, or even a measly aunt to present me with a white rose at the closing

---

4 **cowlick**: *Haarwirbel*   8 **ducktails**: men's hairstyle fashionable in the early 1960s **Vitalis**: product that makes hair shine   9 **hard up** (sl): finding it difficult to get what you want   11 **twinset**: woman's sweater and cardigan worn together 11–12 **plaid kilt** [plæd]: *Schottenrock*   19 **britches** (old fashioned): trousers that end at your knees   20 **clump**: small group of people   21 **scab**: hard cover of a healing wound   22 **gnaw sth.**: keep biting sth.   25 **impersonate sb.**: pretend to be sb.   28 **bar sb.**: prevent sb. from joining sth.   29 **measly**: unimportant

ceremony. Rosaleen doing it was against the rules. I'd cried till I threw up in the sink.

"You're charming enough," Rosaleen had said, washing the vomit out of the sink basin. "You don't need to go to some highfalutin school to get charm."   5

"I do so," I said. "They teach everything. How to walk and pivot, what to do with your ankles when you sit in a chair, how to get into a car, pour tea, take off your gloves …"

Rosaleen blew air from her lips. "Good Lord," she said.

"Arrange flowers in a vase, talk to boys, tweeze your eyebrows,   10
shave your legs, apply lipstick …"

"What about vomit in a sink? They teach a charming way to do that?" she asked.

Sometimes I purely hated her.

The morning after I woke T. Ray, Rosaleen stood in the doorway of   15
my room, watching me chase a bee with a mason jar. Her lip was rolled out so far I could see the little sunrise of pink inside her mouth.

"What are you doing with that jar?" she said.

"I'm catching bees to show T. Ray. He thinks I'm making them   20
up."

"Lord, give me strength." She'd been shelling butter beans on the porch, and sweat glistened on the pearls of hair around her forehead. She pulled at the front of her dress, opening an airway along her bosom, big and soft as couch pillows.   25

The bee landed on the state map I kept tacked on the wall. I watched it walk along the coast of South Carolina on scenic Highway 17. I clamped the mouth of the jar against the wall, trapping it between Charleston and Georgetown. When I slid on the lid, it went into a tailspin, throwing itself against the glass over and   30

4 **highfalutin** (infml): pretentious   6 **pivot**: turn   10 **tweeze sth.**: pull out small
hairs from sth.   16 **mason jar** (AE): *Einmachglas*   22 **shell sth.**: remove the shells
of sth. (e.g. beans)   23 **porch** (AE): small area at the entrance of a house, with a
floor and a roof but no walls   26 **tack sth.**: fix sth. with the help of pins   28 **clamp
sth.**: hold sth. tightly   30 **go into a tailspin**: *ins Schleudern geraten*

over with pops and clicks, reminding me of the hail that landed sometimes on the windows.

I'd made the jar as nice as I could with felty petals, fat with pollen, and more than enough nail holes in the lid to keep the bees from
5 perishing, since for all I knew, people might come back one day as the very thing they killed.

I brought the jar level with my nose. "Come look at this thing fight," I said to Rosaleen.

When she stepped in the room, her scent floated out to me, dark
10 and spicy like the snuff she packed inside her cheek. She held her small jug with its coin-size mouth and a handle for her to loop her finger through. I watched her press it along her chin, her lips fluted out like a flower, then spit a curl of black juice inside it.

She stared at the bee and shook her head. "If you get stung, don't
15 come whining to me," she said, " 'cause I ain't gonna care."

That was a lie.

I was the only one who knew that despite her sharp ways, her heart was more tender than a flower skin and she loved me beyond reason.

20 I hadn't known this until I was eight and she bought me an Easter-dyed biddy from the mercantile. I found it trembling in a corner of its pen, the color of purple grapes, with sad little eyes that cast around for its mother. Rosaleen let me bring it home, right into the living room, where I strewed a box of Quaker Oats on the floor
25 for it to eat and she didn't raise a word of protest.

The chick left dollops of violet-streaked droppings all over the place, due, I suppose, to the dye soaking into its fragile system. We had just started to clean them up when T. Ray burst in, threatening

---

1 **pops and clicks**: sharp explosive sounds   3 **felty petal**: *filziges Blütenblatt*
10 **snuff**: tobacco which is inhaled through the nose or chewed   11 **jug** (AE):
Kanne, Krug   **loop sth.**: push and bend sth. at the same time   12–13 **fluted out**
(adj): (here) pushed together so they open out   13 **curl**: (here) small quantity
15 **whine**: complain in a high-pitched voice   21 **Easter- dyed biddy** (AE infml, old
use): chick that is dyed (= *gefärbt*) a particular colour at Easter   22 **pen**: small area
for keeping an animal   24 **Quaker Oats** (AE): popular breakfast cereal
26 **dollop**: small amount   **violet-streaked droppings**: *Hühnerkot mit violetten
Streifen*

to boil the chick for dinner and fire Rosaleen for being an imbecile.
He started to swoop at the biddy with his tractor-grease hands, but
Rosaleen planted herself in front of him. "There is worse things in
the house than chicken shit," she said and looked him up one side
and down the other. "You ain't touching that chick."   5

His boots whispered *uncle* all the way down the hall. I thought,
She loves me, and it was the first time such a far-fetched idea had
occurred to me.

Her age was a mystery, since she didn't possess a birth certificate.
She would tell me she was born in 1909 or 1919, depending on how   10
old she felt at the moment. She was sure about the place:
McClellanville, South Carolina, where her mama had woven sweet-
grass baskets and sold them on the roadside.

"Like me selling peaches," I'd said to her.

"Not one thing like you selling peaches," she'd said back. "You   15
ain't got seven children you gotta feed from it."

"You've got six brothers and sisters?" I'd thought of her as alone
in the world except for me.

"I did have, but I don't know where a one of them is."

She'd thrown her husband out three years after they married, for   20
carousing. "You put his brain in a bird, the bird would fly backward,"
she liked to say. I often wondered what that bird would do with
Rosaleen's brain. I decided half the time it would drop shit on your
head and the other half it would sit on abandoned nests with its
wings spread wide.   25

I used to have daydreams in which she was white and married
T. Ray, and became my real mother. Other times I was a Negro
orphan she found in a cornfield and adopted. Once in a while I had
us living in a foreign country like New York, where she could adopt
me and we could both stay our natural color.   30

---

1 **imbecile** ['ımbəsl] (n): fool   2 **swoop**: move like a bird   6 **whisper uncle** (AE
infml): admit defeat   7 **far-fetched**: hard to believe   12–13 **sweet-grass**: type of
grass   21 **carouse** [kə'raʊz]: spend time drinking

My mother's name was Deborah. I thought that was the prettiest name I'd ever heard, even though T. Ray refused to speak it. If I said it, he acted like he might go straight to the kitchen and stab something. Once when I asked him when her birthday was and
5 what cake icing she preferred, he told me to shut up, and when I asked him a second time, he picked up a jar of blackberry jelly and threw it against the kitchen cabinet. We have blue stains to this day.

I did manage to get a few scraps of information from him, though, such as my mother was buried in Virginia where her people came
10 from. I got worked up at that, thinking I'd found a grandmother. No, he tells me, my mother was an only child whose mother died ages ago. Naturally. Once when he stepped on a roach in the kitchen, he told me my mother had spent hours luring roaches out of the house with bits of marshmallow and trails of graham-cracker crumbs, that
15 she was a lunatic when it came to saving bugs.

The oddest things caused me to miss her. Like training bras. Who was I going to ask about that? And who but my mother could've understood the magnitude of driving me to junior cheerleader tryouts? I can tell you for certain T. Ray didn't grasp it. But you know
20 when I missed her the most? The day I was twelve and woke up with the rose-petal stain on my panties. I was so proud of that flower and didn't have a soul to show it to except Rosaleen.

Not long after that I found a paper bag in the attic stapled at the top. Inside it I found the last traces of my mother.
25 There was a photograph of a woman smirking in front of an old car, wearing a light-colored dress with padded shoulders. Her expression said, "Don't you dare take this picture," but she wanted it taken, you could see that. You could not believe the stories I saw in that picture, how she was waiting at the car fender for love to come
30 to her, and not too patiently.

---

5 **cake icing**: mixture used to cover and decorate cakes   12 **roach**: *Kakerlake*
13 **lure sb./sth.**: guide sb./sth. into a certain direction   14 **graham cracker**: (in the USA) kind of biscuit   16 **training bra**: *BH für pubertierende Mädchen*
18 **magnitude**: great importance   19 **tryout**: *Probevorstellung*   23 **attic**: room under the roof   25 **smirk**: smile in a silly way to show you are pleased with yourself   29 **fender** (AE): covering over a car wheel

I laid the photograph beside my eighth-grade picture and examined every possible similarity. She was more or less missing a chin, too, but even so, she was above-average pretty, which offered me genuine hope for my future.

The bag contained a pair of white cotton gloves stained the color of age. When I pulled them out, I thought, *Her very hands were inside here*. I feel foolish about it now, but one time I stuffed the gloves with cotton balls and held them through the night.

The end-all mystery inside the bag was a small wooden picture of Mary, the mother of Jesus. I recognized her even though her skin was black, only a shade lighter than Rosaleen's. It looked to me like somebody had cut the black Mary's picture from a book, glued it onto a sanded piece of wood about two inches across, and varnished it. On the back an unknown hand had written "Tiburon, S.C."

For two years now I'd kept these things of hers inside a tin box, buried in the orchard. There was a special place out there in the long tunnel of trees no one knew about, not even Rosaleen. I'd started going there before I could tie my shoelaces. At first it was just a spot to hide from T. Ray and his meanness or from the memory of that afternoon when the gun went off, but later I would slip out there, sometimes after T. Ray had gone to bed, just to lie under the trees and be peaceful. It was my plot of earth, my cubbyhole.

I'd placed her things inside the tin box and buried it out there late one night by flashlight, too scared to leave them hanging around in my room, even in the back of a drawer. I was afraid T. Ray might go up to the attic and discover her things were missing, and turn my room upside down searching for them. I hated to think what he'd do to me if he found them hidden among my stuff.

Now and then I'd go out there and dig up the box. I would lie on the ground with the trees folded over me, wearing her gloves, smiling at her photograph. I would study "Tiburon, S.C." on the back of the black Mary picture, the funny slant of the lettering, and

---

7 **stuff sth.**: fill sth.   9 **end-all** (infml): most important   13 **sanded**: rubbed with sandpaper   **two inches across**: from one side to the other side   **varnish sth.**: *etwas lackieren*   20 **cubbyhole**: small place used as a place of safety for children
22 **flashlight** (AE): *Taschenlampe*   30 **slant of the lettering**: *Neigung der Handschrift*

wonder what sort of place it was. I'd looked it up on the map once, and it wasn't more than two hours away. Had my mother been there and bought this picture? I always promised myself one day, when I was grown-up enough, I would take the bus over there. I wanted to
5 go everyplace she had ever been.

After my morning of capturing bees, I spent the afternoon in the peach stand out on the highway, selling T. Ray's peaches. It was the loneliest summer job a girl could have, stuck in a roadside hut with three walls and a flat tin roof.
10 I sat on a Coke crate and watched pickups zoom by till I was nearly poisoned with exhaust fumes and boredom. Thursday afternoons were usually a big peach day, with women getting ready for Sunday cobblers, but not a soul stopped.

T. Ray refused to let me bring books out here and read, and if I
15 smuggled one out, say, *Lost Horizon*, stuck under my shirt, somebody, like Mrs. Watson from the next farm, would see him at church and say, "Saw your girl in the peach stand reading up a storm. You must be proud." And he would half kill me.

What kind of person is against *reading*? I think he believed it
20 would stir up ideas of college, which he thought a waste of money for girls, even if they did, like me, score the highest number a human being can get on their verbal aptitude test. Math aptitude is another thing, but people aren't meant to be overly bright in everything.

I was the only student who didn't groan and carry on when
25 Mrs. Henry assigned us another Shakespeare play. Well actually, I did *pretend* to groan, but inside I was as thrilled as if I'd been crowned Sylvan's Peach Queen.

Up until Mrs. Henry came along, I'd believed beauty college would be the upper limit of my career. Once, studying her face,

---

10 **crate**: container for carrying things   **zoom**: move fast   11 **exhaust fumes**: *Auspuffgase*   13 **cobbler** (AE): fruit pie   17 **read up a storm**: fully concentrate on reading   20 **stir up ideas**: give sb. the idea of doing sth.   22 **aptitude test**: test that measures a person's knowledge of words   23 **overly** (adv): excessively
24 **carry on**: (here) complain a lot   25 **assign sb. sth.**: give sb. sth. (e.g. a task)
28 **beauty college** (AE): school offering training to be a hairdresser, etc

I told her if she was my customer, I would give her a French twist
that would do wonders for her, and she said – and I quote – "Please,
Lily, you are insulting your fine intelligence. Do you have any idea
how smart you are? You could be a professor or a writer with actual
books to your credit. Beauty school. *Please.*"   5

It took me a month to get over the shock of having life possibilities.
You know how adults love to ask, "So … what are you going to be
when you grow up?" I can't tell you how much I'd hated that
question, but suddenly I was going around volunteering to people,
people who didn't even want to know, that I planned to be a professor   10
and a writer of actual books.

I kept a collection of my writings. For a while everything I wrote
had a horse in it. After we read Ralph Waldo Emerson in class,
I wrote "My Philosophy of Life," which I intended for the start of a
book but could get only three pages out of it. Mrs. Henry said I   15
needed to live past fourteen years old before I would have a
philosophy.

She said a scholarship was my only hope for a future and lent me
her private books for the summer. Whenever I opened one, T. Ray
said, "Who do you think you are, Julius Shakespeare?" The man   20
sincerely thought that was Shakespeare's first name, and if you think
I should have corrected him, you are ignorant about the art of
survival. He also referred to me as Miss Brown-Nose-in-a-Book and
occasionally as Miss Emily-Big-Head-*Diction*. He meant Dickinson,
but again, there are things you let go by.   25

Without books in the peach stand, I often passed the time making
up poems, but that slow afternoon I didn't have the patience for
rhyming words. I just sat out there and thought about how much I
hated the peach stand, how completely and absolutely I hated it.

1 **French twist**: particular hairstyle   9 **volunteer sth. to sb.**: tell sb. sth. without
being asked   13 **Ralph Waldo Emerson** (1803–1882): American author and
philosopher   18 **scholarship**: an amount of money given to sb. by an organization
to help pay for their education   24 **Emily Dickinson** (1830–1886): American poet
25 **let sth. go by**: accept sth. as being unchangeable

The day before I'd gone to first grade, T. Ray had found me in the peach stand sticking a nail into one of his peaches.

He walked toward me with his thumbs jammed into his pockets and his eyes squinted half shut from the glare. I watched his shadow
5 slide over the dirt and weeds and thought he had come to punish me for stabbing a peach. I didn't even know why I was doing it.

Instead he said, "Lily, you're starting school tomorrow, so there are things you need to know. About your mother."

For a moment everything got still and quiet, as if the wind had
10 died and the birds had stopped flying. When he squatted down in front of me, I felt caught in a hot dark I could not break free of.

"It's time you knew what happened to her, and I want you to hear it from me. Not from people out there talking."

We had never spoken of this, and I felt a shiver pass over me. The
15 memory of that day would come back to me at odd moments. The stuck window. The smell of her. The clink of hangers. The suitcase. The way they'd fought and shouted. Most of all the gun on the floor, the heaviness when I'd lifted it.

I knew that the explosion I'd heard that day had killed her. The
20 sound still sneaked into my head once in a while and surprised me. Sometimes it seemed that when I'd held the gun there hadn't been any noise at all, that it had come later, but other times, sitting alone on the back steps, bored and wishing for something to do, or pent up in my room on a rainy day, I felt I *had* caused it, that when I'd
25 lifted the gun, the sound had torn through the room and gouged out our hearts.

It was a secret knowledge that would slip up and overwhelm me, and I would take off running – even if it was raining out, I ran – straight down the hill to my special place in the peach orchard. I'd
30 lie right down on the ground and it would calm me.

Now, T. Ray scooped up a handful of dirt and let if fall out of his hands. "The day she died, she was cleaning out the closet," he said.

---

4 **squint**: look with your eyes partly shut   **glare**: bright light   5 **weed**: *Unkraut*
10 **squat down**: *sich hinhocken*   15 **odd**: strange   20 **sneak**: go or come
secretly   23–24 **pent up**: having feelings that cannot be expressed or released
25 **gouge sth. out** [gaʊdʒ]: cut sth. with a sharp object   27 **slip up**: (here) appear
by mistake   31 **scoop sth. up**: lift sth. up as with a spoon

I could not account for the strange tone of his voice, an unnatural sound, how it was almost, but not quite, *kind*.

Cleaning the closet. I had never considered what she was doing those last minutes of her life, why she was in the closet, what they had fought about.   5

"I remember," I said. My voice sounded small and faraway to me, like it was coming from an ant hole in the ground.

His eyebrows lifted, and he brought his face closer to me. Only his eyes showed confusion. "You *what*?"

"I remember," I said again. "You were yelling at each other."   10

A tightening came into his face. "Is that right?" he said. His lips had started to turn pale, which was the thing I always watched for. I took a step backward.

"Goddamn it, you were four years old!" he shouted. "You don't know what you remember."   15

In the silence that followed, I considered lying to him, saying, *I take it back. I don't remember anything. Tell me what happened*, but there was such a powerful need in me, pent up for so long, to speak about it, to say the words.

I looked down at my shoes, at the nail I'd dropped when I'd seen   20
him coming. "There was a gun."

"Christ," he said.

He looked at me a long time, then walked over to the bushel baskets stacked at the back of the stand. He stood there a minute with his hands balled up before he turned around and came back.   25
"What else?" he said. "You tell me right now what you know."

"The gun was on the floor —"

"And you picked it up," he said. "I guess you remember that." The exploding sound had started to echo around in my head.

I looked off in the direction of the orchard, wanting to break and   30
run.

"I remember picking it up," I said. "But that's all."

23 **bushel** (AE): unit for measuring fruit

He leaned down and held me by the shoulders, gave me a little shake. "You don't remember anything else? You're sure? Now, think."

I paused so long he cocked his head, looking at me, suspicious. "No, sir, that's all."

5 "Listen to me," he said, his fingers squeezing into my arms. "We were arguing like you said. We didn't see you at first. Then we turned around and you were standing there holding the gun. You'd picked it up off the floor. Then it just went off."

He let me go and rammed his hands into his pockets. I could
10 hear his hands jingling keys and nickels and pennies. I wanted so much to grab on to his leg, to feel him reach down and lift me to his chest, but I couldn't move, and neither did he. He stared at a place over my head. A place he was being very careful to study. "The police asked lots of questions, but it was just one of those terrible things.
15 You didn't mean to do it," he said softly. "But if anybody wants to know, that's what happened."

Then he left, walking back toward the house. He'd gone only a little way when he looked back. "And don't stick that nail into my peaches again."

20 It was after 6:00 p.m. when I wandered back to the house from the peach stand, having sold nothing, not one peach, and found Rosaleen in the living room. Usually she would've gone home by now, but she was wrestling with the rabbit ears on top of the TV, trying to fix the snow on the screen. President Johnson faded in and
25 out, lost in the blizzard. I'd never seen Rosaleen so interested in a TV show that she would exert physical energy over it.

"What happened?" I asked. "Did they drop the atom bomb?" Ever since we'd started bomb drills at school, I couldn't help thinking my days were numbered. Everybody was putting fallout shelters in their

---

5 **squeeze**: press firmly with your fingers   10 **jingle sth.**: make a sound with sth. like small bells ringing   **nickel** (AE): coin worth 5 cents   23 **rabbit ears** (AE infml): (formerly) the antennae above a TV   24 **President Johnson**: US president (1963–1969)   26 **exert energy**: (here) do sth. with your hands and body   29 **fallout shelter**: protection against radioactive fallout after an atom bomb explosion

backyards, canning tap water, getting ready for the end of time. Thirteen students in my class made falloutshelter models for their science project, which shows it was not just me worried about it. We were obsessed with Mr. Khrushchev and his missiles.

"No, the bomb hasn't gone off," she said. "Just come here and see ⁵ if you can fix the TV." Her fists were burrowed so deep into her hips they seemed to disappear.

I twisted tin foil around the antennae. Things cleared up enough to make out President Johnson taking his seat at a desk, people all around. I didn't care much for the president because of the way he ¹⁰ held his beagles by the ears. I did admire his wife, Lady Bird, though, who always looked like she wanted nothing more than to sprout wings and fly away.

Rosaleen dragged the footstool in front of the set and sat down, so the whole thing vanished under her. She leaned toward the set, ¹⁵ holding a piece of her skirt and winding it around in her hands. "What is going on?" I said, but she was so caught up in whatever was happening she didn't even answer me. On the screen the president signed his name on a piece of paper, using about ten ink pens to get it done. "Rosaleen –" ²⁰

"Shhh," she said, waving her hand.

I had to get the news from the TV man. "Today, July second, 1964," he said, "the president of the United States signed the Civil Rights Act into law in the East Room of the White House. ..."

I looked over at Rosaleen, who sat there shaking her head, ²⁵ mumbling, "Lord have mercy," just looking so disbelieving and happy, like people on television when they answered the $64,000 Question.

I didn't know whether to be excited for her or worried. All people ever talked about after church were the Negroes and whether they'd ³⁰ get their civil rights. Who was winning – the white people's team or the colored people's team? Like it was a do-or-die contest. When that

---

1 **can tap water**: preserve drinking water in metal canisters   4 **Krushchev**: leader of the Soviet Union (1958–1964) during the Cold War   **missile**: *Rakete*   6 **burrow sth.**: hide sth.   8 **tin foil**: *Alufolie*   11 **beagle**: small dog used for hunting 12–13 **sprout sth.**: grow sth.   23–24 **Civil Rights Act**: cf. p. 304   27–28 **$64,000 Question**: question worth $64,000 on a popular 1950s US game show

minister from Alabama, Reverend Martin Luther King, got arrested
last month in Florida for wanting to eat in a restaurant, the men at
church acted like the white people's team had won the pennant race.
I knew they would not take this news lying down, not in one million
5 years.

"Hallelujah, Jesus," Rosaleen was saying over there on her stool.
Oblivious.

Rosaleen had left dinner on the stove top, her famous smothered
chicken. As I fixed T. Ray's plate, I considered how to bring up the
10 delicate matter of my birthday, something T. Ray had never paid
attention to in all the years of my life, but every year, like a dope,
I got my hopes up thinking *this* year would be the one.

I had the same birthday as the country, which made it even harder
to get noticed. When I was little, I thought people were sending up
15 rockets and cherry bombs because of me – hurray, Lily was born!
Then reality set in, like it always did.

I wanted to tell T. Ray that any girl would love a silver charm
bracelet, that in fact last year I'd been the only girl at Sylvan Junior
High without one, that the whole point of lunchtime was to stand in
20 the cafeteria line jangling your wrist, giving people a guided tour of
your charm collection.

"So," I said, sliding his plate in front of him, "my birthday is this
Saturday."

I watched him pull the chicken meat from around the bone with
25 his fork.

"I was just thinking I would love to have one of those silver
charm bracelets they have down at the mercantile."

The house creaked like it did once in a while. Outside the door
Snout gave a low bark, and then the air grew so quiet I could hear
30 the food being ground up in T. Ray's mouth.

---

3 **pennant race**: (in USA) series of games to decide which teams qualify for the
baseball World Series   8–9 **smothered chicken** (AE): Southern recipe for cooking
chicken   11 **dope** (infml): stupid person   15 **cherry bomb** (AE): kind of fireworks
17–18 **charm bracelet** ['breɪslət]: jewelry worn around the wrist that carries
personal value   30 **grind sth. up**: crush sth. into small pieces

He ate his chicken breast and started on the thigh, looking at me now and then in his hard way.

I started to say, *So then, what about the bracelet?* but I could see he'd already given his answer, and it caused a kind of sorrow to rise in me that felt fresh and tender and had nothing, really, to do with the bracelet. I think now it was sorrow for the sound of his fork scraping the plate, the way it swelled in the distance between us, how I was not even in the room.

That night I lay in bed listening to the flicks and twitters and thrums inside the bee jar, waiting till it was late enough so I could slip out to the orchard and dig up the tin box that held my mother's things. I wanted to lie down in the orchard and let it hold me.

When the darkness had pulled the moon to the top of the sky, I got out of bed, put on my shorts and sleeveless blouse, and glided past T. Ray's room in silence, sliding my arms and legs like a skater on ice. I didn't see his boots, how he'd parked them in the middle of the hall. When I fell, the clatter startled the air so badly T. Ray's snore changed rhythm. At first it ceased altogether, but then the snore started back with three piglet snorts.

I crept down the stairs, through the kitchen. When the night hit my face, I felt like laughing. The moon was a perfect circle, so full of light that all the edges of things had an amber cast. The cicadas rose up, and I ran with bare feet across the grass.

To reach my spot I had to go to the eighth row left of the tractor shed, then walk along it, counting trees till I got to thirty-two.

The tin box was buried in the soft dirt beneath the tree, shallow enough that I could dig it up with my hands.

When I brushed the dirt from the lid and opened it, I saw first the whiteness of her gloves, then the photograph wrapped in waxed paper, just as I'd left it. And finally the funny wooden picture of

9 **flick**: quick movement   **twitter**: short, high sounds   **thrum**: low sound
17 **clatter**: loud noise   **startle sb.**: shock sb., surprise sb.   19 **piglet snort**: loud
noise made by a little pig through its nose   22 **have an amber cast**: *mit Bernstein*
überzogen sein   **cicada**: *Singzikade*   26 **shallow**: not deep

Mary with the dark face. I took everything out, and, stretching out among the fallen peaches, I rested them across my abdomen.

When I looked up through the web of trees, the night fell over me, and for a moment I lost my boundaries, feeling like the sky was
5 my own skin and the moon was my heart beating up there in the dark. Lightning came, not jagged but in soft, golden licks across the sky. I undid the buttons on my shirt and opened it wide, just wanting the night to settle on my skin, and that's how I fell asleep, lying there with my mother's things, with the air making moisture on my chest
10 and the sky puckering with light.

I woke to the sound of someone thrashing through the trees. *T. Ray!* I sat up, panicked, buttoning my shirt. I heard his footsteps, the fast, heavy pant of his breathing. Looking down, I saw my mother's gloves and the two pictures. I stopped buttoning and
15 grabbed them up, fumbling with them, unable to think what to do, how to hide them. I had dropped the tin box back in its hole, too far away to reach.

"Lileeee!" he shouted, and I saw his shadow plunge toward me across the ground.
20 I jammed the gloves and pictures under the waistband of my shorts, then reached for the rest of the buttons with shaking fingers.

Before I could fasten them, light poured down on me and there he was without a shirt, holding a flashlight. The beam swept and zagged, blinding me when it swung across my eyes.
25 "Who were you out here with?" he shouted, aiming the light on my half-buttoned top.

"N-no one," I said, gathering my knees in my arms, startled by what he was thinking. I couldn't look long at his face, how large and blazing it was, like the face of God.
30 He flung the beam of light into the darkness. "Who's out there?" he yelled.

"Please, T. Ray, no one was here but me."

---

2 **abdomen**: part of the body below the chest   6 **jagged**: sharp, distinct form
lick: (here) sudden gentle movement   11 **thrash**: move violently   15 **fumble**:
use your hands in an awkward way   18 **plunge**: move forwards quickly
20 **waistband**: piece of clothing holding up the skirt   24 **zag**: (here) move in
zigzags

"Get up from there," he yelled.

I followed him back to the house. His feet struck the ground so hard I felt sorry for the black earth. He didn't speak till we reached the kitchen and he pulled the Martha White grits from the pantry. "I expect this out of boys, Lily – you can't blame them – but I expect more out of you. You act no better than a slut." 5

He poured a mound of grits the size of an anthill onto the pine floor. "Get over here and kneel down."

I'd been kneeling on grits since I was six, but still I never got used to that powdered-glass feeling beneath my skin. I walked toward them with those tiny feather steps you expect of a girl in Japan, and lowered myself to the floor, determined not to cry, but the sting was already gathering in my eyes. 10

T. Ray sat in a chair and cleaned his nails with a pocketknife. I swayed from knee to knee, hoping for a second or two of relief, but the pain cut deep into my skin. I bit down on my lip, and it was then I felt the wooden picture of black Mary underneath my waistband. I felt the waxed paper with my mother's picture inside and her gloves stuck to my belly, and it seemed all of a sudden like my mother was there, up against my body, like she was bits and pieces of insulation molded against my skin, helping me absorb all his meanness. 15

The next morning I woke up late. The moment my feet touched the floor, I checked under my mattress where I'd tucked my mother's things – just a temporary hiding place till I could bury them back in the orchard. 25

Satisfied they were safe, I strolled into the kitchen, where I found Rosaleen sweeping up grits.

I buttered a piece of Sunbeam bread.

She jerked the broom as she swept, raising a wind. "What happened?" she said. 30

---

4 **pantry**: place where food is kept   20 **insulation**: protection against the cold etc.
21 **mold sth.**: form sth. in a certain shape   26 **stroll**: walk in a relaxed way
28 **Sunbeam**: US brand name of bread

"I went out to the orchard last night. T. Ray thinks I met some boy."

"Did you?"

I rolled my eyes at her. "No."

5   "How long did he keep you on these grits?"

I shrugged. "Maybe an hour."

She looked down at my knees and stopped sweeping. They were swollen with hundreds of red welts, pinprick bruises that would grow into a blue stubble across my skin. "Look at you, child. Look

10 what he's done to you," she said.

My knees had been tortured like this enough times in my life that I'd stopped thinking of it as out of the ordinary; it was just something you had to put up with from time to time, like the common cold. But suddenly the look on Rosaleen's face cut through all that. *Look*

15 *what he's done to you.*

That's what I was doing – taking a good long look at my knees – when T. Ray stomped through the back door.

"Well, look who decided to get up." He yanked the bread out of my hands and threw it into Snout's food bowl. "Would it be too

20 much to ask you to get out to the peach stand and do some work? You're not Queen for a Day, you know."

This will sound crazy, but up until then I thought T. Ray probably loved me some. I could never forget the time he smiled at me in church when I was singing with the hymnbook upside down.

25 Now I looked at his face. It was despising and full of anger.

"As long as you live under my roof, you'll do what I say!" he shouted.

Then I'll find another roof, I thought.

"You understand me?" he said.

30 "Yes, sir, I understand," I said, and I did, too. I understood that a new rooftop would do wonders for me.

---

8 **pinprick**: very small   **bruise**: small mark on the skin after it has been hurt
13 **common cold**: *Erkältung*   17 **stomp**: walk with heavy steps   18 **yank sth.**: pull
sth. quickly

✳

Late that afternoon I caught two more bees. Lying on my stomach across the bed, I watched how they orbited the space in the jar, around and around like they'd missed the exit.

Rosaleen poked her head in the door. "You all right?"

"Yeah, I'm fine." 5

"I'm leaving now. You tell your daddy I'm going into town tomorrow instead of coming here."

"You're going to town? Take me," I said.

"Why do you wanna go?"

"*Please*, Rosaleen." 10

"You're gonna have to walk the whole way."

"I don't care."

"Ain't nothing much gonna be open but firecracker stands and the grocery store."

"I don't care. I just wanna get out of the house some on my 15 birthday."

Rosaleen stared at me, sagged low on her big ankles. "All right, but you ask your daddy. I'll be by here first thing in the morning."

She was out the door. I called after her. "How come you're going to town?" 20

She stayed with her back to me a moment, unmoving. When she turned, her face looked soft and changed, like a different Rosaleen. Her hand dipped into her pocket, where her fingers crawled around for something. She drew out a folded piece of notebook paper and came to sit beside me on the bed. I rubbed my knees while she 25 smoothed out the paper across her lap.

Her name, Rosaleen Daise, was written twenty-five times at least down the page in large, careful cursive, like the first paper you turn in when school starts. "This is my practice sheet," she said. "For the

---

4 **poke sth.**: (here) move sth. in a particular direction   15 **some** (AE non-standard): for a little while   17 **sag**: hang downward because of heavy weight   19 **how come ...?** (infml): used when asking for an explanation   23 **dip into sth.**: put into sth. and move out again   28 **cursive**: (in handwriting) letters joined together

Fourth of July they're holding a voters' rally at the colored church. I'm registering myself to vote."

An uneasy feeling settled in my stomach. Last night the television had said a man in Mississippi was killed for registering to vote, and I myself had overheard Mr. Bussey, one of the deacons, say to T. Ray, "Don't you worry, they're gonna make 'em write their names in perfect cursive and refuse them a card if they forget so much as to dot an i or make a loop in their y."

I studied the curves of Rosaleen's R. "Does T. Ray know what you're doing?"

"T. Ray," she said. "T. Ray don't know nothing."

At sunset he shuffled up, sweaty from work. I met him at the kitchen door, my arms folded across the front of my blouse. "I thought I'd walk to town with Rosaleen tomorrow. I need to buy some sanitary supplies."

He accepted this without comment. T. Ray hated female puberty worse than anything.

That night I looked at the jar of bees on my dresser. The poor creatures perched on the bottom barely moving, obviously pining away for flight. I remembered then the way they'd slipped from the cracks in my walls and flown for the sheer joy of it. I thought about the way my mother had built trails of graham-cracker crumbs and marshmallow to lure roaches from the house rather than step on them. I doubted she would've approved of keeping bees in a jar. I unscrewed the lid and set it aside.

"You can go," I said.

But the bees remained there, like planes on a runway not knowing they'd been cleared for takeoff. They crawled on their stalk legs around the curved perimeters of the glass as if the world had shrunk

1 **rally**: a large public meeting, esp. one which is held to support a particular idea or political party   2 **register yourself to vote**: have your name put on a list so that you are allowed to vote   5 **deacon**: person who is responsible for a church's affairs 8 **loop**: shape like a curve or circle   12 **shuffle up**: walk slowly hardly lifting your feet   14–15 **sanitary supplies**: (here) tampon   19–20 **pine away for flight**: (here) want desperately to fly   28 **stalk leg**: very thin leg

to that jar. I tapped the glass, even laid the jar on its side, but those crazy bees stayed put.

The bees were still in there the next morning when Rosaleen showed up. She was bearing an angel food cake with fourteen candles.

"Here you go. Happy birthday," she said. We sat down and ate ⁵ two slices each with glasses of milk. The milk left a moon crescent on the darkness of her upper lip, which she didn't bother to wipe away. Later I would remember that, how she set out, a marked woman from the beginning.

Sylvan was miles away. We walked along the ledge of the highway, ¹⁰ Rosaleen moving at the pace of a bank-vault door, her spit jug fastened on her finger. Haze hung under the trees, and every inch of air smelled overripe with peaches.

"You limping?" Rosaleen said.

My knees were aching to the point that I was struggling to keep ¹⁵ up with her. "A little."

"Well, why don't we sit down on the side of the road awhile?" she said.

"That's okay," I told her. "I'll be fine."

A car swept by, slinging scalded air and a layer of dust. Rosaleen ²⁰ was slick with heat. She mopped her face and breathed hard.

We were coming to Ebenezer Baptist Church, where T. Ray and I attended. The steeple jutted through a cluster of shade trees; below, the red bricks looked shadowy and cool.

"Come on," I said, turning in the drive. ²⁵

"Where're you going?"

"We can rest in the church."

---

1 **tap sth.**: touch sth. lightly and repeatedly   2 **stay put** (infml): not move from the place where you are   4 **angel food cake**: (USA) light, airy cake
6 **crescent**: *Mondsichel*   10 **ledge**: (here) narrow strip at the side of the highway
11 **bank vault**: room in a bank where the money is kept   12 **haze**: hot thick misty air   20 **sling sth.**: throw sth. carelessly   **scalded**: very hot   21 **slick**: wet from sweating   **mop sth.**: dry sth. with a piece of cloth   23 **steeple**: the pointed tower of the church   **jut**: stick out

The air inside was dim and still, slanted with light from the side
windows, not those pretty stained-glass windows but milky panes
you can't really see through.

I led us down front and sat in the second pew, leaving room for
5 Rosaleen. She plucked a paper fan from the hymnbook holder and
studied the picture on it – a white church with a smiling white lady
coming out the door.

Rosaleen fanned and I listened to little jets of air come off her
hands. She never went to church herself, but on those few times
10 T. Ray had let me walk to her house back in the woods, I'd seen her
special shelf with a stub of candle, creek rocks, a reddish feather,
and a piece of John the Conqueror root, and right in the center a
picture of a woman, propped up without a frame.

The first time I saw it, I'd asked Rosaleen, "Is that you?" since I
15 swear the woman looked exactly like her, with woolly braids, blue-
black skin, narrow eyes, and most of her concentrated in her lower
portion, like an eggplant.

"This is my mama," she said.

The finish was rubbed off the sides of the picture where her
20 thumbs had held it. Her shelf had to do with a religion she'd made
up for herself, a mixture of nature and ancestor worship. She'd
stopped going to the House of Prayer Full Gospel Holiness Church
years ago because it started at ten in the morning and didn't end till
three in the afternoon, which is enough religion to kill a full-grown
25 person, she'd said.

T. Ray said Rosaleen's religion was plain wacko, and for me to
stay out of it. But it drew me to her to think she loved water rocks
and woodpecker feathers, that she had a single picture of her mother
just like I did.

---

2 **stained glass window**: *Bleiglasfenster*   **pane**: piece of glass in a window
4 **pew**: long wooden seat in a church   5 **fan**: *Fächer*   12 **John the Conqueror
root**: a root used in magic spells   13 **prop sth. up**: support sth. so that it does not
fall   15 **braid**: *Zopf*   17 **eggplant** (AE): *Aubergine*   19 **finish**: (here) the last
covering of polish that is put onto the surface to make it shine
26 **wacko** (infml): crazy   28 **woodpecker**: *Specht*

One of the church doors opened and Brother Gerald, our minister, stepped into the sanctuary.

"Well, for goodness' sake, Lily, what are you doing here?" Then he saw Rosaleen and started to rub the bald space on his head with such agitation I thought he might rub down to the skull bone.   5

"We were walking to town and stopped in to cool off."

His mouth formed the word "oh," but he didn't actually say it; he was too busy looking at Rosaleen in his church, Rosaleen who chose this moment to spit into her snuff jug.

It's funny how you forget the rules. She was not supposed to be   10
inside here. Every time a rumor got going about a group of Negroes coming to worship with us on Sunday morning, the deacons stood locked-arms across the church steps to turn them away. We loved them in the Lord, Brother Gerald said, but they had their own places.

"Today's my birthday," I said, hoping to send his thoughts in a   15
new direction.

"Is it? Well, happy birthday, Lily. So how old are you now?"

"Fourteen."

"Ask him if we can have a couple of these fans for your birthday present," said Rosaleen.   20

He made a thin sound, intended for a laugh. "Now, if we let everybody borrow a fan that wanted one, the church wouldn't have a fan left."

"She was just kidding," I said, and stood up. He smiled, satisfied, and walked beside me all the way to the door, with Rosaleen tagging   25
behind.

Outside, the sky had whited over with clouds, and shine spilled across the surfaces, sending motes before my eyes. When we'd cut through the parsonage yard and were back on the highway, Rosaleen produced two church fans from the bosom of her dress, and, doing   30
an impersonation of me gazing up sweet-faced, she said, "Oh, Brother Gerald, she was just kidding."

---

2 **sanctuary**: (here) the area in a church where the minister stands   13 **locked-arms**: with their arms joined tightly together   25–26 **tag behind**: follow   28 **mote**: small piece of dust   30–31 **do an impersonation of sb.**: pretend to be sb. else **gaze**: look for a long time

❈

We came into Sylvan on the worst side of town. Old houses set up on cinder blocks. Fans wedged in the windows. Dirt yards. Women in pink curlers. Collarless dogs.

After a few blocks we approached the Esso station on the corner
5 of West Market and Park Street, generally recognized as a catchall place for men with too much time on their hands.

I noticed that not a single car was getting gas. Three men sat in dinette chairs beside the garage with a piece of plywood balanced on their knees. They were playing cards.

10 "Hit me," one of them said, and the dealer, who wore a Seed and Feed cap, slapped a card down in front of him. He looked up and saw us, Rosaleen fanning and shuffling, swaying side to side. "Well, look what we got coming here," he called out. "Where're you going, nigger?"

15 Firecrackers made a spattering sound in the distance. "Keep walking," I whispered. "Don't pay any attention."

But Rosaleen, who had less sense than I'd dreamed, said in this tone like she was explaining something real hard to a kindergarten student, "I'm going to register my name so I can vote, that's what."

20 "We should hurry on," I said, but she kept walking at her own slow pace.

The man next to the dealer, with hair combed straight back, put down his cards and said, "Did you hear that? We got ourselves a model citizen."

25 I heard a slow song of wind drift ever so slightly in the street behind us and move along the gutter. We walked, and the men pushed back their makeshift table and came right down to the curb to wait for us, like they were spectators at a parade and we were the prize float.

30 "Did you ever see one that black?" said the dealer.

---

2 **cinder block** (AE): *Hohlblockstein* **wedge sth.**: squeeze sth. 5 **catchall** (adj):
used for many purposes 8 **dinette chair** [daɪˈnet]: type of chair **plywood**:
Sperrholz 10 **dealer**: person who deals the cards 10–11 **Seed and Feed**:
US company that sells farming and gardening products 26 **gutter**: *Rinnstein, Gosse*
27 **makeshift**: for temporary use only 29 **float**: *Festzugswagen*

And the man with his combed-back hair said, "No, and I ain't seen one that big either."

Naturally the third man felt obliged to say something, so he looked at Rosaleen sashaying along unperturbed, holding her white-lady fan, and he said, "Where'd you get that fan, nigger?"   5

"Stole it from a church," she said. Just like that.

I had gone once in a raft down the Chattooga River with my church group, and the same feeling came to me now – of being lifted by currents, by a swirl of events I couldn't reverse.

Coming alongside the men, Rosaleen lifted her snuff jug, which   10 was filled with black spit, and calmly poured it across the tops of the men's shoes, moving her hand in little loops like she was writing her name – Rosaleen Daise – just the way she'd practiced.

For a second they stared down at the juice, dribbled like car oil across their shoes. They blinked, trying to make it register. When   15 they looked up, I watched their faces go from surprise to anger, then outright fury. They lunged at her, and everything started to spin. There was Rosaleen, grabbed and thrashing side to side, swinging the men like pocketbooks on her arms, and the men yelling for her to apologize and clean their shoes.   20

"Clean it off!" That's all I could hear, over and over. And then the cry of birds overhead, sharp as needles, sweeping from low-bough trees, stirring up the scent of pine, and even then I knew I would recoil all my life from the smell of it.

"Call the police," yelled the dealer to a man inside.   25

By then Rosaleen lay sprawled on the ground, pinned, twisting her fingers around clumps of grass. Blood ran from a cut beneath her eye. It curved under her chin the way tears do.

When the policeman got there, he said we had to get into the back of his car.   30

---

4 **sashay**: walk in a confident, relaxed way   **unperturbed**: not worried at all
9 **current**: *Strömung*   **swirl**: quick circular movement   17 **outright**: open, direct   19 **pocketbook** (AE, old-fashioned): handbag   22 **bough** [baʊ]: branch
24 **recoil**: turn away quickly because of fear   26 **sprawled**: lying with your arms and legs spread out

"You're under arrest," he told Rosaleen. "Assault, theft, and disturbing the peace." Then he said to me, "When we get down to the station, I'll call your daddy and let him deal with you."

Rosaleen climbed in, sliding over on the seat. I moved after her,
5 sliding as she slid, sitting as she sat.

The door closed. So quiet it amounted to nothing but a snap of air, and that was the strangeness of it, how a small sound like that could fall across the whole world.

1 **assault**: attack

On leaving the old nest, the swarm normally flies only a few metres and settles. Scout bees look for a suitable place to start the new colony. Eventually, one location wins favor and the whole swarm takes to the air.
Bees of the World

Chapter Two

The policeman driving us to jail was Mr. Avery Gaston, but the men at the Esso station called him Shoe. A puzzling nickname since there was nothing remarkable about his shoes, or even his feet so far as I could see. The one thing about him was the smallness of his ears, the ears of a child, ears like little dried apricots. I fixed my eyes on them 5 from the backseat and wondered why he wasn't called Ears.

The three men followed us in a green pickup with a gun rack inside. They drove close to our bumper and blew the horn every few seconds. I jumped each time, and Rosaleen gave my leg a pat. In front of the Western Auto the men started a game of pulling alongside 10 us and yelling things out the window, mostly things we couldn't make out because our windows were rolled up. People in the back of police cars were not given the benefit of door handles or window cranks, I noticed, so we were blessed to be chauffeured to jail in smothering heat, watching the men mouth things we were glad not 15 to know.

Rosaleen looked straight ahead and acted as if the men were insignificant houseflies buzzing at our screen door. I was the only

---

7 **gun rack**: piece of equipment to hold guns   8 **bumper**: *Stoßstange*
9 **give sb. a pat**: touch sb. lightly   10 **pull alongside sb.**: drive beside sb.'s car
13–14 **window crank**: handle to open or shut the window   15 **smothering**: (here) making it difficult to breathe   **mouth sth.**: say sth. which cannot be heard
18 **buzz**: make a continuous low sound   **screen door** (AE): door with a net to keep insects out

one who could feel the way her thighs trembled, the whole backseat like a vibrating bed.

"Mr. Gaston," I said, "those men aren't coming with us, are they?"

His smile appeared in the rearview mirror. "I can't say what men
5 riled up like that will do."

Before Main Street they tired of the amusement and sped off. I breathed easier, but when we pulled into the empty lot behind the police station, they were waiting on the back steps. The dealer tapped a flashlight against the palm of his hand. The other two held
10 our church fans, waving them back and forth.

When we got out of the car, Mr. Gaston put handcuffs on Rosaleen, fastening her arms behind her back. I walked so close to her I felt heat vapor trailing off her skin.

She stopped ten yards short of the men and refused to budge.
15 "Now, look here, don't make me get out my gun," Mr. Gaston said. Usually the only time the police in Sylvan got to use their guns was when they got called out to shoot rattlesnakes in people's yards.

"Come on, Rosaleen," I said. "What can they do to you with a policeman right here?"

20 That was when the dealer lifted the flashlight over his head, then down, smashing it into Rosaleen's forehead. She dropped to her knees.

I don't remember screaming, but the next thing I knew, Mr. Gaston had his hand clamped over my mouth. "Hush," he said.
25 "Maybe now you feel like apologizing," the dealer said.

Rosaleen tried to get to her feet, but without her hands it was hopeless. It took me and Mr. Gaston both to pull her up.

"Your black ass is gonna apologize one way or another," the dealer said, and he stepped toward Rosaleen.

30 "Hold on now, Franklin," said Mr. Gaston, moving us toward the door. "Now's not the time."

---

4 **rearview mirror**: *Rückspiegel*   5 **riled up** (AE infml): very angry   6 **speed off**:
drive away quickly   7 **lot**: area of land   11 **handcuffs**: *Handschellen*   13 **vapor**:
very small drops of liquid in the air   **trail off sth.**: (here) evaporate from sth.
14 **budge**: move   17 **rattlesnake**: *Klapperschlange*

"I'm not resting till she apologizes."

That's the last I heard him yell before we got inside, where I had an overpowering impulse to kneel down and kiss the jailhouse floor.

♣

The only image I had for jails was from westerns at the movies, and this one was nothing like that. For one thing, it was painted pink 5 and had flower-print curtains in the window. It turned out we'd come in through the jailer's living quarters. His wife stepped in from the kitchen, greasing a muffin tin.

"Got you two more mouths to feed," Mr. Gaston said, and she went back to work without a smile of sympathy. 10

He led us around to the front, where there were two rows of jail cells, all of them empty. Mr. Gaston removed Rosaleen's handcuffs and handed her a towel from the bathroom. She pressed it against her head while he filled out papers at a desk, followed by a period of poking around for keys in a file drawer. 15

The jail cells smelled with the breath of drunk people. He put us in the first cell on the first row, where somebody had scratched the words "Shit Throne" across a bench attached to one wall. Nothing seemed quite real. *We're in jail*, I thought. *We're in* jail.

When Rosaleen pulled back the towel, I saw an inch-long gash 20 across a puffy place high over her eyebrow. "Is it hurting bad?" I asked.

"Some," she said. She circled the cell two or three times before sinking down onto the bench.

"T. Ray will get us out," I said. 25

"Uh-huh."

She didn't speak another word till Mr. Gaston opened the cell door about a half hour later. "Come on," he said. Rosaleen looked hopeful for a moment. She actually started to lift herself up. He shook his head. "You ain't going anywhere. Just the girl." 30

---

7 **living quarters**: the part of a building where people live   8 **grease sth.**: rub fat or butter onto sth.   **tin**: *Backblech*   15 **poke around for sth.** (infml): search for sth.
file drawer: *Schublade mit Akten*   20 **gash**: large cut in the skin
21 **puffy**: swollen   23 **some** (AE infml): a little

At the door I held on to a cell bar like it was the long bone in Rosaleen's arm. "I'll be back. All right? … All right, Rosaleen?"

"You go on, I'll manage."

The caved-in look of her face nearly did me in.

5 The speedometer needle on T. Ray's truck wiggled so badly I couldn't make out whether it pointed to seventy or eighty. Leaning into the steering wheel, he jammed his foot onto the accelerator, let off, then jammed it again. The poor truck was rattling to the point I expected the hood to fly off and decapitate a couple of pine trees.

10 I imagined that T. Ray was rushing home so he could start right away constructing pyramids of grits all through the house – a torture chamber of food staples, where I would go from one pile to the next, kneeling for hours on end with nothing but bathroom breaks. I didn't care. I couldn't think of anything but Rosaleen back there in 15 jail.

I squinted at him sideways. "What about Rosaleen? You have to get her out –"

"You're lucky I got *you* out!" he yelled.

"But she can't stay there –"

20 "She dumped snuff juice on three white men! What the hell was she thinking? And on Franklin Posey, for Christ's sake. She couldn't pick somebody normal? He's the meanest nigger-hater in Sylvan. He'd as soon kill her as look at her."

"But not really," I said. "You don't mean he would *really* kill her."

25 "What I mean is, I wouldn't be surprised if he flat-out killed her."

---

1 **cell bar**: *Gitterstab der Gefängniszelle*   4 **caved-in** (adj): showing hopelessness
do sb. in (infml): kill sb.   5 **speedometer**: *Tacho*   **wiggle**: move quickly and
abruptly   7 **jam sth.**: press sth. (esp. your foot) with force   9 **hood** (AE): *Haube*
decapitate sb./sth.: cut the head off sb./sth.   11–12 **torture chamber**:
Folterkammer   12 **food staple**: basic type of food that is used a lot   **pile**: heap
13 **for hours on end**: for several hours without interruption   **bathroom break**:
pause to use the toilet   20 **dump sth. on sb./sth.**: drop sth. down on sb./sth. in a
careless way   23 **as soon do sth. as do sth. else** (infml): be equally happy to do
sth. as sth. else   25 **flat-out** (adv, AE infml): straight away and completely

My arms felt weak in their sockets. Franklin Posey was the man with the flashlight, and he was gonna kill Rosaleen. But then, hadn't I known this inside even before T. Ray ever said it?

He followed me up the stairs. I moved with deliberate slowness, anger suddenly building in me. How could he leave Rosaleen in jail like that? 5

As I stepped inside my room, he stopped at the doorway. "I have to go settle the payroll for the pickers," he said. "Don't you leave this room. You understand me? You sit here and think about me coming back and dealing with you. Think about it real hard." 10

"You don't scare me," I said, mostly under my breath.

He'd already turned to leave, but now he whirled back. "What did you say?"

"You don't scare me," I repeated, louder this time. A brazen feeling had broken loose in me, a daring *something* that had been 15 locked up in my chest.

He stepped toward me, raising the back of his hand like he might bring it down across my face. "You better watch your mouth."

"Go ahead, try and hit me!" I yelled.

When he swung, I turned my face. It was a clean miss. 20

I ran for the bed and scrambled onto the middle of it, breathing hard. "My mother will never let you touch me again!" I shouted.

"*Your mother?*" His face was bright red. "You think that goddamn woman gave a shit about you?"

"My mother loved me!" I cried. 25

He threw back his head and let out a forced, bitter laugh.

"It's – it's not funny," I said.

He lunged toward the bed then, pressing his fists into the mattress, bringing his face so close I could see the tiny holes where his whiskers grew. I slid backward, toward the pillows, shoving my 30 back into the headboard.

---

1 **socket**: (here) hollow area in the bone   4 **deliberate**: done on purpose   8 **settle the payroll for the pickers**: *die Pfirsischpflücker auszahlen*   12 **whirl**: move around quickly   14 **brazen** [ˈbreɪzən]: without shame but with self-confidence   15 **break loose**: become free   **daring**: risky and brave   30 **whiskers**: hair growing on a man's face   31 **headboard**: the board at the top of the bed

"Not funny?" he yelled. "*Not funny?* Why, it's the funniest goddamn thing I ever heard: you thinking your mother is your guardian angel." He laughed again. "The woman could have cared less about you."

5 "That's not true," I said. "It's *not*."

"And how would you know?" he said, still leaning toward me. A leftover smile pulled the corners of his mouth.

"I hate you!" I screamed.

That stopped his smiling instantly. He stiffened. "Why, you little
10 bitch," he said. The color faded from his lips.

Suddenly I felt ice cold, as if something dangerous had slipped into the room. I looked toward the window and felt a tremor slide along my spine.

"You listen to me," he said, his voice deadly calm. "The truth is,
15 your sorry mother ran off and left you. The day she died, she'd come back to get her things, that's all. You can hate me all you want, but *she's* the one who left you."

The room turned absolutely silent.

He brushed at something on his shirtfront, then walked to the
20 door.

After he left, I didn't move except to trace the bars of light on the bed with my finger. The sound of his boots banging down the stairs drifted away, and I took the pillows from underneath the bedspread and placed them around me like I was making an inner tube that
25 might keep me afloat. I could understand her leaving him. But leaving me? This would sink me forever.

The bee jar sat on the bedside table, empty now. Sometime since this morning the bees had finally gotten around to flying off. I reached over and took the jar in my hands, and out came the tears
30 I'd been holding on to, it seemed like for years.

Your sorry mother ran off and left you. The day she died, she'd come back to get her things, that's all.

3–4 **could have cared less** (usu. **couldn't have cared less**): not care at all
12 **tremor**: a slight shaking movement   13 **spine**: *Wirbelsäule*   15 **sorry** (adj): very bad, deserving pity   23 **bedspread**: decorative cover of a bed   25 **keep sb. afloat**: prevent sb. from sinking   28 **get around to doing sth.**: find the time to do sth.

God and Jesus, you make him take it back.

The memory settled over me. The suitcase on the floor. The way they'd fought. My shoulders began to shake in a strange, uncontrollable way. I held the jar pressed between my breasts, hoping it would steady me, but I couldn't stop shaking, couldn't 5 stop crying, and it frightened me, as though I'd been struck by a car I hadn't seen coming and was lying on the side of the road, trying to understand what had happened.

I sat on the edge of the bed, replaying his words over and over. Each time there was a wrench in what felt like my heart.   10

I don't know how long I sat there feeling broken to pieces. Finally I walked to the window and gazed out at the peach trees stretching halfway to North Carolina, the way they held up their leafy arms in gestures of pure beseeching. The rest was sky and air and lonely space.   15

I looked down at the bee jar still clutched in my hand and saw a teaspoon of teardrops floating in the bottom. I unfastened the window screen and poured it out. The wind lifted it on her skirt tails and shook it over the blistered grass. *How could she have left me?* I stood there several minutes looking out on the world, trying to 20 understand. Little birds were singing, so perfect.

That's when it came to me: *What if my mother leaving wasn't true? What if T. Ray had made it up to punish me?*

I felt almost dizzy with relief. That was it. That had to be it. I mean, my father was Thomas Edison when it came to inventing 25 punishments. Once after I'd back-talked him, he'd told me my rabbit, Mademoiselle, had died, and I'd cried all night before I discovered her the next morning healthy as anything in her pen. He had to be making this up, too. Some things were not possible in this world. Children did not have two parents who refused to love them. 30 One, maybe, but for pity's sake, not two.

---

10 **wrench**: pain you feel when you have to leave a person or place you love
12 **gaze at sth.**: look at sth. for a long time   14 **beseeching**: (here) asking for pity
18 **skirt tails**: lower part of a skirt   19 **blistered** (adj): (here) *ausgetrocknet*
24 **dizzy**: unsteady   25 **Thomas Edison** (1847–1939): American inventor
26 **back-talk sb.**: answer sb. rudely   31 **for pity's sake**: used for emphasis

It had to be like he'd said before: she was cleaning out the closet the day of the accident. People cleaned out closets all the time.

I took a breath to steady myself.

You could say I'd never had a true religious moment, the kind
5   where you know yourself spoken to by a voice that seems other than yourself, spoken to so genuinely you see the words shining on trees and clouds. But I had such a moment right then, standing in my own ordinary room. I heard a voice say, *Lily Melissa Owens, your jar is open.*

10   In a matter of seconds I knew exactly what I had to do – *leave.* I had to get away from T. Ray, who was probably on his way back this minute to do Lord-knows-what to me. Not to mention I had to get Rosaleen out of jail.

The clock read 2:40. I needed a solid plan, but I didn't have the
15   luxury of sitting down to think one up. I grabbed my pink canvas duffel bag, the one I'd planned to use for overnights the minute anyone asked me. I took the thirty-eight dollars I'd earned selling peaches and stuffed it into the bag with my seven best pairs of panties, the ones that had the days of the week printed across the
20   backside. I dumped in socks, five pairs of shorts, tops, a night-gown, shampoo, brush, toothpaste, toothbrush, rubber bands for my hair, all the time watching the window. *What else?* Catching sight of the map tacked on the wall, I snatched it down, not bothering to pry out the tacks.

25   I reached under the mattress and pulled out my mother's picture, the gloves, and the wooden picture of black Mary, and tucked them down in the bag, too.

Tearing a sheet of paper from last year's English notebook, I wrote a note, short and to the point: "Dear T. Ray, Don't bother looking for
30   me. Lily. P.S. People who tell lies like you should rot in hell."

---

6 **genuine**: true, authentic   15 **think sth. up**: invent sth., create sth. in your mind
16 **duffel bag**: *Seesack*   **overnight** (n): act of staying at a friend's house for the
night   20 **top** (n): piece of clothing worn on the upper part of the body
23–24 **pry out the tacks**: *die Reißbrettstifte rausziehen*

When I checked the window, T. Ray was coming out of the orchard toward the house, fists balled, head plowed forward like a bull wanting to gore something.

I propped the note on my dresser and stood a moment in the center of the room, wondering if I'd ever see it again. "Goodbye," I said, and there was a tiny sprig of sadness pushing up from my heart. 5

Outside, I spied the broken space in the latticework that wrapped around the foundation of the house. Squeezing through, I disappeared into violet light and cobwebbed air. 10

T. Ray's boots stomped across the porch.

"Lily! Li-leeeee!" I heard his voice sailing along the floorboards of the house.

All of a sudden I caught sight of Snout sniffing at the spot where I'd crawled through. I backed deeper into the darkness, but she'd caught my scent and started barking her mangy head off. 15

T. Ray emerged with my note crumpled in his hand, yelled at Snout to shut the hell up, and tore out in his truck, leaving plumes of exhaust all along the driveway.

Walking along the weedy strip beside the highway for the second time that day, I was thinking how much older fourteen had made me. In the space of a few hours I'd become forty years old. 20

The road stretched empty as far as I could see, with heat shimmer making the air seem wavy in places. If I managed to get Rosaleen free – an "if" so big it could have been the planet Jupiter – just where did I think we'd go? 25

Suddenly I stood still. *Tiburon, South Carolina.* Of course. The town written on the back of the black Mary picture. Hadn't I been planning to go there one of these days? It made such perfect sense: my mother had been there. Or else she knew people there who'd 30

---

2 **head plowed forward** (AE spelling): *mit dem Kopf in Angriffsstellung*   3 **gore sth.**: hit and wound sth. with a horn   6 **sprig**: *Zweig*   8 **latticework**: (here) *Gitterzaun*   16 **mangy**: dirty and in a bad condition   18 **tear out** (**tore – torn**): drive away quickly   **plume**: small cloud

cared enough to send her a nice picture of Jesus' mother. And who would ever think to look for us there?

I squatted beside the ditch and unfolded the map. Tiburon was a pencil dot beside the big red star of Columbia. T. Ray would check the bus station, so Rosaleen and I would have to hitchhike. How hard could that be? You stand there with your thumb out and a person takes pity on you.

A short distance past the church, Brother Gerald whizzed by in his white Ford. I saw his brake lights flicker. He backed up.

"I thought that was you," he said through the window.

"Where're you headed?"

"Town."

"Again? What's the bag for?"

"I'm … I'm taking some things to Rosaleen. She's in jail."

"Yeah, I know," he said, flinging open the passenger door.

"Get in, I'm heading there myself."

I'd never been inside a preacher's car before. It's not that I expected a ton of Bibles stacked on the backseat, but I was surprised to see that, inside, it was like anybody else's car.

"You're going to see Rosaleen?" I said.

"The police called and asked me to press charges against her for stealing church property. They say she took some of our fans. You know anything about that?"

"It was only two fans —"

He jumped straight into his pulpit voice. "In the eyes of God it doesn't matter whether it's two fans or two hundred. Stealing is stealing. She asked if she could take the fans, I said no, in plain English. She took them anyway. Now that's sin, Lily."

Pious people have always gotten on my nerves.

"But she's deaf in one ear," I said. "I think she just mixed up what you said. She's always doing that. T. Ray will tell her, 'Iron my *two* shirts,' and she'll iron the *blue* shirts."

---

3 **ditch**: a long channel at the side of the road to hold the rainwater   4 **dot**: small round mark   **Columbia**: the capital of South Carolina   8 **whizz**: move quickly 9 **back up**: drive a car backwards   18 **stack sth.**: arrange sth. one on top of each other   21 **press charges**: *Strafanzeige erstatten*

"A hearing problem. Well, I didn't know that," he said.

"Rosaleen would never steal a thing."

"They said she'd assaulted some men at the Esso station."

"It wasn't like that," I said. "See, she was singing her favorite hymn, 'Were you there when they crucified my Lord?' I don't believe those men are Christians, Brother Gerald, because they yelled at her to shut up with that blankety-blank Jesus tune. Rosaleen said, 'You can curse me, but don't blaspheme the Lord Jesus.' But they kept right on. So she poured the juice from her snuff cup on their shoes. Maybe she was wrong, but in her mind she was standing up for Jesus." I was sweating through my top and all along the backs of my thighs.

Brother Gerald dragged his teeth back and forth across his lip. I could tell he was actually weighing what I'd said.

Mr. Gaston was in the station alone, eating boiled peanuts at his desk, when Brother Gerald and I came through the door. Being the sort of person he was, Mr. Gaston had shells all over the floor.

"Your colored woman ain't here," he said, looking at me. "I took her to the hospital for stitches. She took a fall and hit her head."

Took a fall, my rear end. I wanted to throw his boiled peanuts against the wall.

I could not keep myself from shouting at him. "What do you mean, she fell and hit her head?"

Mr. Gaston looked over at Brother Gerald, that all-knowing look men give each other when a female acts the least bit hysterical. "Settle down, now," he said to me.

"I can't settle down till I know if she's all right," I said, my voice calmer but still shaking a little.

"She's fine. It's only a little concussion. I expect she'll be back here later this evening. The doctor wanted her watched for a few hours."

3 **assault sb.**: attack sb.   7 **blankety-blank** (infml): used in the place of a swear word like "damned"   8 **blaspheme**: speak about God or religion in an offensive way   10–11 **stand up for sb.**: defend sb.   17 **shell**: hard outer part of a nut 19 **for stitches**: *um genäht zu werden*   20 **my rear end** (infml): expression indicating disbelief (**rear**: bottom, backside)   29 **concussion**: *Gehirnerschütterung*

While Brother Gerald was explaining how he couldn't sign the warrant papers seeing as how Rosaleen was nearly deaf, I started for the door.

Mr. Gaston shot me a warning look. "We got a guard on her at the
5   hospital, and he's not letting anybody see her, so you go on back home. You understand?"

"Yes, sir. I'm going home."

"You do that," he said. "'Cause if I hear you've been anywhere near that hospital, I'm calling your daddy again."

10   Sylvan Memorial Hospital was a low brick building with one wing for whites and one for blacks.

I stepped into a deserted corridor clogged with too many smells. Carnations, old people, rubbing alcohol, bathroom deodorizer, red Jell-O. Air conditioners poked out from the windows in the white
15   section, but back here there was nothing but electric fans moving the hot air from one place to another.

At the nurses' station a policeman leaned on the desk. He looked like somebody just out of high school, who'd flunked PE and hung out with the shop boys smoking at recess. He was talking to a girl in
20   white. A nurse, I guess, but she didn't look much older than I was. "I get off at six o'clock," I heard him say. She stood there smiling, tucking a piece of hair behind her ear.

At the opposite end of the hall an empty chair sat outside one of the rooms. It had a policeman's hat underneath it. I hurried down
25   there to find a sign on the door. NO VISITORS. I went right in.

There were six beds, all empty, except the farthest one over by the window. The sheets rose up, trying hard to accommodate the occupant. I plopped my bag on the floor. "Rosaleen?"

2 **warrant**: *Haftbefehl*   4 **shoot sb. a look**: look at sb. quickly and intensely
10 **wing**: part of a large building   12 **be clogged with sth.**: become too full of sth.
13 **carnation**: *Nelke*   14 **Jell-O** (AE): *Wackelpudding*   **poke out**: stick out
18 **flunk sth.** (AE infml): fail sth. (esp. a school subject)   **PE**: Physical Education
18–19 **hang out with sb.** (infml): spend time with sb.   19 **shop boy**: boy who works
in a factory or shop   **recess** ['ri:ses] (AE): break   21 **get off**: (here) stop working
27 **accommodate sb.**: provide enough space for sb.   28 **plop sth.**: drop sth.

A gauze bandage the size of a baby's diaper was wrapped around her head, and her wrists were tied to the bed railing.

When she saw me standing there, she started to cry. In all the years she'd looked after me, I'd never seen a tear cross her face. Now the levee broke wide open. I patted her arm, her leg, her cheek, her hand.

When her tear glands were finally exhausted, I said, "What happened to you?"

"After you left, that policeman called Shoe let those men come in for their apology."

"They hit you again?"

"Two of them held me by the arms while the other one hit me – the one with the flashlight. He said, 'Nigger, you say you're sorry.' When I didn't, he came at me. He hit me till the policeman said that was enough. They didn't get no apology, though."

I wanted those men to die in hell begging for ice water, but I felt mad at Rosaleen, too. *Why couldn't you just apologize? Then maybe Franklin Posey would let you off with just a beating.* All she'd done was guarantee they'd come back.

"You've got to get out of here," I said, untying her wrists.

"I can't just *leave,*" she said. "I'm still in jail."

"If you stay here, those men are gonna come back and kill you. I'm serious. They're gonna kill you, like those colored people in Mississippi got killed. Even T. Ray said so."

When she sat up, the hospital gown rode up her thighs. She tugged it toward her knees, but it slid right back like a piece of elastic. I found her dress in the closet and handed it to her.

"This is crazy –" she said.

"Put on the dress. Just do it, all right?"

She pulled it over her head and stood there with the bandage sloped over her forehead.

---

1 **gauze bandage** [gɑːz]: *Mullverband*   **diaper** ['daɪpər]: *Windel*   2 **bed railing**: *Bettrahmen*   5 **levee**: dam   7 **gland**: *Drüse*   **exhaust sth.**: use sth. up so nothing is left   18 **let sb. off with sth.**: not punish sb. but give them sth. as a light punishment   25 **gown**: piece of clothing that is worn over other clothes to protect them, esp. in a hospital   **ride up**: (of clothing) move gradually upwards

"That bandage has got to go," I said. I eased it off to find two rows of catgut stitches. Then, signaling her to be quiet, I cracked the door to see if the policeman was back at his chair.

He was. Naturally it was too much to hope he'd stay off flirting
5 long enough for us to float out of here. I stood there a couple of minutes, trying to think up some kind of scheme, then opened my bag, dug into my peach money, and took out a couple of dimes. "I'm gonna try and get rid of him. Get in the bed, in case he looks in here."

10 She stared at me, her eyes shrunk to mere dots. "Baby *Jesus*," she said.

When I stepped out into the hall, he jumped up. "You weren't supposed to be in there!"

"Don't I know it," I said. "I'm looking for my aunt. I could have
15 sworn they told me Room One-oh-two, but there's a colored woman in there." I shook my head, trying to look confused.

"You're lost, all right. You need to go to the other side of the building. You're in the colored section."

I smiled at him. "Oh."

20 Over on the white side of the hospital I found a pay phone next to a waiting area. I got the hospital number from Information and dialed it up, asking for the nurses' station in the colored wing.

I cleared my throat. "This is the jailer's wife over at the police station," I said to the girl who answered. "Mr. Gaston wants you to
25 send the policeman that we've got over there back to the station. Tell him the preacher is on his way in to sign some papers, and Mr. Gaston can't be here 'cause he had to leave just now. So if you could tell him to get over here right away …"

Part of me was saying these actual words, and part of me was
30 listening to myself say them, thinking how I belonged in a reform school or a juvenile delinquent home for girls, and would probably soon be in one.

---

1 **ease sth. off**: remove sth. gently   2 **catgut**: thin strong string made from animal intestines (= *Darm*)   **crack sth.**: (here) open sth.   5 **float**: move   7 **dime** (AE): coin worth ten cents   15 **one-oh-two**: 102   23 **clear your throat**: cough so that you can speak clearly   30–31 **reform school**: (in the USA) place to educate young criminals   31 **juvenile delinquent**: young criminal

She repeated it all back to me, making sure she had it straight. Her sigh passed over the receiver. "I'll tell him."

She'll tell him. I couldn't believe it.

I crept back to the colored side and hunched over the water fountain as the girl in white relayed all this to him, using a lot of hand gestures. I watched as the policeman put on his hat and walked down the corridor and out the door.

When Rosaleen and I stepped from her room, I looked left, then right. We had to go past the nurses' desk to get to the door, but the girl in white seemed preoccupied, sitting with her head down, writing something.

"Walk like a visitor," I told Rosaleen.

Halfway to the desk, the girl stopped writing and stood up. "Shitbucket," I said. I grabbed Rosaleen's arm and pulled her into a patient's room.

A tiny woman was perched in the bed, old and birdlike, with a blackberry face. Her mouth opened when she saw us, and her tongue curled out like a misplaced comma. "I need a little water," she said. Rosaleen went over and poured some from a pitcher and gave the woman the glass, while I held my duffel bag at my chest and peeped out the door.

I watched the girl disappear into a room a few doors down carrying some sort of glass bottle. "Come on," I said to Rosaleen.

"Y'all leaving already?" said the tiny woman.

"Yeah, but I'll probably be back before the day's out," said Rosaleen, more for my benefit than the woman's.

This time we didn't walk like visitors, we tore out of there. Outside, I took Rosaleen's hand and tugged her down the side-walk. "Since you got everything else figured out, I guess you know where we're going," she said, and there was a tone in her voice.

---

1 **have sth. straight**: understand sth. correctly   4 **hunch over sth.**: bend over sth.
5 **relay sth.**: narrate sth.   10 **preoccupied**: busy doing sth.   14 **shitbucket**: swear
word   24 **Y'all** (southern AE infml): you all (used when addressing more than one person)

"We're going to Highway Forty and thumb a ride to Tiburon, South Carolina. At least we're gonna try."

I took us the back way, cutting through the city park, down a little alley to Lancaster Street, then three blocks over to May Pond
5   Road, where we slipped into the vacant lot behind Glenn's Grocery.

We waded through Queen Anne's lace and thick-stalked purple flowers, into dragonflies and the smell of Carolina jasmine so thick I could almost see it circling in the air like golden smoke. She didn't ask me why we were going to Tiburon, and I didn't tell her. What
10 she did ask was "When did you start saying 'shitbucket'?"

I'd never resorted to bad language, though I'd heard my share of it from T. Ray or else read it in public restrooms. "I'm fourteen now. I guess I can say it if I want to." And I wanted to, right that minute. "Shitbucket," I said.

15 "Shitbucket, hellfire, damnation, and son of a mother bitch," said Rosaleen, laying into each word like it was sweet potatoes on her tongue.

We stood on the side of Highway 40 in a patch of shade provided by a faded billboard for Lucky Strike cigarettes. I stuck out my thumb
20 while every car on the highway sped up the second they saw us.

A colored man driving a beat-up Chevy truck full of cantaloupes had mercy on us. I climbed in first and kept having to scoot over as Rosaleen settled herself by the window.

The man said he was on his way to visit his sister in Columbia,
25 that he was taking the cantaloupes to the state farmers' market. I told him I was going to Tiburon to visit my aunt and Rosaleen was coming to do housework for her. It sounded lame, but he accepted it.

"I can drop you three miles from Tiburon," he said.

---

1 **thumb a ride** (AE infml): hitchhike   6 **wade through sth.**: *durch etwas waten*
Queen Anne's lace: type of plant   **stalk**: *Stängel*   7 **dragonfly**: *Libelle*
Carolina jasmine: a flowering plant   11 **resort to sth.**: make use of sth. (usu. bad)
to achieve sth.   12 **restroom** (AE): toilet   16 **lay into sb./sth.** (infml): attack sb./
sth.   21 **beat-up** (adj): old and in bad condition   **cantaloupe**: type of melon with
orange flesh   27 **lame** (infml): unconvincing

Sunset is the saddest light there is. We rode a long time in the glow of it, everything silent except for the crickets and the frogs who were revving up for twilight. I stared through the windshield as the burned lights took over the sky.

The farmer flicked on the radio and the Supremes blared through 5 the truck cab with "Baby, baby, where did our love go?" There's nothing like a song about lost love to remind you how everything precious can slip from the hinges where you've hung it so careful. I laid my head against Rosaleen's arm. I wanted her to pat life back into place, but her hands lay still in her lap. 10

Ninety miles after we'd climbed in his truck, the farmer pulled off the road beside a sign that read TIBURON 3 MILES. It pointed left, toward a road curving away into silvery darkness. Climbing out of the truck, Rosaleen asked if we could have one of his cantaloupes for our supper. 15

"Take yourself two," he said.

We waited till his taillights turned to specks no bigger than lightning bugs before we spoke or even moved. I was trying not to think how sad and lost we really were. I was not so sure it was an improvement over living with T. Ray, or even life in prison. There 20 wasn't a soul anywhere to help us. But still, I felt painfully alive, like every cell in my body had a little flame inside it, burning so brightly it hurt.

"At least we got a full moon," I told Rosaleen.

We started walking. If you think the country is quiet, you've 25 never lived in it. Tree frogs alone make you wish for earplugs.

We walked along, pretending it was a regular day. Rosaleen said it looked like that farmer who'd driven us here had had a good crop of cantaloupes. I said it was amazing the mosquitoes weren't out.

When we came to a bridge with water running beneath, we 30 decided we would pick our way down to the creek bed and rest for the night. It was a different universe down there, the water shining

---

3 **rev up**: accelerate, speed up   5 **The Supremes**: female pop group popular in the 1960s   **blare**: be played loudly   8 **precious**: of great value   **slip**: fall   **hinge**: *Scharnier*   17 **taillight**: red light at the back of a car or truck   **speck**: little spot   18 **lightning bug** (AE): *Glühwürmchen*   26 **earplug**: *Ohrenstöpsel*   31 **creek**: small river

with flecks of moving light and kudzu vines draped between the
pine trees like giant hammocks. It reminded me of a Grimm Brothers
forest, drawing up the nervous feelings I used to get when I stepped
into the pages of fairy tales where unthinkable things were likely –
5 you just never knew.

Rosaleen broke open the cantaloupes, pounding them against a
creek stone. We ate them down to their skins, then scooped water
into our hands and drank, not caring about algae or tadpoles or
whether the cows used the creek for their toilet. Then we sat on the
10 bank and looked at each other.

"I just wanna know, of all the places on this earth, why you
picked Tiburon," Rosaleen said. "I've never even heard of it."

Even though it was dark, I pulled the black Mary picture out of
my bag and handed it to her. "It belonged to my mother. On the
15 back it says Tiburon, South Carolina."

"Let me get this straight. You picked Tiburon 'cause your mother
had a picture with that town written on the back – *that's it?*"

"Well, think about it," I said. "She must have been there sometime
in her life to have owned this picture. And if she was, a person might
20 remember her, you never know."

Rosaleen held it up to the moonlight to see it better. "Who's this
supposed to be?"

"The Virgin Mary," I said.

"Well, if you ain't noticed, she's colored," said Rosaleen, and I
25 could tell it was having an effect on her by the way she kept gazing
at it with her mouth parted. I could read her thought: *If Jesus' mother
is black, how come we only know about the white Mary?* This would be
like women finding out Jesus had had a twin sister who'd gotten half
God's genes but none of the glory.

30 She handed it back. "I guess I can go to my grave now, because
I've seen it all."

---

1 **fleck**: spot   **kudzu vine**: *subtropische Kletterpflanze*   **drape**: hang loosely
2 **hammock**: *Hängematte*   3 **draw up sth.**: (here) *zu Tage fördern*   6 **pound sth.**:
hit sth. hard   8 **tadpole**: *Kaulquappe*   12 **pick sth.**: choose sth.   26 **parted** (adj):
(here) open

I pushed the picture down in my pocket. "You know what T. Ray said about my mother?" I asked, wanting finally to tell her what had happened. "He said she left me and him way before she died. That she'd just come back for her things the day the accident happened."

I waited for Rosaleen to say how ridiculous that was, but she 5
squinted straight ahead as if weighing the possibility.

"Well, it's not true," I said, my voice rising like something had seized it from below and was shoving it up into my throat. "And if he thinks I'm going to believe that story, he has a hole in his so-called brain. He only made it up to punish me. I know he did." 10

I could have added that mothers have instincts and hormones that prevent them leaving their babies, that even pigs and opossums didn't leave their offspring, but Rosaleen, having finally pondered the matter, said, "You're probably right. Knowing your daddy, he could do a thing like that." 15

"And my mother could never do what he said she did," I added.

"I didn't know your mama," Rosaleen said. "But I used to see her from a distance sometimes when I came out of the orchard from picking. She'd be hanging clothes on the line or watering her plants, and you'd be right there beside her, playing. I only saw her one time 20
when you weren't under her feet."

I had no idea Rosaleen had ever seen my mother. I felt suddenly light-headed, not knowing if it was from hunger or tiredness or this surprising piece of news. "What was she doing that time you saw her alone?" I asked. 25

"She was out behind the tractor shed, sitting on the ground, staring off at nothing. When we walked by, she didn't even notice us. I remember thinking she looked a little sad."

"Well, who wouldn't be sad living with T. Ray?" I said.

I saw the lightbulb snap on in Rosaleen's face then, the flash of 30
recognition.

---

13 **offspring**: child, children   **ponder sth.**: think about sth.   23 **light-headed**: dizzy and unable to think clearly   26 **shed**: small simple building   30 **I saw the lightbulb snap on**: *Ich sah wie das Licht anging*   **flash**: sudden appearance of an emotion

"Oh," she said. "I get it. You ran off 'cause of what your daddy said about your mother. It didn't have nothing to do with me in jail. And here you got me worrying myself sick about you running away and getting in trouble over me, and you would've run off anyway.
5 Well, ain't it nice of you to fill me in."

She poked out her lip and looked up toward the road, making me wonder if she was about to walk back the way we came. "So what are you planning to do?" she said. "Go from town to town asking people about your mother? Is that your bright idea?"

10 "If I needed somebody to criticize me around the clock, I could've brought T. Ray along!" I shouted. "And for your information, I don't exactly have a plan."

"Well, you sure had one back at the hospital, coming in there saying we're gonna do this and we're gonna do that, and I'm
15 supposed to follow you like a pet dog. You act like you're my keeper. Like I'm some dumb nigger you gonna save." Her eyes were hard and narrow.

I rose to my feet. "That's not fair!" Anger sucked the air from my lungs.

20 "You meant well enough, and I'm glad to be away from there, but did you think once to ask me?" she said.

"Well, you are dumb!" I yelled. "You have to be dumb to pour your snuff juice on those men's shoes like that. And then dumber not to say you're sorry, if saying it will save your life. They were
25 gonna come back and kill you, or worse. I got you out of there, and this is how you thank me. Well, fine."

I stripped off my Keds, grabbed my bag, and waded into the creek. The coldness cut sharp circles around my calves. I didn't want to be on the same planet with her, much less the same side of the
30 creek.

"You find your own way from now on!" I yelled over my shoulder.

---

5 **fill sb. in**: inform sb.   15 **keeper**: person responsible for another person
16 **dumb** (infml): stupid   18 **suck sth.**: *etwas aufsaugen*   27 **Keds**: brand of shoes,
sneakers   28 **calf**: *Wade*

On the opposite side I plopped onto the mossy dirt. We stared across the water at each other. In the dark she looked like a boulder shaped by five hundred years of storms. I lay back and closed my eyes.

In my dream I was back on the peach farm, sitting out behind the tractor shed, and even though it was broad daylight, I could see a huge, round moon in the sky. It looked so perfect up there. I gazed at it awhile, then leaned against the shed and closed my eyes. Next I heard a sound like ice breaking, and, looking up, I saw the moon crack apart and start to fall. I had to run for my life.

I woke with my chest hurting. I searched for the moon and found it all in one piece, still spilling light over the creek. I looked across the water for Rosaleen. She was gone.

My heart did flip-flops.

Please, God. I didn't mean to treat her like a pet dog. I was trying to save her. That's all.

Fumbling to get my shoes on, I felt the same old grief I'd known in church every single Mother's Day. *Mother, forgive.*

Rosaleen, where are you? I gathered up my bag and ran along the creek toward the bridge, hardly aware I was crying. Tripping over a dead limb, I sprawled through the darkness and didn't bother to get up. I could picture Rosaleen miles from here, tearing down the highway, mumbling, *Shitbucket, damn fool girl.*

Looking up, I noticed that the tree I'd fallen beneath was practically bald. Only little bits of green here and there, and lots of gray moss dangling to the ground. Even in the dark I could see that it was dying, and doing it alone in the middle of all these unconcerned pines. That was the absolute way of things. Loss takes up inside of everything sooner or later and eats right through it.

Humming drifted out of the night. It wasn't a gospel tune exactly, but it carried all the personality of one. I followed the sound and

1 **plop**: fall, making a short sound   **mossy**: *mit Moos überzogen*   2 **boulder**: huge stone or rock   12 **spill sth.**: (here) send out sth.   14 **do flip-flops**: (here) *sich überschlagen*   17 **grief**: sorrow   21 **limb**: (here) branch   **sprawl**: (here) fall forward moving your arms and legs   22 **tear down**: run quickly   26 **dangle**: hang or swing   27 **unconcerned**: *gleichgültig*   30 **humming** (n): a low, continuous sound

found Rosaleen in the middle of the creek, not a stitch of clothes on her body. Water beaded across her shoulders, shining like drops of milk, and her breasts swayed in the currents. It was the kind of vision you never really get over. I couldn't help it, I wanted to go and
5 lick the milk beads from her shoulders.

I opened my mouth. I wanted something. Something, I didn't know what. *Mother, forgive.* That's all I could feel. That old longing spread under me like a great lap, holding me tight.

Off came my shoes, my shorts, my top. I hesitated with my
10 underpants, then worked them off, too.

The water felt like a glacier melting against my legs. I must have gasped at the iciness, because Rosaleen looked up and seeing me come naked through the water, started to laugh. "Look at you strutting out here. Jiggle-tit and all."

15 I eased down beside her, suspending my breath at the water's sting. "I'm sorry," I said.

"I know," she said. "Me, too." She reached over and patted the roundness of my knee like it was biscuit dough.

Thanks to the moon, I could see clear down to the creek bottom,
20 all the way to a carpet of pebbles. I picked one up – reddish, round, a smooth water heart. I popped it into my mouth, sucking for whatever marrow was inside it.

Leaning back on my elbows, I slid down till the water sealed over my head. I held my breath and listened to the scratch of river against
25 my ears, sinking as far as I could into that shimmering, dark world. But I was thinking about a suitcase on the floor, about a face I could never quite see, about the sweet smell of cold cream.

1–2 **not a stitch of clothes on her body**: completely naked   2 **bead** (v): form small drops   4 **get over sth.**: *über etwas hinwegkommen*   8 **spread**: extend and open up **lap**: *Schoß*   12 **gasp**: take a quick, deep breath   14 **strut**: walk majestically **jiggle** (infml): move up and down   15 **suspend sth.**: stop or hold sth.   18 **dough**: *Teig*   22 **marrow**: soft substance in bones   23 **slide down** (**slid – slid**): move slowly down   **seal over sth.**: close over sth.   24 **scratch**: (here) sound 25 **shimmer**: shine with a soft light

New beekeepers are told that the way to find the elusive queen is by first locating her circle of attendants.

The Queen Must Die: And Other Affairs of Bees and Men

Chapter Three

Next to Shakespeare I love Thoreau best. Mrs. Henry made us read portions of *Walden Pond*, and afterward I'd had fantasies of going to a private garden where T. Ray would never find me. I started appreciating Mother Nature, what she'd done with the world. In my mind she looked like Eleanor Roosevelt.   5

I thought about her the next morning when I woke beside the creek in a bed of kudzu vines. A barge of mist floated along the water, and dragonflies, iridescent blue ones, darted back and forth like they were stitching up the air. It was such a pretty sight for a second I forgot the heavy feeling I'd carried since T. Ray had told me   10 about my mother. Instead I was at Walden Pond. *Day one of my new life*, I said to myself. *That's what this is.*

Rosaleen slept with her mouth open and a long piece of drool hanging from her bottom lip. I could tell by the way her eyes rolled under her lids she was watching the silver screen where dreams   15 come and go. Her swollen face looked better, but in the bright of day

elusive: difficult to find   **locate sb./sth.**: find the exact position of sb./sth.
attendant: person serving another person   1 **Henry David Thoreau** (1817–1862):
US writer and poet, who lived a simple life for two years in a small wooden house
and then wrote about this in his book **Walden** (1854)   5 **Eleanor Roosevelt**
(1884–1962): wife of US President Franklin D.Roosevelt, who was known for
supporting the rights of women and minority groups   7 **barge**: large boat
mist: *Nebel*   8 **iridescent**: having many bright colours that constantly change
13 **drool**: *Speichel*

I noticed purple bruises on her arms and legs as well. Neither one of us had a watch on, but going by the sun we had slept more than half the morning away.

I hated to wake Rosaleen, so I pulled the wooden picture of Mary
5 out of my bag and propped it against a tree trunk in order to study it properly. A ladybug had crawled up and sat on the Holy Mother's cheek, making the most perfect beauty mark on her. I wondered if Mary had been an outdoor type who preferred trees and insects over the churchy halo she had on.

10 I lay back and tried to invent a story about why my mother had owned a black Mary picture. I drew a big blank, probably due to my ignorance about Mary, who never got much attention at our church. According to Brother Gerald, hell was nothing but a bonfire for Catholics. We didn't have any in Sylvan – only Baptists
15 and Methodists – but we got instructions in case we met them in our travels. We were to offer them the five-part plan of salvation, which they could accept or not. The church gave us a plastic glove with each step written on a different finger. You started with the pinkie and worked over to the thumb. Some ladies carried their
20 salvation gloves in their purse in case they ran into a Catholic unexpectedly.

The only Mary story we talked about was the wedding story – the time she persuaded her son, practically against his will, to manufacture wine in the kitchen out of plain water. This had been a
25 shock to me, since our church didn't believe in wine or, for that matter, in women having a lot of say about things. All I could really figure was my mother had been mixed up with the Catholics somehow, and – I have to say – this secretly thrilled me.

I stuffed the picture into my pocket while Rosaleen slept on,
30 blowing puffs of air that vibrated her lips. I decided she might sleep into tomorrow, so I shook her arm till her eyes slit open.

---

2 **go by sth.**: judge from sth.   6 **ladybug**: *Marienkäfer*   7 **beauty mark**:
Schönheitsfleck   9 **halo**: *Heiligenschein*   11 **draw a blank**: not have any ideas
14 **bonfire**: large public fire   19 **pinkie**: smallest finger

"Lord, I'm stiff," she said. "I feel like I've been beaten with a stick."

"You have been beaten, remember?"

"But not with a stick," she said.

I waited till she got to her feet, a long, unbelievable process of ⁵ grunts and moans and limbs coming to life.

"What did you dream?" I asked when she was upright.

She gazed at the treetops, rubbing her elbows. "Well, let's see. I dreamed the Reverend Martin Luther King, Jr., knelt down and painted my toenails with the spit from his mouth, and every nail was ¹⁰ red like he'd been sucking on red hots."

I considered this as we set off for Tiburon, Rosaleen walking like she was on anointed feet, like her ruby toes owned the whole countryside.

We drifted by gray barns, cornfields in need of irrigation, and ¹⁵ clumps of Hereford cows, chewing in slow motion, looking very content with their lives. Squinting into the distance, I could see farmhouses with wide porches and tractor-tire swings suspended from ropes on nearby tree branches; windmills sprouted up beside them, their giant silver petals creaking a little when the breezes rose. ²⁰ The sun had baked everything to perfection; even the gooseberries on the fence had fried to raisins.

The asphalt ran out, turned to gravel. I listened to the sound it made scraping under our shoes. Perspiration puddled in the notch where Rosaleen's collarbones came together. I didn't know whose ²⁵ stomach was carrying on more about needing food, mine or hers, and since we'd started walking, I'd realized it was Sunday, when the stores were closed up. I was afraid we'd end up eating dandelions, digging wild turnips and grubs out of the ground to stay alive.

---

6 **grunt**: noise that a pig makes   **moan**: deep sound expressing unhappiness
11 **red hot** (n): chili pepper   13 **anointed**: *gesalbt*   15 **irrigation**: water that is
supplied by channels or pipes   19 **sprout up**: grow quickly   20 **breeze**: light wind
21 **gooseberry**: *Stachelbeere*   23 **gravel**: *Kies*   24 **scrape**: make an unpleasant noise
puddle (v): form a small surface of water   **notch**: *Mulde*   25 **collarbone**:
Schlüsselbein   26 **carry on**: (here) *sich bemerkbar machen*   28 **dandelion**
['dændilaɪən]: *Löwenzahn*   29 **grub**: insect in the form of a fat white worm

The smell of fresh manure floated out from the fields and took care of my appetite then and there, but Rosaleen said, "I could eat a mule."

"If we can find some place open when we get to town, I'll go in
5 and get us some food," I told her.

"And what're we gonna do for beds?" she said.

"If they don't have a motel, we'll have to rent a room."

She smiled at me then. "Lily, child, there ain't gonna be any place that will take a colored woman. I don't care if she's the Virgin Mary,
10 nobody's letting her stay if she's colored."

"Well, what was the point of the Civil Rights Act?" I said, coming to a full stop in the middle of the road. "Doesn't that mean people have to let you stay in their motels and eat in their restaurants if you want to?"

15 "That's what it means, but you gonna have to drag people kicking and screaming to do it."

I spent the next mile in deep worry. I had no plan, no prospects of a plan. Until now I'd mostly believed we would stumble upon a window somewhere and climb through it into a brand-new life.
20 Rosaleen, on the other hand, was out here biding time till we got caught. Counting it as summer vacation from jail.

What I needed was a sign. I needed a voice speaking to me like I'd heard yesterday in my room saying, *Lily Melissa Owens, your jar is open.*

25 *I'll take nine steps and look up. Whatever my eyes light on, that's my sign.* When I looked up, I saw a crop duster plunging his little plane over a field of growing things, behind him a cloud of pesticides parachuting out. I couldn't decide what part of this scene represented: the plants about to be rescued from the bugs or the
30 bugs about to be murdered by the spray. There was an off chance I was really the airplane zipping over the earth creating rescue and doom everywhere I went.

---

1 **manure**: waste matter of animals spread over the fields   1–2 **take care of sth.**:
(here) *etwas erledigen*   20 **bide time**: pass time   25 **light on sth.**: see sth. by
chance   26 **crop duster**: (here) *Pilot eines Sprühflugzeugs*   27 **pesticide** ['pestɪsaɪd]:
chemical used for killing pests, esp. insects   30 **off chance**: unlikely chance
31 **zip**: move quickly   32 **doom**: death or destruction

I felt miserable.

The heat had been gathering as we walked, and it now dripped down Rosaleen's face.

"Too bad there's not a church around here where we could steal some fans," she said.   5

From far away the store on the edge of town looked about a hundred years old, but when we got up to it, I saw it was actually older. A sign over the door said FROGMORE STEW GENERAL STORE AND RESTAURANT. SINCE 1854.

General Sherman had probably ridden by here and decided to   10
spare it on the basis of its name, because I'm sure it hadn't been on looks. The whole front of it was a forgotten bulletin board: Studebaker Service, Live Bait, Buddy's Fishing Tournament, Rayford Brothers' Ice Plant, Deer Rifles $45, and a picture of a girl wearing a Coca-Cola bottle cap on her head. A sign announced a gospel sing at   15
the Mount Zion Baptist Church that took place back in 1957, if anyone wanted to know.

My favorite thing was the fine display of car tags nailed up from different states. I would like to have read every single one, if I'd had the time.   20

In the side yard a colored man lifted the top of a barbecue pit made from an oil drum, and the smell of pork lathered in vinegar and pepper drew so much saliva from beneath my tongue I actually drooled onto my blouse.

A few cars and trucks were parked out front, probably belonging   25
to people who cut church and came here straight from Sunday school.

"I'll go in and see if I can buy some food," I said.

"And snuff. I need some snuff," said Rosaleen.

---

10 **General Sherman** (1820–1891): military commander of the Northern states during the Civil War   11 **spare sth.**: *etwas verschonen*   12 **bulletin board**: noticeboard   13 **bait**: *Köder*   18 **car tag** (AE): licence plate   21 **pit**: sunken enclosed area   22 **oil drum**: *Ölfass*   **lather sth. in sth.**: (here) bathe sth. in sth.
26 **cut church**: not go to church when you should go

While she slumped on a bench near the barbecue drum, I stepped through the screen door into the mingled smells of pickled eggs and sawdust, beneath dozens of sugar-cured hams dangling from the ceiling. The restaurant was situated in a section at the back while the
5 front of the store was reserved for selling everything from sugarcane stalks to turpentine.

"May I help you, young lady?" A small man wearing a bow tie stood on the other side of a wooden counter, nearly lost behind a barricade of scuppernong jelly and Sweet Fire pickles. His voice was
10 high-pitched, and he had a soft, delicate look to him. I could not imagine him selling deer rifles.

"I don't believe I've seen you before," he said.

"I'm not from here. I'm visiting my grandmother."

"I like it when children spend time with their grandparents," he
15 said. "You can learn a lot from older folks."

"Yes, sir," I said. "I learned more from my grandmother than I did the whole eighth grade."

He laughed like this was the most comical thing he'd heard in years. "Are you here for lunch? We have a Sunday-plate special –
20 barbecue pork."

"I'll take two of them to go," I said. "And two Coca-Colas, please."

While I waited for our lunch, I wandered along the store aisles, stocking up for supper. Packages of salted peanuts, buttermilk cookies, two pimiento-cheese sandwiches in plastic, sour balls, and
25 a can of Red Rose snuff. I piled it on the counter.

When he returned with the plates and drink bottles, he shook his head. "I'm sorry, but it's Sunday. I can't sell anything from the store, just the restaurant. Your grandma ought to know that. What's her name anyway?"

30 "Rose," I said, reading it off the snuff can.

"Rose Campbell?"

---

1 **slump**: sit heavily   2 **pickled**: preserved in vinegar   3 **sugar-cured ham**: ham treated with sugar   5–6 **sugarcane stalk**: *Zuckerrohrstängel*   6 **turpentine**: *Terpentin*   7 **bow tie**: *Fliege*   9 **scuppernong**: grape variety in the southeastern USA   22 **aisle** [aɪl]: passage between rows of shelves in a supermarket   23 **stock up**: buy a lot for later use   24 **pimiento**: red pepper with a mild taste   **sour balls**: type of sweet

"Yes, sir. Rose Campbell."

"I thought she only had grandboys."

"No, sir, she's got me, too."

He touched the bag of sour balls. "Just leave it all here. I'll put it back."   5

The cash register pinged, and the drawer banged out. I rummaged in my bag for the money and paid him.

"Could you open the Coke bottles for me?" I asked, and while he walked back toward the kitchen, I dropped the Red Rose snuff in my bag and zipped it up.   10

Rosaleen had been beaten up, gone without food, slept on the hard ground, and who could say how long before she'd be back in jail or even killed? She deserved her snuff.

I was speculating how one day, years from now, I would send the store a dollar in an envelope to cover it, spelling out how guilt had   15
dominated every moment of my life, when I found myself looking at a picture of the black Mary. I do not mean a picture of just any black Mary. I mean the identical, very same, exact one as my mother's. She stared at me from the labels of a dozen jars of honey. BLACK MADONNA HONEY, they said.   20

The door opened, and a family came in fresh from church, the mother and daughter dressed alike in navy with white Peter Pan collars. Light streamed in the door, hazy, warped, blurred with drizzles of yellow. The little girl sneezed, and her mother said, "Come here, let's wipe your nose."   25

I looked again at the honey jars, at the amber lights swimming inside them, and made myself breathe slowly.

I realized it for the first time in my life: there is nothing but mystery in the world, how it hides behind the fabric of our poor, browbeat days, shining brightly, and we don't even know it.   30

I thought about the bees that had come to my room at night, how they'd been part of it all. And the voice I'd heard the day before,

---

6 **cash register**: *Ladenkasse*   **pinge**: make a high sound   **rummage**: search with
your fingers   10 **zip sth. up**: *Reißverschluss von etwas zuziehen*   15 **spell sth. out**:
explain sth. clearly   22–23 **Peter Pan collar**: a small, closefitting collar with ends
rounded at the front   23 **warped**: not straight, bent   24 **drizzle**: light, fine rain
29 **fabric**: basic structure   30 **browbeat** (n): frightening, intimidating

saying, *Lily Melissa Owens, your jar is open*, speaking as plain and clear as the woman in navy speaking to her daughter.

"Here's your Coca-Colas," the bow-tied man was saying. I pointed to the honey jars. "Where did you get those?"

5 He thought the tone of shock in my voice was really consternation. "I know what you mean. A lot of folks won't buy it 'cause it's got the Virgin Mary pictured as a colored woman, but see, that's because the woman who makes the honey is colored herself."

"What's her name?"

10 "August Boatwright," he said. "She keeps bees all over the county." Keep breathing, keep breathing. "Do you know where she lives?"

"Oh, sure, it's the darndest house you ever saw. Painted like Pepto-Bismol. Your grandmother surely's seen it – you go through town on Main Street till it turns into the highway to Florence."

15 I walked to the door. "Thanks."

"You tell your grandma hello for me," he said.

Rosaleen's snores were making the bench slats tremble. I gave her a shake. "Wake up. Here's your snuff, but put it in your pocket, 'cause I didn't exactly pay for it."

20 "You stole it?" she said.

"I had to, 'cause they don't sell items from the store on Sunday."

"Your life has gone straight to hell," she said.

I spread our lunch out like a picnic on the bench but couldn't eat a bite of it till I told her about the black Mary on the honey jar and 25 the beekeeper named August Boatwright.

"Don't you think my mother must've known her?" I said. "It couldn't be just a coincidence."

She didn't answer, so I said louder, "Rosaleen? Don't you think so?"

30 "I don't know what I think," she said. "I don't want you getting your hopes up too much, is all." She reached over and touched my cheek. "Oh, Lily, what have we gone and done?"

---

5 **consternation**: worried feeling after a sad surprise   12 **darndest**: mild swear word used to emphasize sth.   13 **Pepto-Bismol**: (US brandname) pink liquid medicine for stomach problems   17 **slat**: thin piece of wood used in furniture
27 **coincidence**: pure chance   32 **go and do sth.**: do sth. (usually stupid)

✹

Tiburon was a place like Sylvan, minus the peaches. In front of the
domed courthouse someone had stuck a Confederate flag in the
mouth of their public cannon. South Carolina was Dixie first,
America second. You could not get the pride of Fort Sumter out of
us if you tried.   5

Strolling down Main Street, we moved through long blue shadows
cast from the two-story buildings that ran the length of the street. At
a drugstore, I peered through the plate glass at a soda fountain with
chrome trim, where they sold cherry Cokes and banana splits,
thinking that soon it would not be just for white people anymore.   10

We walked past Worth Insurance Agency, Tiburon County Rural
Electric office, and the Amen Dollar Store, which had Hula Hoops,
swim goggles, and boxes of sparklers in the window with SUMMER
FUN spray-painted across the glass. A few places, like the Farmers
Trust Bank, had GOLDWATER FOR PRESIDENT signs in their windows,   15
sometimes with a bumper sticker across the bottom saying
AFFIRMATION VIETNAM.

At the Tiburon post office I left Rosaleen on the sidewalk and
stepped inside to where the post office boxes and the Sunday
newspapers were kept. As far as I could tell, there were no wanted   20
posters in there of me and Rosaleen, and the front-page headline in
the Columbia paper was about Castro's sister spying for the CIA and

---

2 **Confederate** (adj): of the Southern states which left the USA in 1860–1861
3 **Dixie** (AE infml): name for the Southern states of the USA   4 **Fort Sumter**: the
US fort in the harbor of Charleston, South Carolina, where the Civil War began and
which was the first Confederate victory   8 **peer**: look carefully   **plate glass**: thick,
clear glass   **soda fountain** (AE, old use): place where drinks and ice-cream are
sold   9 **trim**: *Verzierung*   **banana split**: type of dessert   12 **Hula Hoop**: large
plastic ring that you spin around your waist by moving your hips   13 **swim
goggles** (pl): *Schwimmbrille*   **sparkler**: *Wunderkerze*   15 **Barry Goldwater**
(1909–1998): Republican presidential candidate in the 1964 US election
16 **bumper sticker**: sign with a message on it that people stick on the bumper of
their car   17 **Affirmation Vietnam**: sign indicating support for American policy in
Vietnam   20–21 **wanted poster**: *Fahndungsplakat*   22 **Fidel Castro** (born 1926):
the communist leader of Cuba, whose sister first supported the 1959 Cuban
Revolution but then opposed it and left the country

not a word about a white girl breaking a Negro woman out of jail in Sylvan.

    I dropped a dime into the slot and took one of the papers, wondering if the story was inside somewhere. Rosaleen and I
5 squatted on the ground in an alley and spread out the paper, opening every page. It was full of Malcolm X, Saigon, the Beatles, tennis at Wimbledon, and a motel in Jackson, Mississippi, that closed down rather than accept Negro guests, but nothing about me and Rosaleen.

    Sometimes you want to fall on your knees and thank God in
10 heaven for all the poor news reporting that goes on in the world.

6 **Malcolm X** (1925–1965): African-American leader who promoted the cause of black supremacy and black nationalism   **Saigon**: (now: Ho Chi Minh City) capital of South Vietnam until 1975   10 **poor**: (here) of bad quality

Honeybees are social insects and live in colonies. Each colony is a family unit, comprising a single, egg-laying female or queen and her many sterile daughters called workers. The workers cooperate in the food-gathering, nest-building and rearing the offspring. Males are reared only at the times of year when their presence is required.

Bees of the World

Chapter Four

The woman moved along a row of white boxes that bordered the woods beside the pink house, a house so pink it remained a scorched shock on the back of my eyelids after I looked away. She was tall, dressed in white, wearing a pith helmet with veils that floated across her face, settled around her shoulders, and trailed down her back. 5 She looked like an African bride.

Lifting the tops off the boxes, she peered inside, swinging a tin bucket of smoke back and forth. Clouds of bees rose up and flew wreaths around her head. Twice she disappeared in the fogged billows, then gradually reemerged like a dream rising up from the 10 bottom of the night.

We stood across the road, Rosaleen and I, temporarily mute. Me out of awe for the mystery playing out and Rosaleen because her lips were sealed with Red Rose snuff.

"She's the woman who makes the Black Madonna Honey," I said. 15 I was unable to take my eyes off her, the Mistress of Bees, the portal into my mother's life. *August.*

---

comprise sth.: have sth. as a part   2–3 **scorched shock**: (here) a strong impression caused by seeing sth.   4 **pith helmet**: a large, light hard hat   **veil**: thin transparent covering to protect the face   9 **wreath**: (here) circle   10 **billow**: moving cloud of smoke   12 **mute**: not speaking   13 **awe** [ɑː]: feeling of respect and fear
16 **portal**: gate, doorway

Rosaleen, wilting, spit a stream of black juice, then wiped away the mustache of perspiration above her lip. "I hope she makes honey better than she picks out paint."

"I like it," I announced.

5   We waited till she went inside, then crossed the highway and opened the gate in the picket fence that was about to topple over from the weight of Carolina jasmine. Add that to all the chive, dillweed, and lemon balm growing around the porch and the smell could knock you over.

10   We stood on the porch in the pink light shining off the house. June bugs flickered all around, and music notes floated from inside, sounding like a violin, only a lot sadder.

My heart kicked in. I asked Rosaleen if she could hear it beating, it was that loud.

15   "I don't hear nothing but the Good Lord asking me what I'm doing here." She spit what I hoped was the last of her snuff.

I knocked on the door while she muttered a slew of words under her breath: *Give me strength … Baby Jesus … Lost our feeble minds.*

The music stopped. In the corner of my eye I caught a slight
20   movement at the window, a venetian blind slit open, then closed.

When the door opened, it was not the woman in white but another one wearing red, her hair cut so short it resembled a little gray, curlicue swim cap pulled tight over her scalp. Her face stared at us, suspicious and stern. I noticed she carried a musical bow tucked
25   under her arm like a riding whip. It crossed my mind she might use it on us.

"Yes?"

"Are you August Boatwright?"

"No, I'm June Boatwright," she said, her eyes sweeping over the
30   stitches on Rosaleen's forehead. "August Boatwright is my sister. You came to see her?"

---

1 **wilt** (v): become weak due to heat   6 **picket**: a pointed piece of wood that is fixed in the ground   **topple over**: fall down   7 **chive**: *Schnittlauch*   8 **dillweed**: *Dill*   **lemon balm**: *Zitronenmelisse*   11 **June bug**: type of flying beetle   13 **kick in**: start to react   17 **slew of sth.**: large number of sth.   20 **venetian blind**: *Jalousie*   23 **curlicue swim cap**: *Badekappe mit dekorativen Motiven*   24 **musical bow**: *Geigenbogen*   25 **cross your mind**: come into your mind

I nodded, and simultaneously another woman appeared, with bare feet. She wore a green-and-white sleeveless gingham dress and short braids that stuck straight out all over her head.

"I'm May Boatwright," she said. "I'm August's sister, too." She smiled at us, one of those odd grins that let you know she was not an   5 altogether normal person.

I wished June with her whip would grin, too, but she only looked annoyed.

"Is August expecting you?" she said, directing her words to Rosaleen.   10

Of course Rosaleen jumped in ready to spill the whole story. "No, see, Lily has this picture –"

I broke in. "I saw a honey jar back at the store, and the man said …"

"Oh, you've come for honey. Well, why didn't you say so? Come   15 on in the front parlor. I'll get August."

I shot a look at Rosaleen that said, *Are you crazy? Don't tell them about the picture.* We were going to have to get our stories straight, that was for sure.

Some people have a sixth sense, and some are duds at it. I believe   20 I must have it, because the moment I stepped into the house I felt a trembling along my skin, a traveling current that moved up my spine, down my arms, pulsing out from my fingertips. I was practically radiating. The body knows things a long time before the mind catches up to them. I was wondering what my body knew that   25 I didn't.

I smelled furniture wax everywhere. Somebody had gone over the entire parlor with it, a big room with fringed throw rugs, an old piano with a lace runner, and cane-bottom rockers draped with afghans. Each chair had its own little velvet stool sitting before it.   30 *Velvet.* I went over and rubbed my hand across one of them.

---

1 **simultaneous** [ˌsaɪməlˈteɪniəs]: at the same time   2 **gingham**: kind of cotton
11 **spill sth.**: tell sth. that is supposed to be secret   16 **parlor**: room for
entertaining visitors   20 **be a dud at sth.** (infml): be bad at sth.   28 **fringed throw
rug**: *kleiner Teppich mit Fransen*   29 **lace runner**: *Spitzenläufer*   **cane-bottom
rocker**: *Schaukelstuhl mit geflochtenem Sitz*   **drape sth. with sth.**: hang sth. loosely
over sth.   30 **afghan**: type of blanket   **velvet**: *Samt*

Next I walked over to a drop-leaf table and sniffed a beeswax candle that smelled precisely like the furniture wax. It sat in a star-shaped holder next to a jigsaw puzzle in progress, though I couldn't tell what picture it would make. A wide-mouthed milk bottle filled
5 with gladiolus was perched on another table under the window. The curtains were organdy, not your average white organdy but silver-gray, so the air came through with a slightly smoky shimmer.

Imagine walls with nothing on them but mirrors. I counted five of them, each one with a big brass frame around it.

10 Then I turned around and looked back toward the door where I'd come in. Over in the corner was a carving of a woman nearly three feet tall. She was one of those figures that had leaned out from the front of a ship in olden times, so old she could have been on the *Santa Maria* with Columbus for all I knew.

15 She was black as she could be, twisted like driftwood from being out in the weather, her face a map of all the storms and journeys she'd been through. Her right arm was raised, as if she was pointing the way, except her fingers were closed in a fist. It gave her a serious look, like she could straighten you out if necessary.

20 Even though she wasn't dressed up like Mary and didn't resemble the picture on the honey jar, I knew that's who she was. She had a faded red heart painted on her breast and a yellow crescent moon, worn down and crooked, painted where her body would have blended into the ship's wood. A candle inside a tall red glass threw
25 glints and glimmers across her body. She was a mix of mighty and humble all in one. I didn't know what to think, but what I *felt* was magnetic and so big it ached like the moon had entered my chest and filled it up.

The only thing I could compare it to was the feeling I got one
30 time when I walked back from the peach stand and saw the sun spreading across the late afternoon, setting the top of the orchard on

---

1 **drop-leaf table**: table with a section that can be dropped   **6 organdy**: stiff cotton cloth   11 **carving**: object made by cutting away material from wood   15 **twisted**: not straight   **driftwood**: wood that floats on the sea   19 **straighten sb. out**: make sb. behave better   22 **faded**: not bright   23 **crooked** ['krʊkɪd]: not straight, twisted   24 **blend into sth.**: mix with sth. unnoticeably   25 **glint**: flash of light

fire while darkness collected underneath. Silence had hovered over
my head, beauty multiplying in the air, the trees so transparent I felt
I could see through to something pure inside them. My chest had
ached then, too, this very same way.

The lips on the statue had a beautiful, bossy half smile, the sight   5
of which caused me to move both my hands up to my throat.
Everything about that smile said, *Lily Owens, I know you down to the
core.*

I felt she knew what a lying, murdering, hating person I really
was. How I hated T. Ray, and the girls at school, but mostly myself   10
for taking away my mother.

I wanted to cry, but then, in the next instant, I wanted to laugh,
because the statue also made me feel like Lily the Smiled-Upon, like
there was goodness and beauty in me, too. Like I really had all that
fine potential Mrs. Henry said I did.   15

Standing there, I loved myself and I hated myself. That's what the
black Mary did to me, made me feel my glory and my shame at the
same time.

I stepped closer to her and caught the faint scent of honey coming
from the wood. May walked over and stood beside me, and I could   20
smell nothing then but the pomade on her hair, onions on her
hands, vanilla on her breath. Her palms were pink like the bottoms
of her feet, her elbows darker than the rest of her, and for some
reason the sight of them filled me with tenderness.

August Boatwright entered, wearing a pair of rimless glasses and   25
a lime green chiffon scarf tied onto her belt. "Who've we got here?"
she said, and the sound of her voice snapped me back to my ordinary
senses.

She was almond-buttery with sweat and sun, her face corrugated
with a thousand caramel wrinkles and her hair looking flour dusted,   30
but the rest of her seemed decades younger.

---

1 **hover**: stay in the air in one place   7–8 **to the core**: completely, to your
innermost self   21 **pomade**: liquid that is put on the hair to make it look shiny
26 **chiffon**: type of fine transparent cloth made from silk   27 **snap sb. back to sth.**:
bring sb.'s thoughts back to sth. quickly   29 **almond-buttery** ['ɑːlmənd]: *mit
Mandelbutter eingerieben*   **corrugated**: (here) *zerfurcht*   30 **wrinkle**: *Falte*

"I'm Lily, and that's Rosaleen," I said, hesitating as June appeared in the doorway behind her. I opened my mouth without any sense of what I would say next. What came out couldn't have surprised me more. "We ran away from home and don't have any place to go,"
5 I told her.

Any other day of my life I could have won a fibbing contest hands down, and that, *that* is what I came up with: the pathetic truth. I watched their faces, especially August's. She took off her glasses and rubbed the depressions on each side of her nose. It was so quiet
10 I could hear a clock ticking in another room.

August replaced her glasses, walked to Rosaleen, and examined the stitches on her forehead, the cut under her eye, the bruises along her temple and arms. "You look like you've been beaten."

"She fell down the front steps when we were leaving," I offered,
15 returning to my natural fibbing habit.

August and June traded looks while Rosaleen narrowed her eyes, letting me know I'd done it again, speaking for her like she wasn't even there.

"Well, you can stay here till you figure out what to do. We can't
20 have you living on the side of the road," said August.

The intake of June's breath nearly sucked the air from the room. "But, August —"

"They'll stay here," she repeated in a way that let me know who the big sister was and who the little sister was. "It'll be all right.
25 We've got the cots in the honey house."

June flounced out, her red skirt flashing around the door. "Thank you," I said to August.

"You're welcome. Now, sit down. I'll get some orangeade." We got situated in the cane-bottom rockers while May stood guard, grinning
30 her crazy-woman grin. She had great big muscles in her arms, I noticed.

---

6 **fib**: lie   **contest**: competition   6–7 **hands down**: easily   7 **pathetic**: sad
25 **cot** (AE): *Feldbett*   26 **flounce out**: leave suddenly and in a rush

"How come y'all have names from a calendar?" Rosaleen asked her.

"Our mother loved spring and summer," May said. "We had an April, too, but … she died when she was little." May's grin dissolved, and out of nowhere she started humming "Oh! Susanna" like her life depended on it.

Rosaleen and I stared at her as her humming turned into hard crying. She cried like April's death had happened only this second.

Finally August returned with a tray of four jelly glasses, orange slices stuck real pretty on the rims. "Oh, May, honey, you go on out to the wall and finish your cry," she said, pointing her to the door and giving her a nudge.

August acted like this was the sort of normal behavior happening in every household in South Carolina. "Here you go – orangeade."

I sipped. Rosaleen, however, downed hers so fast she let out a belch that the boys in my old junior high would have envied. It was unbelievable.

August pretended she didn't hear it while I stared at the velvet footstool and wished Rosaleen could be more *cultured*.

"So you're Lily and Rosaleen," August said. "Do you have last names?"

"Rosaleen … Smith, and Lily … Williams," I lied and then launched in. "See, my mother died when I was little, and then my father died in a tractor accident last month on our farm in Spartanburg County. I don't have any other kin around here, so they were going to send me to a home."

August shook her head. Rosaleen shook hers, too, but for a different reason.

"Rosaleen was our housekeeper," I went on. "She doesn't have any family but me, so we decided to go up to Virginia to find my aunt. Except we don't have any money, so if you have any work for

---

4 **dissolve**: (here) disappear   12 **nudge**: a gentle push   15 **down sth.**: drink sth. quickly   16 **belch**: *Rülpser*   23 **launch in**: start to add sth. in an enthusiastic way 25 **kin**: relatives

us to do while we're here, maybe we could earn a little before heading on. We aren't really in a hurry to get to Virginia."

Rosaleen glared at me. For a minute there was nothing but ice clinking in our glasses. I hadn't realized how sweltering the room
5 was, how stimulated my sweat glands had gotten. I could actually smell myself. I cut my eyes over to the black Mary in the corner and back to August.

She put down her glass. I had never seen eyes that color, eyes the purest shade of ginger.

10 "I'm from Virginia myself," she said, and for some reason this stirred up the current that had moved in my limbs when I'd first entered the room. "All right, then. Rosaleen can help May in the house, and you can help me and Zach with the bees. Zach is my main helper, so I can't pay you anything, but at least you'll have a
15 room and some food till we call your aunt and see about her sending some bus money."

"I don't exactly know her whole name," I said. "My father just called her Aunt Bernie; I never met her."

"Well, what were you planning to do, child, go door to door in
20 Virginia?"

"No, ma'am, just Richmond."

"I see," said August. And the thing was, she did. She saw right through it.

That afternoon, heat built up in the skies over Tiburon; finally it
25 gave way to a thunderstorm. August, Rosaleen, and I stood on the screen porch that jutted off the back of the kitchen and watched the clouds bruise dark purple over the treetops and the wind whip the branches. We were waiting for a let-up so August could show us our new quarters in the honey house, a converted garage in the back

---

6 **cut your eyes over to sth.**: look at sth. quickly   9 **ginger**: *Ingwer*   11 **stir sth. up**: bring sth. to life   26 **porch** (AE): small area at the entrance of a house, with a floor and a roof but no walls   27 **bruise** (v): (here) develop the color of a bruise (*blauer Fleck*)   28 **let-up** (n): period of time when sth. becomes weaker

corner of the yard painted the same hot-flamingo shade as the rest of the house.

Now and then sprays of rain flew over and misted our faces. Every time I refused to wipe away the wetness. It made the world seem so alive to me. I couldn't help but envy the way a good storm 5 got everyone's attention.

August went back into the kitchen and returned with three aluminum pie pans and handed them out. "Come on. Let's make a run for it. These will keep our heads dry, at least."

August and I dashed into the downpour, holding the pans over 10 our heads. Glancing back, I saw Rosaleen holding the pie pan in her hand, missing the whole point.

When August and I reached the honey house, we had to huddle in the door and wait on her. Rosaleen glided along, gathering rain in the pan and flinging it out like a child would do. She walked on 15 puddles like they were Persian carpets, and when a clap of thunder boomed around us, she looked up at the drowned sky, opened her mouth, and let the rain fall in. Ever since those men had beaten her, her face had been so pinched and tired, her eyes dull like they'd had the light knocked out of them. Now I could see she was returning to 20 herself, looking like an all-weather queen out there, like nothing could touch her.

If only she could get some manners.

The inside of the honey house was one big room filled with strange honey-making machines – big tanks, gas burners, troughs, 25 levers, white boxes, and racks piled with waxy honeycombs. My nostrils nearly drowned in the scent of sweetness.

Rosaleen made gigantic puddles on the floor while August ran for towels. I stared at a side wall that was covered with shelves of mason jars. Pith helmets with netting, tools, and wax candles hung from 30 nails near the front door, and a thin veneer of honey lay across everything. The soles of my shoes stuck slightly as I walked.

---

8 **pie pan** (AE): tin for baking   10 **downpour**: heavy rain   13 **huddle**: gather closely together   15 **fling sth. out**: throw sth. away   19 **pinched** (adj): looking unhealthy   25 **trough** [trɔːf]: long open container for liquids   26 **lever**: a handle used to operate a piece of machinery   31 **veneer**: layer

August led us to a tiny corner room in the back with a sink, a full-length mirror, one curtainless window, and two wooden cots made up with clean white sheets. I placed my bag on the first cot. "May and I sleep out here sometimes when we're harvesting honey round
5 the clock," August said. "It can get hot, so you'll need to turn the fan on."

Rosaleen reached up to where it sat on a shelf along the back wall and flipped the switch, causing cobwebs to blow off the blades and fly all over the room. She had to pick them off her cheekbones.

10 "You need dry clothes," August told her.

"I'll air-dry," Rosaleen said, and she stretched out on the cot, making the legs on it bow.

"You'll have to come into the house to use the bathroom," August said. "We don't lock the doors, so just come on in."

15 Rosaleen's eyes were closed. She had already drifted off and was making little puff noises with her mouth.

August lowered her voice. "So she fell down the steps?"

"Yes, ma'am, she went down headfirst. Caught her foot in the rug at the top of the stairs, the one my mother hooked herself."

20 The secret of a good lie is don't overly explain, and throw in one good detail.

"Well, Miss Williams, you can start work tomorrow," she said. I stood there wondering who she was talking to, who was Miss Williams, when I remembered I was Lily Williams now. That's the
25 other secret to lying – you have to keep your stories straight. "Zach will be away for a week," she was saying. "His family has gone down to Pawley's Island to visit his mama's sister."

"If you don't mind me asking, what will I be doing?"

"You'll work with Zach and me, making the honey, doing
30 whatever needs doing. Come on, I'll give you the tour."

We walked back to the large room with all the machines. She led me to a column of white boxes stacked one on top of the other.

---

8 **flip a switch**: *Schalter umdrehen*   15 **drift off**: (here) start to sleep   19 **hook a rug**: *Teppichvorleger häkeln*   20 **overly**: excessively

"These are called supers," she said, setting one on the floor in front of me and removing the lid.

From the outside it looked like a regular old drawer pulled out of the dresser, but inside it were frames of honeycomb hung in a neat row. Each frame was filled with honey and sealed over with beeswax.   5

She pointed her finger. "That's the uncapper over there, where we take the wax off the comb. Then it goes through the wax melter over here."

I followed her, stepping over bits and pieces of honeycomb, which is what they had instead of dust bunnies. She stopped at the   10
big metal tank in the center of the room.

"This is the spinner," she said, patting the side like it was a good dog. "Go on up there and look in."

I climbed up the two-step ladder and peered over the edge, while August flipped a switch and an old motor on the floor sputtered and   15
cranked. The spinner started slowly, gaining speed like the cotton-candy machine at the fair, until it was sending heavenly smells into the atmosphere.

"It separates out the honey," she said. "Takes out the bad stuff, leaves in the good. I've always thought how nice it would be to have   20
spinners like this for human beings. Just toss them in and let the spinner do its work."

I looked back at her, and she was staring at me with her ginger-cake eyes. Was I paranoid to think that when she'd said human beings, what she really meant was me?   25

She turned off the motor, and the humming stopped with a series of ticking sounds. Bending over the brown tube leading from the spinner, she said, "From here it goes into the baffle tank, then over to the warming pan, and finally into the settling tank. That's the honey gate, where we fill the buckets. You'll get the hang of it."   30

1–12 **super, frame, uncapper, spinner**: cf. p. 305–306   10 **dust bunny**: small ball of dust   15 **sputter**: make short explosive sounds   16 **crank**: make loud noises
21 **toss sth.**: throw sth.   28 **baffle tank**: container with panels that control the flow of liquid   30 **get the hang of sth.**: learn how to do sth.

I doubted it. I'd never seen such a complex situation in my life. "Well, I imagine you'll want to rest up like Rosaleen. Supper is at six. You like sweet-potato biscuits? That's May's specialty."

When she left, I lay on the empty cot while rain crashed on the tin roof. I felt like I'd been traveling for weeks, like I'd been dodging lions and tigers on a safari through the jungle, trying to get to the Lost Diamond City buried in the Congo, which happened to be the theme of the last matinee I'd seen in Sylvan before leaving. I felt that somehow I belonged here, I really did, but I *could* have been in the Congo for how unfamiliar it felt. Staying in a colored house with colored women, eating off their dishes, lying on their sheets – it was not something I was against, but I was brand-new to it, and my skin had never felt so white to me.

T. Ray did not think colored women were smart. Since I want to tell the whole truth, which means the worst parts, I thought they could be smart, but not as smart as me, me being white. Lying on the cot in the honey house, though, all I could think was *August is so intelligent, so cultured*, and I was surprised by this. That's what let me know I had some prejudice buried inside me.

When Rosaleen woke from her nap, before she had a chance to raise her head off the pillow, I said, "Do you like it here?"

"I guess I do," she said, working to get herself to a sitting position. "So far."

"Well, I like it, too," I said. "So I don't want you saying anything to mess it up, okay?"

She crossed her arms over her belly and frowned. "Like what?"

"Don't say anything about the black Mary picture I got in my bag, okay? And don't mention my mother."

She reached up and started twisting some of her loose braids back together. "Now, how come you wanna keep that a secret?"

I hadn't had time to sort out my reasons. I wanted to say, *Because I just want to be normal for a little while – not a refugee girl looking for*

---

5 **dodge sb./sth.**: avoid sb./sth.   8 **matinee**: performance of a film or play in the afternoon

her mother, but a regular girl paying a summer visit to Tiburon, South Carolina. I want time to win August over, so she won't send me back when she finds out what I've done. And those things were true, but even as they crossed my mind, I knew they didn't completely explain why talking to August about my mother made me so uneasy.   5

I went over and began helping Rosaleen with her braids. My hands, I noticed, were shaking a little. "Just tell me you aren't gonna say anything," I said.

"It's your secret," she said. "You do what you want with it."

The next morning I woke early and walked outside. The rain had   10
stopped and the sun glowed behind a bank of clouds.

Pinewoods stretched beyond the honey house in every direction. I could make out about fourteen beehives tucked under the trees in the distance, the tops of them postage stamps of white shine.

The night before, during dinner, August had said she owned   15
twenty-eight acres left to her by her granddaddy. A girl could get lost on twenty-eight acres in a little town like this. She could open a trapdoor and disappear.

Light spilled through a crack in a red-rimmed cloud, and I walked toward it along a path that led from the honey house into the   20
woods. I passed a child's wagon loaded with garden tools. It rested beside a plot growing tomatoes tied to wooden stakes with pieces of nylon hose. Mixed in with them were orange zinnias and lavender gladiolus that dipped toward the ground.

The sisters loved birds, I could see. There was a concrete birdbath   25
and tons of feeders – hollowed-out gourds and rows of big pinecones sitting everywhere, each one smeared with peanut butter.

Where the grass gave way to the woods, I found a stone wall crudely cemented together, not even knee high but nearly fifty yards long. It curved on around the property and abruptly stopped. It   30

---

14 **shine**: *Glanz*   16 **acre** [ˈeɪkər]: unit for measuring an area of land
(ca. 4000 square metres)   18 **trapdoor**: small door in a floor   22 **stake**: wooden
post   23 **hose** (AE): stocking   **zinnia**: *Zinnie*   24 **dip**: bend downwards
26 **gourd** [gɔːrd]: round fruit with a hard shell   **pinecone**: *Tannenzapfen*

didn't seem to have any purpose to it. Then I noticed tiny pieces of folded-up paper stuck in the crevices around the stones. I walked the length of the fence, and it was the same all the way, hundreds of these bits of paper.

5   I pulled one out and opened it, but the writing was too blurred from rain to make out. I dug out another one. *Birmingham, Sept 15, four little angels dead.*

     I folded it and put it back, feeling like I'd done something wrong.

     Stepping over the wall, I moved into the trees, picking my way
10 through little ferns with their blue-green feathers, careful not to tear the designs the spiders had worked so hard on all morning. It was like me and Rosaleen really had discovered the Lost Diamond City.

     As I walked, I began to hear the sound of running water. It's impossible to hear that sound and not go searching for the source.
15 I pushed deeper into the woods. The growth turned thick, and sticker bushes snagged my legs, but I found it – a little river, not much bigger than the creek where Rosaleen and I had bathed. I watched the currents meander, the lazy ripples that once in a while broke along the surface.

20   Taking off my shoes, I waded in. The bottom turned mushy, squishing up through my toes. A turtle plopped off a rock into the water right in front of me, nearly scaring the Lord Jesus out of me. There was no telling what other invisible creatures I was out here socializing with – snakes, frogs, fish, a whole river world of biting
25 bugs, and I could have cared less.

     When I put on my shoes and headed back, the light poured down in shafts, and I wanted it to always be like this – no T. Ray, no Mr. Gaston, nobody wanting to beat Rosaleen senseless. Just the rain-cleaned woods and the rising light.

---

2 **crevice**: small crack or opening   6 **Birmingham**: reference to the bombing of a black church   10 **fern**: *Farn*   16 **sticker bush**: bush with thorns   **snag sth.**: scratch sth.   18 **ripple**: small wave   20 **mushy**: soft and wet   21 **squish**: make a soft wet sucking sound   27 **shaft**: beam

Let's imagine for a moment that we are tiny enough to follow a bee into a hive. Usually the first thing we would have to get used to is the darkness.
Exploring the World of Social Insects

Chapter Five

The first week at August's was a consolation, a pure relief. The world will give you that once in a while, a brief timeout; the boxing bell rings and you go to your corner, where somebody dabs mercy on your beat-up life.

All that week no one brought up my father, supposedly dead in a tractor accident, or my long-lost aunt Bernie in Virginia. The calendar sisters just took us in.

The first thing they did was take care of Rosaleen's clothes. August got into her truck and went straight to the Amen Dollar Store, where she bought Rosaleen four pairs of panties, a pale blue cotton nightgown, three waistless, Hawaiian-looking dresses, and a bra that could have slung boulders.

"This ain't charity," said Rosaleen when August spread them across the kitchen table. "I'll pay it all back."

"You can work it off," said August.

May came in with witch hazel and cotton balls and began to clean up Rosaleen's stitches.

1 **consolation**: feeling of happiness after a period of sadness
3–4 **dab sth. on sb**.: put sth. on sb. with light movements   10 **panties** (AE):
women's underwear   16 **witch hazel**: liquid used for treating injuries on the skin

"Somebody knocked the daylights out of you," she said, and a moment later she was humming "Oh! Susanna" at that same frantic speed she'd hummed it before.

June jerked her head up from the table, where she was inspecting
5 the purchases. "You're humming the song again," she said to May. "Why don't you excuse yourself?"

May dropped her cotton ball on the table and left the room. I looked at Rosaleen, and she shrugged. June finished cleaning the stitches herself; it was distasteful to her, I could tell by the way she
10 held her mouth, how it drew into a tight buttonhole.

I slipped out to find May. I was going to say, *I'll sing "Oh! Susanna" with you start to finish*, but I couldn't find her.

It was May who taught me the honey song:

Place a beehive on my grave
15 *and let the honey soak through.*
When I'm dead and gone,
that's what I want from you.
The streets of heaven are gold and sunny,
but I'll stick with my plot and a pot of honey.
20 *Place a beehive on my grave*
and let the honey soak through.

I loved the silliness of it. Singing made me feel like a regular person again. May sang the song in the kitchen when she rolled dough or sliced tomatoes, and August hummed it when she pasted
25 labels on the honey jars. It said everything about living here.

We lived for honey. We swallowed a spoonful in the morning to wake us up and one at night to put us to sleep. We took it with every meal to calm the mind, give us stamina, and prevent fatal disease.

2 **frantic**: mad   28 **stamina**: strength that lasts a long time   **fatal**: deadly

We swabbed ourselves in it to disinfect cuts or heal chapped lips. It went in our baths, our skin cream, our raspberry tea and biscuits. Nothing was safe from honey. In one week my skinny arms and legs began to plump out and the frizz in my hair turned to silken waves. August said honey was the ambrosia of the gods and the shampoo of the goddesses.

I spent my time in the honey house with August while Rosaleen helped May around the house. I learned how to run a steamheated knife along the super, slicing the wax cap off the combs, how to load them just so into the spinner. I adjusted the flame under the steam generator and changed the nylon stockings August used to filter the honey in the settling tank. I caught on so fast she said I was a marvel. Those were her very words: *Lily, you are a* marvel.

My favorite thing was pouring beeswax into the candle molds. August used a pound of wax per candle and pressed tiny violets into them, which I collected in the woods. She had a mail-order business to stores in places as far away as Maine and Vermont. People up there bought so many of her candles and jars of honey she couldn't keep up with it, and there were tins of Black Madonna All-Purpose Beeswax for her special customers. August said it could make your fishing line float, your button thread stronger, your furniture shinier, your stuck window glide, and your irritated skin glow like a baby's bottom. Beeswax was a miracle cure for everything.

May and Rosaleen hit it off right away. May was simpleminded. I don't mean retarded, because she was smart in some ways and read cookbooks nonstop. I mean she was naive and unassuming, a grown-up and a child at the same time, plus she was a touch crazy. Rosaleen liked to say May was a bona fide candidate for the nuthouse, but she still took to her. I would come into the kitchen and they would be standing shoulder to shoulder at the sink, holding ears of

---

1 **swab**: clean with soft material   4 **plump up**: become larger   **frizz**: dry curls
5 **ambrosia**: favourite food   12 **settling tank**: cf. p. 306: storage tank
marvel: (here) wonderful person   14 **mold**: *Gussform*   15 **violet**: *Veilchen*
21 **thread**: *Zwirn*   26 **unassuming**: modest   28 **bona fide** [,bəʊnə ˈfaɪdi]:
perfect   **nuthouse**: (infml) mental hospital   29 **take to sb.**: start liking sb.

corn they couldn't get shucked for talking. Or they'd be dabbing pinecones with peanut butter for the birds.

It was Rosaleen who figured out the mystery of "Oh! Susanna." She said if you kept things on a happy note, May did fine, but bring
5   up an unpleasant subject – like Rosaleen's head full of stitches or the tomatoes having rot-bottom – and May would start humming "Oh! Susanna." It seemed to be her personal way of warding off crying. It worked for things like tomato rot, but not for much else.

A few times she cried so bad, ranting and tearing her hair, that
10 Rosaleen had to come get August from the honey house. August would calmly send May out back to the stone wall. Going out there was about the only thing that could bring her around.

May didn't allow rat traps in the house, as she couldn't even bear the thought of a suffering rat. But what really drove Rosaleen crazy
15 was May catching spiders and carrying them out of the house in the dustpan. I liked this about May, since it reminded me of my bug-loving mother. I went around helping May catch granddaddy longlegs, not just because a smashed bug could send her over the edge but because I felt I was being loyal to my mother's wishes.

20 May had to have a banana every morning, and this banana absolutely could not have a bruise on it. One morning I watched her peel seven bananas in a row before she found one without a bad place. She kept tons of bananas around the kitchen, stoneware bowls chock-full; next to honey, they were the most plentiful thing in the
25 house. May could go through five or more every morning looking for the ideal, flawless banana, the one that hadn't gotten banged up by the grocery world.

Rosaleen made banana pudding, banana cream pie, banana Jell-O, and banana slices on lettuce leaf till August told her it was all
30 right, just throw the blooming things away.

---

1 **shuck sth.**: remove the shell of sth.   6 **rot-bottom**: plant disease
7 **ward sth. off**: protect yourself against sth.   9 **rant**: behave like a mad person
12 **bring sb. around**: (here): bring sb. back to their senses
16 **dustpan**: *Handschaufel*   17–18 **granddaddy longlegs**: type of spider
18–19 **send sb. over the edge**: make sb. go crazy   30 **blooming**: mild swear word

The one it was hard to get a fix on was June. She taught history and English at the colored high school, but what she really loved was music. If I got finished early in the honey house, I went to the kitchen and watched May and Rosaleen cook, but really I was there to listen to June play the cello.   5

She played music for dying people, going to their homes and even to the hospital to serenade them into the next life. I had never heard of such a thing, and I would sit at the table drinking sweet iced tea, wondering if this was the reason June smiled so little. Maybe she was around death too much.   10

I could tell she was still bristled at the idea of me and Rosaleen staying; it was the one sore point about our being here.

I overheard her talking to August one night on the back porch as I was coming across the yard to go to the bathroom in the pink house. Their voices stopped me beside the hydrangea bush.   15

"You know she's lying," said June.

"I know," August told her. "But they're in some kind of trouble and need a place to stay. Who's gonna take them in if we don't – a white girl and a Negro woman? Nobody around here." For a second neither spoke. I heard the moths landing against the porch lightbulb. 20

June said, "We can't keep a runaway girl here without letting somebody know."

August turned toward the screen and looked out, causing me to step deeper into the shadows and press my back against the house. "Let who know?" she said. "The police? They would only haul her 25 off someplace. Maybe her father really did die. If so, who better is she gonna stay with for the time being than us?"

"What about this aunt she mentioned?"

"There's no aunt and you know it," said August.

June's voice sounded exasperated. "What if her father *didn't* die in 30 this so-called tractor accident? Won't he be looking for her?"

---

11 **bristled**: annoyed, offended   12 **sore**: (here) unpleasant
15 **hydrangea** [haɪˈdreɪndʒə]: *Hortensie*   25–26 **haul sb. off**: take sb. away
30 **exasperated**: annoyed, stressed

A pause followed. I crept closer to the edge of the porch. "I just have a feeling about this, June. Something tells me not to send her back to some place she doesn't want to be. Not yet, at least. She has some reason for leaving. Maybe he mistreated her. I believe we can
5 help her."

"Why don't you just ask her point-blank what kind of trouble she's in?"

"Everything in time," August said. "The last thing I want is to scare her off with a lot of questions. She'll tell us when she's ready.
10 Let's be patient."

"But she's *white*, August."

This was a great revelation – not that I was white but that it seemed like June might not want me here because of my skin color. I hadn't known this was possible – to reject people for being *white*. A
15 hot wave passed through my body. "Righteous indignation" is what Brother Gerald called it. Jesus had righteous indignation when he turned over the tables in the temple and drove out the thieving moneychangers. I wanted to march up there, flip a couple of tables over, and say, *Excuse me, June Boatwright, but you don't even* know *me!*
20 "Let's see if we can help her," August said as June disappeared from my line of sight. "We owe her that."

"I don't see that we owe her anything," June said. A door slammed. August flipped off the light and let out a sigh that floated into the darkness.

25 I walked back toward the honey house, feeling ashamed that August had seen through my hoax but relieved, too, that she wasn't planning on calling the police or sending me back – *yet. Yet*, she'd said.

Mostly I felt resentment at June's attitude. As I squatted on the
30 grass at the edge of the woods, the pee felt hot between my legs. I watched it puddle in the dirt, the smell of it rising into the night. There was no difference between my piss and June's. That's what I thought when I looked at the dark circle on the ground. Piss was piss.

---

15 **righteous indignation**: the right to be angry   18–19 **flip sth. over**: turn sth. over   26 **hoax**: dishonest plan or action   30 **pee** (infml): urine

🐝

Every evening after supper we sat in their tiny den around the television set with the ceramic bee planter on top. You could hardly see the screen for the philodendron vines that dangled around the news pictures.

I liked the way Walter Cronkite looked, with his black glasses 5 and his voice that knew everything worth knowing. Here was a man who was not against books, that was plain. Take everything T. Ray was not, shape it into a person, and you would get Walter Cronkite.

He filled us in on an integration parade in St. Augustine that got attacked by a mob of white people, about white vigilante groups, fire 10 hoses, and teargas. We got all the totals. Three civil rights workers killed. Two bomb blasts. Three Negro students chased with ax handles.

Since Mr. Johnson signed that law, it was like somebody had ripped the side seams out of American life. We watched the lineup of 15 governors coming on the TV screen asking for "calm and reason." August said she was afraid it was only a matter of time before we saw things like that happen right here in Tiburon.

I felt white and self-conscious sitting there, especially with June in the room. Self-conscious and ashamed. 20

Usually May didn't watch, but one night she joined us, and midway through she started to hum "Oh! Susanna." She was upset over a Negro man named Mr. Raines, who was killed by a shotgun from a passing car in Georgia. They showed a picture of his widow, holding her children, and suddenly May started to sob. Of course 25 everybody jumped up like she was an unpinned grenade and tried to quiet her, but it was too late.

May rocked back and forth, slapping her arms and scratching at her face. She tore open her blouse so the pale yellow buttons went flying like popped corn. I had never seen her like this, and it 30 frightened me.

1 **den** (AE): (here) living room   2 **bee planter**: flower pot with plants that attract bees   5 **Walter Cronkite**: US television journalist, presented the national CBS Evening News from 1962 to 1981   9 **St. Augustine**: city in Florida
10 **vigilante** [ˌvɪdʒɪ'lænti] **group**: *Bürgerwehr*   12 **blast**: explosion
26 **unpinned grenade**: grenade ready to explode

August and June each took one of May's elbows and guided her through the door in a movement so smooth it was plain they'd done it before. A few moments later I heard water filling the clawfooted tub where twice I'd bathed in honey water. One of the sisters had
5 put a pair of red socks on two of the tub's feet – who knows why. I supposed it was May, who didn't need a reason.

Rosaleen and I crept to the door of the bathroom. It was cracked open enough for us to see May sitting in the tub in a little cloud of steam, hugging her knees. June scooped up handfuls of water and
10 drizzled them slowly across May's back. Her crying had eased off now into sniffling.

August's voice came from behind the door. "That's right, May. Let all that misery slide right off you. Just let it go."

Each night after the news, we all knelt down on the rug in the parlor
15 before black Mary and said prayers to her, or rather the three sisters and I knelt and Rosaleen sat on a chair. August, June, and May called the statue "Our Lady of Chains," for no reason that I could see.

Hail Mary, full of grace, the Lord is with thee. Blessed art thou among women ...

20 The sisters held strands of wooden beads and moved them in their fingers. In the beginning Rosaleen refused to join in, but soon she was going right along with the rest of us. I had the words memorized after the first evening. That's because we said the same thing over and over till it went on repeating itself in my head long
25 after I stopped mouthing it.

It was some kind of Catholic saying, but when I asked August if they were Catholic, she said, "Well, yes and no. My mother was a good Catholic – she went to mass twice a week at St. Mary's in Richmond, but my father was an Orthodox Eclectic."

3–4 **claw-footed tub**: a bathtub on four feet that resemble animal feet and claws
11 **sniffle**: quiet, pathetic breath   20 **strand of wooden beads**: *Holzperlenkette*

I had no idea what sort of denomination Orthodox Eclectic was, but I nodded like we had a big group of them back in Sylvan.

She said, "May and June and I take our mother's Catholicism and mix in our own ingredients. I'm not sure what you call it, but it suits us."   5

When we finished saying Hail Mary about three hundred times, we said our personal prayers silently, which was kept to a minimum, since our knees would be killing us by then. I shouldn't complain, since it was nothing compared to kneeling on the Martha Whites. Finally the sisters would cross themselves from their foreheads to   10
their navels, and it would be over.

One evening, after they had crossed themselves and everyone had left the room but me and August, she said, "Lily, if you ask Mary's help, she'll give it."

I didn't know what to say to that, so I shrugged.   15

She motioned me to sit next to her in the rocking chair. "I want to tell you a story," she said. "It's a story our mother used to tell us when we got tired of our chores or out of sorts with our lives."

"I'm not tired of my chores," I said.

"I know, but it's a good story. Just listen."   20

I situated myself in the chair and rocked back and forth, listening to the creaking sounds that rocking chairs are famous for. "A long time ago, across the world in Germany, there was a young nun named Beatrix who loved Mary. She got sick and tired of being a nun, though, what with all the chores she had to do and the rules   25
she had to go by. So one night when it got too much for her, she took off her nun outfit, folded it up, and laid it on her bed. Then she crawled out the convent window and ran away."

Okay, I could see where we were headed.

"She thought she was in for a wonderful time," August said. "But   30
life wasn't what she thought it'd be for a runaway nun. She roamed around feeling lost, begging in the streets. After a while she wished

18 **out of sorts**: sick or upset   25 **what with**: considering   28 **convent**: place
where nuns live   30 **be in for sth.**: be about to experience sth.
31–32 **roam around**: wander aimlessly

she could return to the convent, but she knew they'd never take her back."

We weren't talking about Beatrix the nun, that was plain as day. We were talking about me.

5 "What happened to her?" I asked, trying to sound interested. "Well, one day, after years of wandering and suffering, she disguised herself and went back to her old convent, wanting to visit one last time. She went into the chapel and asked one of her old sisters, 'Do you remember the nun Beatrix, who ran away?'

10 'What do you mean?' the sister said. 'The nun Beatrix didn't run away. Why, there she is over near the altar, sweeping.' Well, you can imagine how this floored the real Beatrix. She marched over to the sweeping woman to get a look at her and discovered it was none other than Mary. Mary smiled at Beatrix, then led her back to her

15 room and gave her back her nun outfit. You see, Lily, all that time Mary had been standing in for her."

The creaking in my rocker died away as I slowed to a stop. Just what was August trying to say? That Mary would stand in for me back home in Sylvan so T. Ray wouldn't notice I was gone? That was

20 too outlandish even for the Catholics. I think she was telling me, *I know you've run away – everybody gets the urge to do that sometime – but sooner or later you'll want to go home. Just ask Mary for help.*

I excused myself, glad to be out of the spotlight. After that I started asking Mary for her special help – not to take me home,

25 though, like the poor nun Beatrix. No, I asked her to see to it that I never went back. I asked her to draw a curtain around the pink house so no one would ever find us. I asked this daily, and I sure couldn't get over that it seemed to be working. No one knocked on the door and dragged us off to jail. Mary had made us a curtain of

30 protection.

12 **floor sb.**: utterly surprise sb.   16 **stand in for sb.**: take sb.'s place
20 **outlandish**: unusual and strange

On our first Friday evening there, after prayers were finished and orange and pink swirls still hung in the sky from sunset, I went with August to the bee yard.

I hadn't been out to the hives before, so to start off she gave me a lesson in what she called "bee yard etiquette." She reminded me that 5 the world was really one big bee yard, and the same rules worked fine in both places: Don't be afraid, as no life-loving bee wants to sting you. Still, don't be an idiot; wear long sleeves and long pants. Don't swat. Don't even think about swatting. If you feel angry, whistle. Anger agitates, while whistling melts a bee's temper. Act like 10 you know what you're doing, even if you don't. Above all, send the bees love. Every little thing wants to be loved.

August had been stung so many times she had immunity. They barely hurt her. In fact, she said, stings helped her arthritis, but since I didn't have arthritis, I should cover up. She made me put on one of 15 her long-sleeved white shirts, then placed one of the white helmets on my head and adjusted the netting.

If this was a man's world, a veil took the rough beard right off it. Everything appeared softer, nicer. When I walked behind August in my bee veil, I felt like a moon floating behind a night cloud. 20

She kept 48 hives strewn through the woods around the pink house, and another 280 were parceled out on various farms, in river yards and upland swamps. The farmers loved her bees, thanks to all the pollinating they did, how they made the watermelons redder and the cucumbers bigger. They would have welcomed her bees for 25 free, but August paid every one of them with five gallons of honey

She was constantly checking on her hives, driving her old flatbed truck from one end of the county to the other. The "honey wagon" was what she called it. Bee patrol was what she did in it.

I watched her load the red wagon, the one I'd seen in the 30 backyard, with brood frames, those little slats that slip down in the hives for the bees to deposit honey on.

---

2 **swirl**: pattern that twists in circles   5 **etiquette**: rules of accepted behaviour
9 **swat**: hit, especially with a flat object   10 **melt sb.'s temper**: make sb. become
gentler, less angry   21 **strewn** (past participle of strew): scatter   23 **upland**:
elevated area   **swamp**: land covered with water   24 **pollinate**: *befruchten*
29 **bee patrol**: checking the beehives are functioning well

"We have to make sure the queen has plenty of room to lay her eggs, or else we'll get a swarm," she said.

"What does that mean, a swarm?"

"Well, if you have a queen and a group of independentminded
5 bees that split off from the rest of the hive and look for another place to live, then you've got a swarm. They usually cluster on a limb somewhere."

It was clear she didn't like swarms.

"So," she said, getting down to business, "what we have to do is
10 take out the frames filled with honey and put in empty ones." August pulled the wagon while I walked behind it carrying the smoker stuffed with pine straw and tobacco leaves. Zach had placed a brick on top of each hive telling August what to do. If the brick was at the front, it meant the colony had nearly filled the combs and needed
15 another super. If the brick was at the back, there were problems like wax moths or ailing queens. Turned on its side, the brick announced a happy bee family, no Ozzie, just Harriet and her ten thousand daughters.

August struck a match and lit the grass in the smoker. I watched
20 her face flare with light, then recede into the dimness. She waved the bucket, sending smoke into the hive. The smoke, she said, worked better than a sedative.

Still, when August removed the lids, the bees poured out in thick black ropes, breaking into strands, a flurry of tiny wings moving
25 around our faces. The air rained bees, and I sent them love, just like August said.

She pulled out a brood frame, a canvas of whirling blacks and grays, with rubbings of silver. "There she is, Lily, see her?" said August. "That's the queen, the large one."

30 I made a curtsy like people do for the queen of England, which made August laugh.

---

6 **limb**: branch of a tree   11 **smoker**: cf. p. 306   17 **Ozzie and Harriet**: Ozzie
and Harriet Nelson, popular couple on US television between 1952 and 1966
22 **sedative**: *Beruhigungsmittel*   24 **flurry**: sudden, short movement   27 **brood
frame**: cf. p. 306   28 **rubbing of sth.**: (here) shade of sth.   30 **make a curtsy**:
bend your knee as a sign of respect

I wanted to make her love me so she would keep me forever. If I could make her love me, maybe she would forget about Beatrix the nun going home and let me stay.

When we walked back to the house, darkness had settled in and fireflies sparked around our shoulders. I could see Rosaleen and May   5
through the kitchen window finishing the dishes.

August and I sat in collapsible lawn chairs beside a crepe myrtle that kept dropping blossoms all over the ground. Cello music swelled out from the house, rising higher and higher until it lifted off the earth, sailing toward Venus.   10

I could see how such music drew the ghosts out of dying people, giving them a ride to the next life. I wished June's music could've seen my mother out.

I gazed at the stone wall that edged the backyard.

"There are pieces of paper in the wall out there," I said, as if   15
August didn't know this.

"Yes, I know. It's May's wall. She made it herself."

"May did?" I tried to picture her mixing cement, carrying rocks around in her apron.

"She gets a lot of the stones from the river that runs through the   20
woods back there. She's been working on it ten years or more."

So that's where she got her big muscles – rock lifting. "What are all those scraps of paper stuck in it?"

"Oh, it's a long story," August said. "I guess you've noticed – May is special."   25

"She sure does get upset easy," I said.

"That's because May takes in things differently than the rest of us do." August reached over and laid her hand on my arm. "See, Lily, when you and I hear about some misery out there, it might make us feel bad for a while, but it doesn't wreck our whole world. It's like we   30

---

5 **firefly**: *Leuchtkäfer*   7 **crepe** [kreɪp] **myrtle**: small tree with pleasant smell
12 **give sb. a ride**: take sb. somewhere   13 **see sb. out**: (here) be with sb. as they
die   14 **edge sth.**: be on the edge of sth.

have a built-in protection around our hearts that keeps the pain from overwhelming us. But May – she doesn't have that. Everything just comes into her – all the suffering out there – and she feels as if it's happening to her. She can't tell the difference."

5 Did this mean if I told May about T. Ray's mounds of grits, his dozens of small cruelties, about my killing my mother – that hearing it, she would feel everything I did? I wanted to know what happened when *two* people felt it. Would it divide the hurt in two, make it lighter to bear, the way feeling someone's joy seemed to double it?

10 Rosaleen's voice drifted from the kitchen window, followed by May's laughter. May sounded so normal and happy right then, I couldn't imagine how she'd gotten the way she was – one minute laughing and the next overrun with everybody's misery. The last thing I wanted was to be like that, but I didn't want to be like T. Ray
15 either, immune to everything but his own selfish life. I didn't know which was worse.

"Was she born like that?" I asked.

"No, she was a happy child at first."

"Then what happened to her?"

20 August focused her eyes on the stone wall. "May had a twin. Our sister April. The two of them were like one soul sharing two bodies. I never saw anything like it. If April got a toothache, May's gum would plump up red and swollen just like April's. Only one time did our father use a belt strap on April, and I swear to you, the welts rose
25 on May's legs, too. Those two had no separation between them."

"The first day we were here May told us that April died."

"And that's when it all started with May," she said, then looked at me like she was trying to decide whether to go on. "It's not a pretty story."

30 "My story's not pretty either," I said, and she smiled.

"Well, when April and May were eleven, they walked to the market with a nickel each to buy an ice cream. They'd seen the white

---

5 **mound**: small hill   22 **gum**: *Zahnfleisch*   24 **belt strap**: a belt's leather band

children in there licking their cones and looking at cartoon books. The man who owned the market gave them the cones but said they had to go outside to eat them. April was headstrong and told him she wanted to look at the cartoon books. She argued with the man for her own way, like she used to do with Father, and finally the man took her arm and pulled her to the door, and her ice cream dropped to the floor. She came home screaming that it wasn't fair. Our father was the only colored dentist in Richmond, and he'd seen more than his share of unfairness. He told April, 'Nothing's fair in this world. You might as well get that straight right now.' " 10

I was thinking how I myself had gotten that straight long before I was eleven. I blew a puff of air across my face, bending my neck to behold the Big Dipper. June's music poured out, serenading us.

"I think most children might have let that roll on by, but it did something to April," August said. "She got deflated about life, 15 I suppose you'd say. It opened her eyes to things she might not have noticed, being so young. She started having stretches when she didn't want to go to school or do anything. By the time she was thirteen, she was having terrible depressions, and of course the whole time, whatever she was feeling, May was feeling. And then, 20 when April was fifteen, she took our father's shotgun and killed herself."

I hadn't expected that. I sucked in my breath, then felt my hand go up and cover my mouth.

"I know," said August. "It's terrible to hear something like that." 25 She paused a moment. "When April died, something in May died, too. She never was normal after that. It seemed like the world itself became May's twin sister."

August's face was blending into the tree shadows. I slid up in my chair so I could still see her. 30

"Our mother said she was like Mary, with her heart on the outside of her chest. Mother was good about taking care of her, but when

---

1 **cone** (here): *Eiswaffel*   13 **Big Dipper**: *Großer Wagen*   15 **deflated**: disillusioned   17 **stretch**: period of time

she died, it fell to me and June. We tried for years to get May some help. She saw doctors, but they didn't have any idea what to do with her except put her away. So June and I came up with this idea of a wailing wall."

5   "A what kind of wall?"

"Wailing wall," she said again. "Like they have in Jerusalem. The Jewish people go there to mourn. It's a way for them to deal with their suffering. See, they write their prayers on scraps of paper and tuck them in the wall."

10   "And that's what May does?"

August nodded. "All those bits of paper you see out there stuck between the stones are things May has written down – all the heavy feelings she carries around. It seems like the only thing that helps her."

15   I looked in the direction of the wall, invisible now in the darkness. *Birmingham, Sept 15, four little angels dead.*

"Poor May," I said.

"Yes," said August. "Poor May." And we sat in the sorrow for a while, until the mosquitoes collected around us and chased us

20   indoors.

In the honey house Rosaleen was on her cot with the lights out and the fan going full blast. I stripped down to my panties and sleeveless top, but it was still too hot to move.

My chest hurt from feeling things. I wondered if T. Ray was

25   pacing the floors feeling as injured as I hoped he did. Maybe he was telling himself what a rotten excuse for a father he was for not treating me better, but I doubted it. Thinking up ways to kill me was more like it.

I turned my pillow over and over for the coolness, thinking about

30   May and her wall and what the world had come to that a person

---

22 **full blast**: at maximum capacity

needed something like that. It gave me the willies to think what
might be stuffed in among those rocks. The wall brought to my
mind the bleeding slabs of meat Rosaleen used to cook, the gashes
she made up and down them, stuffing them with pieces of wild,
bitter garlic.   5

The worst thing was lying there wanting my mother. That's how
it had always been; my longing for her nearly always came late at
night when my guard was down. I tossed on the sheets, wishing
I could crawl into bed with her and smell her skin. I wondered: Had
she worn thin nylon gowns to bed? Did she bobby-pin her hair?   10
I could just see her, propped in bed. My mouth twisted as I pictured
myself climbing in beside her and putting my head against her
breast. I would put it right over her beating heart and listen. *Mama*,
I would say. And she would look down at me and say, *Baby, I'm right
here.*   15

I could hear Rosaleen trying to turn over on her cot. "You awake?"
I said.

"Who can sleep in this oven?" she said.

I wanted to say, *You can*, as I'd seen her sleeping that day outside
the Frogmore Stew General Store and Restaurant, and it had been at   20
least this hot. She had a fresh Band-Aid on her forehead. Earlier,
August had boiled her tweezers and fingernail scissors in a pot on
the stove and used them to pluck out Rosaleen's stitches.

"How's your head?"

"My head is just fine." The words came out like stiff little jabs in 25
the air.

"Are you mad or something?"

"Why would I be mad? Just 'cause you spend all your time with
August now ain't no reason for me to care. You pick who you want
to talk with, it's not my business."   30

I couldn't believe it; Rosaleen sounded jealous.

"I don't spend *all* my time with her."

---

1 **give sb. the willies**: frighten sb.   3 **slab**: thick slice   8 **your guard is down**:
you are not careful enough to protect yourself   10 **bobby-pin your hair** (AE):
use a u-shaped pin to hold your hair   21 **Band-Aid** (AE): plaster   22 **tweezers**:
Pinzette   23 **pluck sth. out**: pull sth. out with tweezers   25 **jab**: sudden, strong
punch

"Pretty much," she said.

"Well, what do you expect? I work in the honey house with her. I have to spend time with her."

"What about tonight? You out there working on honey sitting on
5 the lawn?"

"We were just talking."

"Yeah, I know," she said, and then she rolled toward the wall, turning her back into a great hump of silence.

"Rosaleen, don't act like that. August might know things about
10 my mother."

She raised up on her elbow and looked at me. "Lily, your mama's gone," she said softly. "And she ain't coming back."

I sat straight up. "How do you know she isn't alive right in this very town? T. Ray could've lied about her being dead, just like he
15 lied about her leaving me."

"Oh, Lily. Girl. You got to stop all this."

"I feel her here," I said. "She's been here, I know it."

"Maybe she was. I can't say. I just know some things are better left alone."

20 "What do you mean? That I shouldn't find out what I can about my own mother?"

"What if – " She paused and rubbed the back of her neck. "What if you find out something you don't wanna know?"

What I heard her say was *Your mother left you, Lily. Let it alone.* I
25 wanted to yell how stupid she was, but the words bunched in my throat. I started hiccuping instead.

"You think T. Ray was telling me the truth about her leaving me, don't you?"

"I don't have any idea about that," Rosaleen said. "I just don't
30 want you getting yourself hurt."

I lay back on the bed. In the silence my hiccups ricocheted around the room.

---

8 **hump**: large mass   24 **let sth. alone**: stop talking or thinking about sth.
25 **bunch**: remain stuck   26 **hiccup**: *Schluckauf haben*   31 **ricochet**: (here) echo

"Hold your breath, pat your head, and rub your tummy," Rosaleen said.

I ignored her. Eventually I heard her breathing shift to a deeper place.

I pulled on my shorts and sandals and crept to the desk where   5
August filled honey orders. I tore a piece of paper from a tablet and wrote my mother's name on it. Deborah Owens.

When I looked outside, I knew I would have to make my way by starlight. I crept across the grass, back to the edge of the woods, to May's wall. Hiccuping all the way. Placing my hands on the stones,   10
all I wanted was not to ache so much.

I wanted to let go of my feelings for a little while, to pull in my moat bridge. I pressed the paper with her name into a cranny that seemed right for her, giving her to the wailing wall. Somewhere along the way my hiccups disappeared.   15

I sat on the ground with my back against the stones and my head tilted back so I could see the stars with all the spy satellites mixed in. Maybe one of them was taking my picture this very minute. They could spot me even in the dark. Nothing was safe. I would have to remember that.   20

I started thinking maybe I should find out what I could about my mother, before T. Ray or the police came for us. But where to start? I couldn't just pull out the black Mary picture and show it to August without the truth wrecking everything, and she would decide – might decide, would decide, I couldn't say – that she was obliged to   25
call T. Ray to come get me. And if she knew that Rosaleen was a true fugitive, wouldn't she *have* to call the police?

The night seemed like an inkblot I had to figure out. I sat there and studied the darkness, trying to see through it to some sliver of light.

---

13 **moat**: protective water channel around a castle   **cranny**: very small opening
27 **fugitive**: person running away to avoid being caught   28 **inkblot**: *Tintenklecks*

The queen must produce some substance that attracts the workers and that can be obtained from her only by direct contact. This substance evidently stimulates the normal working behavior in the hive. This chemical messenger has been called "queen substance." Experiments have shown that the bees obtain it directly from the body of the queen.

Man and Insects

Chapter Six

The next morning, inside the honey house, I woke to banging in the yard. When I pulled myself off the cot and wandered outside, I found the tallest Negro man I'd ever seen working on the truck, bent over the motor, tools scattered around his feet. June handed
5 him wrenches and what-have-you, cocking her head and beaming at him.

In the kitchen May and Rosaleen were working on pancake batter. I didn't like pancakes that much, but I didn't say so. I was just thankful it wasn't grits. After kneeling on them half your life, you
10 don't care to eat them.

The trash can was full of banana peels, and the electric percolator bubbled into the tiny glass nozzle on top of it. *Bloop, bloop.* I loved the way it sounded, the way it smelled.

"Who's the man out there?" I asked.
15   "That's Neil," said May. "He's sweet on June."

"It looks to me like June is sweet on him, too."

"Yeah, but she won't say so," said May. "She's kept that poor man strung along for years. Won't marry him and won't let him go."

---

5 **wrench**: *Schraubschlüssel*   **what-have-you** (infml): other things
cock your head: hold your head at an angle   **beam**: smile   7 **batter**: *Backteig*
11 **percolator** (AE): coffee-maker   12 **nozzle**: *Ausguss*
18 **string sb. along**: keep sb. waiting

May drizzled batter on the griddle in the shape of a big L. "This one's yours," she said. L for Lily.

Rosaleen set the table and warmed the honey in a bowl of hot water. I poured orange juice into the jelly glasses.

"How come June won't get married to him?" I asked.   5

"She was supposed to get married to somebody else a long time ago," said May. "But he didn't show up for the wedding."

I looked at Rosaleen, afraid this situation of jilted love might be unfortunate enough to send May into one of her episodes, but she was intent on my pancake. It struck me for the first time how odd it   10 was that none of them were married. Three unmarried sisters living together like this.

I heard Rosaleen make a sound like *Hmmmph*, and I knew she was thinking about her own sorry husband, wishing he hadn't shown up for *their* ceremony.   15

"June swore off men and said she would never get married, and then she met Neil when he came to be the new principal at her school. I don't know what happened to his wife, but he didn't have one anymore after he moved here. He has tried every which way to get June to marry him, but she won't do it. Me and August can't   20 convince her either."

A wheeze welled up from May's chest, and then out came "Oh! Susanna." *Here we go.*

"Lord, not again," said Rosaleen.

"I'm sorry," May said. "I just can't help it."   25

"Why don't you go out to the wall?" I said, prying the spatula out of her hand. "It's okay."

"Yeah," Rosaleen told her. "You do what you gotta do." We watched from the screen door as May cut past June and Neil.

A few minutes later June came in with Neil behind her. I worried   30 that his head wouldn't clear the door.

---

1 **griddle**: iron plate for frying food   8 **jilted love**: relationship abruptly ended
10 **be intent on**: be concentrated on   19 **every which way** (infml): using any
means   22 **wheeze**: high sound from the chest   **well up**: rise   26 **pry sth.**: try to
get sth. with force   29 **cut past sb./sth.**: walk past sb./sth.   31 **clear the door**:
walk through the door without touching it

"What started May off?" June wanted to know. Her eyes followed a roach that darted beneath the refrigerator. "You didn't step on a roach in front of her, did you?"

"No," I said. "We didn't even see a roach."

5 She opened the cabinet under the sink and dug into the back for a pump can of bug killer. I thought about explaining to her my mother's ingenious method of ridding the house of roaches – cracker crumbs and marshmallow – but then I thought, *This is June, forget it.*

"Well, what upset her, then?" June asked.

10 I hated to come out and say it with Neil standing right there, but Rosaleen didn't have any problem with it. "She's upset you won't marry Neil."

I had never considered until then that colored people could blush, or maybe it was anger that turned June's face and ears such a 15 dark plum color.

Neil laughed. "See there. You should marry me and quit upsetting your sister."

"Oh, get out of here," she said, and gave him a push.

"You promised me pancakes, and I'm gonna have them," he said. 20 He wore blue jeans and an undershirt with grease smears on it, along with horn-rimmed glasses. He looked like a very studious mechanic.

He smiled at me and then Rosaleen. "So are you gonna introduce me or keep me in the dark?"

I have noticed that if you look carefully at people's eyes the first 25 five seconds they look at you, the truth of their feelings will shine through for just an instant before it flickers away. June's eyes turned dull and hard when she looked at me.

"This is Lily and Rosaleen," she said. "They're visiting for a while."

"Where do you come from?" he asked me. This is the number one 30 most-asked question in all of South Carolina. We want to know if you are one of us, if your cousin knows our cousin, if your little sister went to school with our big brother, if you go to the same

---

5 **cabinet**: piece of furniture with doors and drawers   6 **pump can** (AE): *Spraydose*
7 **ingenious**: very clever   8 **crumb**: *Krümel*   14 **blush**: turn red in the face out of shame   15 **plum color**: dark reddish, purple

Baptist church as our ex-boss. We are looking for ways our stories fit together. It was rare, though, for Negroes to ask white people where they're from, because there was nothing much to be gained from it, as their stories weren't that likely to link up.

"Spartanburg County," I said, having to pause and remember 5 what I'd said earlier.

"And you?" he said to Rosaleen.

She stared at the copper Jell-O molds that hung on either side of the window over the sink. "Same place as Lily."

"What's that burning?" said June. 10

Smoke poured off the griddle. The L-shaped pancake had burned to a crisp. June yanked the spatula from my fingers, scraped up the mess, and dropped it into the trash.

"How long are you planning on staying?" Neil asked.

June stared at me. Waiting. Her lips pinched tight along her teeth. 15

"A while longer," I answered, looking over into the garbage can. L for Lily.

I could feel the questions gathering in him, knew I could not face them.

"I'm not hungry," I said, and walked out the back door. Crossing 20 the back porch, I heard Rosaleen say to him, "Have you registered yourself to vote?"

On Sunday I thought they would go to church, but no, they held a special service in the pink house, and people came to them. It was a group called the Daughters of Mary, which August had organized. 25

The Daughters of Mary started showing up in the parlor before 10:00 a.m. First was an old woman named Queenie and her grown daughter, Violet. They were dressed alike in bright yellow skirts and white blouses, though they wore different hats, at least. Next came

4 **link up**: establish a connection   11–12 **burn sth. to a crisp**: burn sth. very badly
12 **spatula**: kitchen tool

Lunelle, Mabelee, and Cressie, who wore the fanciest hats I'd ever laid eyes on.

It turned out Lunelle was a hatmaker without the least bit of shyness. I'm talking about purple felt the size of a sombrero with
5 fake fruit on the back. That was Lunelle's.

Mabelee wore a creation of tiger fur wrapped with gold fringe, but it was Cressie who carried the day in a crimson smokestack with black netting and ostrich feathers.

If this was not enough, they wore clip-on earbobs of various
10 colored rhinestones and circles of rouge on their brown cheeks. I thought they were beautiful.

In addition to all these Daughters, it turned out Mary had one son besides Jesus, a man named Otis Hill, with stubby teeth, in an oversize navy suit, so technically the group was the Daughters and
15 Son of Mary. He'd come with his wife, who was known to everyone as Sugar-Girl. She wore a white dress, turquoise cotton gloves, and an emerald green turban on her head.

August and June, hatless, gloveless, earbobless, looked practically poverty-stricken next to them, but May, good old May, had tied on a
20 bright blue hat with the brim up on one side and down on the other.

August had brought in chairs and arranged them in a semicircle facing the wooden statue of Mary. When we were all seated, she lit the candle and June played the cello. We said the Hail Marys together, Queenie and Violet moving strings of wooden beads
25 through their fingers.

August stood up and said she was glad me and Rosaleen were with them; then she opened a Bible and read, "And Mary said … Behold, from henceforth all generations shall call me blessed. For he that is mighty hath done to me great things. … He hath scattered the
30 proud. … He hath put down the mighty from their seats, and exalted them of low degree. He hath filled the hungry with good things; and the rich he hath sent empty away."

1 **fancy** (adj): impressive   7 **carry the day**: win first prize   **crimson**: dark red
smokestack: tall chimney   8 **ostrich**: *Vogel Strauß*   9 **earbob**: earring
10 **rhinestone**: glass jewel   13 **stubby**: short   16 **turquoise** ['tɜːkwɔɪz]:
greenish-blue   20 **brim**: *Rand*   28 **behold** (old use): look   **from henceforth**:
from now on   30 **hath** (old use): has   **exalt sb.**: make sb. more important

Laying the Bible in her chair, she said, "It's been a while since we've told the story of Our Lady of Chains, and since we have visitors who've never heard the story of our statue, I thought we'd tell it again."

One thing I was starting to understand was that August loved to   5
tell a good story.

"Really, it's good for all of us to hear it again," she said. "Stories have to be told or they die, and when they die, we can't remember who we are or why we're here."

Cressie nodded, making the ostrich feathers wave through the air   10
so you had the impression of a real bird in the room. "That's right. Tell the story," she said.

August pulled her chair close to the statue of black Mary and sat facing us. When she began, it didn't sound like August talking at all but like somebody talking through her, someone from another time   15
and place. All the while her eyes looked off toward the window, like she was seeing the drama play out in the sky.

"Well," she said, "back in the time of slaves, when the people were beaten down and kept like property, they prayed every day and every night for deliverance.   20

"On the islands near Charleston, they would go to the praise house and sing and pray, and every single time someone would ask the Lord to send them rescue. To send them consolation. To send them freedom."

I could tell she had repeated those opening lines a thousand   25
times, that she was saying them the exact way she'd heard them coming from the lips of some old woman, who'd heard them from the lips of an even older one, the way they came out like a song, with rhythms that rocked us to and fro till we had left the premises and were, ourselves, on the islands of Charleston looking for rescue.   30

"One day," August said, "a slave named Obadiah was loading bricks onto a boat that would sail down the Ashley River, when he

20 **deliverance**: rescue, salvation   29 **premises**: *Grundstück*

saw something washed up on the bank. Coming closer, he saw it was the wooden figure of a woman. Her body was growing out of a block of wood, a black woman with her arm lifted out and her fist balled up."

5 At this point August stood up and struck the pose herself. She looked just like the statue standing there, her right arm raised and her hand clutched into a fist. She stayed like that for a few seconds while we sat, spellbound.

"Obadiah pulled the figure out of the water," she went on, "and 10 struggled to set her upright. Then he remembered how they'd asked the Lord to send them rescue. To send them consolation. To send them freedom. Obadiah knew the Lord had sent this figure, but he didn't know who she was.

"He knelt down in the marsh mud before her and heard her voice 15 speak plain as day in his heart. She said, 'It's all right. I'm here. I'll be taking care of you now.' "

This story was ten times better than Beatrix the nun. August glided back and forth across the room as she spoke. "Obadiah tried to pick up the waterlogged woman who God had sent to take care of 20 them, but she was too heavy, so he went and got two more slaves, and between them they carried her to the praise house and set her on the hearth.

"By the time the next Sunday came, everyone had heard about the statue washing up from the river, how it had spoken to Obadiah. 25 The praise house was filled with people spilling out the door and sitting on the window ledges. Obadiah told them he knew the Lord God had sent her, but he didn't know who she was."

"He didn't know who she was!" cried Sugar-Girl, breaking in to the story. Then all the Daughters of Mary broke loose, saying over 30 and over, *"Not one of them knew."*

I looked over at Rosaleen, who I hardly recognized for the way she leaned forward in her chair, chanting along with them.

---

8 **spellbound**: with undivided attention   19 **waterlogged**: full of water
22 **hearth**: fireplace   26 **window ledge**: flat shelf below a window

When everything had quieted down, August said, "Now, the oldest of the slaves was a woman named Pearl. She walked with a stick, and when she spoke, everyone listened. She got to her feet and said, 'This here is the mother of Jesus.'

"Everyone knew the mother of Jesus was named Mary, and that 5
she'd seen suffering of every kind. That she was strong and constant and had a mother's heart. And here she was, sent to them on the same waters that had brought them here in chains. It seemed to them she knew everything they suffered."

I stared at the statue, feeling the fractured place in my heart.   10

"And so," August said, "the people cried and danced and clapped their hands. They went one at a time and touched their hands to her chest, wanting to grab on to the solace in her heart. "They did this every Sunday in the praise house, dancing and touching her chest, and eventually they painted a red heart on her breast so the people 15
would have a heart to touch.

"Our Lady filled their hearts with fearlessness and whispered to them plans of escape. The bold ones fled, finding their way north, and those who didn't lived with a raised fist in their hearts. And if ever it grew weak, they would only have to touch her heart again.   20

"She grew so powerful she became known even to the master. One day he hauled her off on a wagon and chained her in the carriage house. But then, without any human help, she escaped during the night and made her way back to the praise house. The master chained her in the barn fifty times, and fifty times she loosed 25
the chains and went home. Finally he gave up and let her stay there."

The room grew quiet as August stood there a minute, letting everything sink in. When she spoke again, she raised her arms out beside her. "The people called her Our Lady of Chains. They called her that not because she *wore* chains …"   30

"*Not because she wore chains,*" the Daughters chanted.

---

10 **fractured**: broken   13 **solace**: comfort   23 **carriage house** (AE): farm building where horses were kept   25 **barn**: farm building

"They called her Our Lady of Chains because *she broke them.*"

June wedged the cello between her legs and played "Amazing Grace," and the Daughters of Mary got to their feet and swayed together like colorful seaweed on the ocean floor.

5   I thought this was the grand finale, but no, June switched over to the piano and banged out a jazzed-up version of "Go Tell It on the Mountain." That's when August started a conga line. She danced over to Lunelle, who latched on to August's waist. Cressie hooked on to Lunelle, followed by Mabelee, and off they went around the room,
10 causing Cressie to grab hold of her crimson hat. When they swung back by, Queenie and Violet joined them, then Sugar-Girl. I wanted to be part of it, too, but I only watched, and so did Rosaleen and Otis.

June seemed to play faster and faster. I fanned my face, trying to
15 get a little air, feeling light-headed.

When the dance ended, the Daughters stood panting in a half circle before Our Lady of Chains, and what they did next took my breath away. One at a time they went and touched the statue's fading red heart.

20 Queenie and her daughter went together and rubbed their palms against the wood. Lunelle pressed her fingers to Mary's heart, then kissed each one of them in a slow, deliberate way, a way that brought tears to my eyes.

Otis pressed his forehead to the heart, standing there the longest
25 time of them all, head to heart, like he was filling up his empty tank.

June kept playing while each of them came, until there was only Rosaleen and me left. May nodded to June to keep on with the music and took Rosaleen's hand, pulling her to Our Lady of Chains, so even Rosaleen got to touch Mary's heart.

30 I wanted to touch her vanishing red heart, too, as much as anything I'd ever wanted. As I rose from my chair, my head was still swimming some. I walked toward black Mary with my hand lifted.

---

6 **bang sth. out**: play sth. with a lot of energy   7 **conga line**: line of dancers
8 **latch on to sb./sth.** (infml): take hold of sb./sth.   16 **pant**: breathe quickly

But just as I was about to reach her, June stopped playing. She stopped right in the middle of the song, and I was left in the silence with my hand stretched out.

Drawing it back, I looked around me, and it was like seeing everything through a train's thick window. A blur passed before me. 5 A moving wave of color. *I am not one of you*, I thought.

My body felt numb. I thought how nice it would be to grow smaller and smaller – until I was a dot of nothing.

I heard August scolding, "June, what got into you?" but her voice was so distant. 10

I called to the Lady of Chains, but maybe I wasn't really saying her name out loud, only hearing myself call on the inside. That's the last I remember. Her name echoing through the empty spaces.

When I woke, I was lying on August's bed across the hall with an ice-cold washcloth folded over my forehead and August and 15 Rosaleen staring down at me. Rosaleen had pulled up the skirt of her dress and was fanning me with it, showing most of her thighs. "Since when have you started fainting?" she said, and sat down on the edge of the bed, causing me to roll into her side. She scooped me into her arms. For some reason this caused my chest to fill with more sadness 20 than I could bear, and I wrestled myself free, claiming I needed a drink of water.

"Maybe it was the heat," August said. "I should've turned on the fans. It must've been ninety degrees in there."

"I'm all right," I told them, but to tell the truth, I was bewildered 25 at myself.

I felt I'd stumbled upon an amazing secret – it was possible to close your eyes and exit life without actually dying. You just had to faint. Only I didn't know how to make it happen, how to pull the plug so I could drain away when I needed to. 30

---

7 **numb**: without feeling   9 **scold sb.**: speak angrily to sb.   15 **washcloth** (AE): *Waschlappen*   25 **bewildered**: confused   27 **stumble on sth.**: accidentally come across sth.   29–30 **pull the plug**: *Stöpsel rausziehen*   30 **drain away**: *weggespült werden*

My fainting spell had broken up the Daughters of Mary and sent May to the wailing wall. June had gone upstairs to her room and locked the door, while the Daughters huddled in the kitchen.

We chalked it up to heat. Heat, we said. Heat would make
5 a person do strange things.

You should have seen how August and Rosaleen fussed over me the rest of the evening. You want some root beer, Lily? How about a feather pillow? Here, swallow this spoon of honey.

We sat in the den, where I ate supper off a tray, which was
10 a privilege in itself. June was still in her room, not answering August's calls at the door, and May, who wasn't allowed near the TV because she'd already spent way too much time today at the wall, was in the kitchen clipping recipes from *McCall's* magazine.

On the television Mr. Cronkite said they were going to send
15 a rocket ship to the moon. "On July twenty-eighth, the United States of America will launch *Ranger Seven* from Cape Kennedy, Florida," he said. It was going to take a 253,665-mile flight before it crash-landed onto the moon. The whole point was to take pictures of the surface and send them back.

20 "Well, baby Jesus," said Rosaleen. "A rocket to the moon." August shook her head. "Next they'll be walking around up there."

We had all thought President Kennedy was off his rocker when he declared we'd land a man on the moon. The Sylvan newspaper had called it a "Luna-tic Vision." I took the article to class for the
25 current-events bulletin board. We all said, A man on the moon. *Right.*

But you can never underestimate the power of cutthroat competition. We wanted to beat the Russians – that was what made the world go around for us. Now it looked like we would.

30 August cut off the TV set. "I need some air."

---

6 **fuss over sb./sth.**: give a lot of attention to sb./sth.   7 **root beer**: sweet soft drink
13 **McCall's magazine**: monthly American women's magazine
22 **be off your rocker** (infml): be crazy   27 **cutthroat**: aggressive

We all went, Rosaleen and August holding on to my elbows in case I started to keel over again.

It was the in-between time, before day leaves and night comes, a time I've never been partial to because of the sadness that lingers in the space between going and coming. August gazed at the sky where 5 the moon was rising, large and ghostly silver.

"Look at her good, Lily," she said, " 'cause you're seeing the end of something."

"I am?"

"Yes, you are, because as long as people have been on this earth, 10 the moon has been a mystery to us. Think about it. She is strong enough to pull the oceans, and when she dies away, she always comes back again. My mama used to tell me Our Lady lived on the moon and that I should dance when her face was bright and hibernate when it was dark." 15

August stared at the sky a long moment and then, turning toward the house, said, "Now it won't ever be the same, not after they've landed up there and walked around on her. She'll be just one more big science project."

I thought about the dream I'd had that night Rosaleen and I slept 20 by the pond, how the moon had cracked to pieces.

August disappeared into the house, and Rosaleen headed for her cot in the honey house, but I stayed on and stared at the sky, imagining *Ranger 7* blasting away for it.

I knew one day I would go back into the parlor when no one was 25 around and touch the Lady's heart. Then I would show August the picture of my mother and see if the moon broke loose and fell out of the sky.

---

2 **keel over**: collapse   4 **be partial to sth.**: like sth.   **linger**: stay for some time
15 **hibernate**: spend the winter in a state like deep sleep   24 **blast away**: move at
full speed

How did bees ever become equated with sex? They do not live a riotous sex life themselves. A hive suggests cloister more than bordello.

The Queen Must Die: And Other Affairs of Bees and Men

Chapter Seven

I jumped every time I heard a siren. It might have been an ambulance off in the distance or a police chase on television – it didn't matter. Part of me was always braced for T. Ray or Mr. Shoe Gaston to drive up and end my charmed life. We had been at August's house eight
5 whole days. I didn't know how long black Mary could keep the curtain drawn.

On Monday morning, July 13, I was walking back to the honey house after breakfast when I noticed a strange black Ford parked in the driveway. I lost my breath for a moment, till I remembered Zach
10 was coming back to work today.

It would be me and August *and* Zach. I'm not proud of it, but I resented the intrusion.

He was not what I expected. I found him inside holding a honey drizzle like a microphone, singing, "I found my thrill on Blueberry
15 Hill." I watched unseen from the doorway, not making a sound, but when he launched into "Viva Las Vegas," slinging his hips around Elvis-style, I broke out laughing.

He whirled around, knocking over a tray of brood frames, which made a great big mess all over the floor.

---

riotous: noisy and exciting **cloister**: convent
3 **be braced for sb./sth.**: be prepared for sb./sth.   12 **intrusion**: *Einmischung*

"I was just singing," he said, like this was news to me. "Who are you anyway?"

"Lily," I said. "I'm staying with August and them for a while."

"I'm Zachary Taylor," he said.

"Zachary Taylor was a president," I told him.   5

"Yeah, so I've heard." He fished out a dogtag suspended on a chain under his shirt and held it up to my nose. "See right there. Zachary Lincoln Taylor." He smiled then, and I saw he had a one-side dimple. It's a feature that has always gotten to me.

He went and got a towel and cleaned up the floor. "August told   10
me about you being here and helping us out, but she didn't say anything about you being … white."

"Yep, I'm white, all right," I said. "White as can be."

There was nothing white about Zachary Lincoln Taylor. Even the whites of his eyes weren't exactly white. He had broad shoulders and   15
a narrow waist and short-cropped hair like most of the Negro boys wore, but it was his face I couldn't help staring at. If he was shocked over me being white, I was shocked over him being handsome.

At my school they made fun of colored people's lips and noses. I myself had laughed at these jokes, hoping to fit in. Now I wished   20
I could pen a letter to my school to be read at opening assembly that would tell them how wrong we'd all been. You should see Zachary Taylor, I'd say.

I wondered how August could forget to tell him a thing like the fact that I was white. She'd told *me* plenty about *him*. I knew she was   25
his godmother. That his daddy had left him when he was small, that his mama worked as a lunchroom lady at the same school where June taught. He was about to be a junior at the black high school, where he made all A's and played halfback on the football team. She'd said he ran like the wind, which might be his ticket to a college   30

---

5 **Zachary Taylor**: US President (1849–50)   6 **dogtag**: piece of metal with your name on it   9 **dimple**: small hollow place in the skin   **get to sb.** (infml): have an effect on sb.   16 **short-cropped**: cut very short   21 **opening assembly**: daily ceremony before school

up north. This had struck me as better than I would manage, since
I was probably headed for beauty school now.

I said, "August went out to the Satterfield farm to check on some
hives. She said I should help you in here. What do you want me to
5 do?"

"Grab some frames from the hive boxes over there and help me
load the uncapper, I guess."

"So who do you like best, Fats Domino or Elvis?" I asked,
dropping in the first frame.

10 "Miles Davis," he said.

"I don't know who that is."

"Of course you don't. But he's the best trumpet player in the
world. I'd give anything to play like him."

"Would you give up football?"

15 "How do you know I play football?"

"I know things," I said, and smiled at him.

"I can see that." He was trying not to smile back.

I thought, *We're going to be friends.*

He flipped the switch, and the extractor started to spin, building
20 speed. "So how come you're staying here?"

"Me and Rosaleen are on our way to Virginia to live with my aunt.
My daddy died in a tractor accident, and I haven't had a mother
since I was little, so I'm trying to get to my family up there before
I get put in an orphanage or something."

25 "But how come you're *here*?"

"Oh, you mean at August's. We were hitchhiking and got let out
at Tiburon. We knocked on August's door, and she gave us a bed.
That's it."

He nodded like this made some kind of actual sense.

30 "How long have you worked here?" I asked, happy to change the
subject.

1 **strike sb. as sth.**: give sb. a certain impression

"All through high school. I come after school when it's not football season, every Saturday and all summer. I bought a car with the money I made last year."

"That Ford out there?"

"Yeah, it's a '59 Ford Fairlane," he said.   5

He flipped the switch on the extractor again, and the machine groaned while it came to a stop. "Come on, I'll show you."

I could see my face in the surface of it. I figured he stayed up nights polishing it with his undershirts. I walked along giving it the white-glove inspection.   10

"You can teach me to drive," I said.

"Not in this car."

"Why not?"

"Because you look like the kind of girl who'll wreck something for sure."   15

I turned to face him, ready to defend myself, and saw he was grinning. And there was the one-side dimple again.

"For sure," he said. "Wreck something for sure."

Every day Zach and I worked in the honey house. August and Zach had already extracted most of the honey from her bee yards, but   20
there were still several stacks of supers on pallets sitting around.

We ran the warmer and caught the wax in a tin tub, then loaded the frames into the extractor and filtered the honey through brand-new nylon hose. August liked to keep a little pollen in her honey because it was good for people, so we saw to that, too. Sometimes   25
we broke off pieces of comb and pushed them down into the jars before we filled them. You had to make sure they were new combs with no brood eggs in them, since nobody wanted to have baby bee larvae in their honey.

---

10 **white-glove** (adj): (here) thorough   21 **stack of sth.**: *Stapel*   22 **warmer**: piece of equipment to heat sth.   29 **larva, pl. – ae**: insect at the worm stage

And if we weren't doing all that, we were filling candle molds with beeswax and washing mason jars till my hands turned stiff as corn husk from detergent.

The only part of the day I dreaded was dinner, when I had to be
5 around June. You'd think anybody who played music for dying people would be a nicer person. I couldn't understand why she resented me so much. Somehow even me being white and imposing on their hospitality didn't seem enough reason.

"How are things coming with you, Lily?" she'd say every night at
10 the table. Like she'd rehearsed this in the mirror.

I'd say, "Things are coming fine. And how are they coming with you, June?"

She would glance at August, who would be following all this like she was overcome with interest. "Fine," June would say.

15 Having gotten that out of the way, we would shake out our napkins and do our best to ignore each other the rest of the meal. I knew that August was trying to correct June's rudeness toward me, but I wanted to say to her, *Do you think me and June Boatwright give a damn how each other is coming? Just give up.*

20 One night after the Hail Marys, August said, "Lily, if you wish to touch Our Lady's heart, you're welcome, isn't she, June?"

I glanced at June, who gave me a forced smile.

"Maybe some other time," I said.

I'm here to tell you, if I was dying on my cot in the honey house
25 and the only thing that could save me was June's change of heart, I would meet my death and shoot straight to heaven. Or maybe hell. I wasn't even sure anymore.

The best meal was lunch, which Zach and I ate under the cool of the pine trees. May fixed us bologna sandwiches nearly every single
30 day. We could also count on candlestick salad, which meant half a banana standing up in a pineapple slice. "Let me light your candle," she'd say, and strike an imaginary match. Then she'd fasten a bottled

---

3 **husk**: *Schrot*   **detergent**: washing powder   7 **impose on sth.**: exploit sth.
29 **bologna**: type of sausage that is put in sandwiches   32 **bottle sth.**: put sth. in a
bottle to preserve it

cherry on the tip of the banana with a toothpick. Like Zach and I were still in kindergarten. But we'd go along with her, acting all excited over her lighting the banana. For dessert we crunched cubes of lime Kool-Aid, which she'd frozen in ice trays.

One day we sat on the grass after lunch, listening to the wind 5 snap the sheets Rosaleen had hung on the clothesline.

"What's your favorite subject in school?" Zach asked.

"English."

"I bet you like to write themes," he said, rolling his eyes.

"As a matter of fact I do. I was planning on being a writer and an 10 English teacher in my spare time."

"*Was* planning?" he said.

"I don't think I have much of a future now, being an orphan." What I meant was being a fugitive from the law. Considering the state of things, I didn't know if I'd even get back to high school. 15

He studied his fingers. I could smell the sharp scent of his sweat. He had patches of honey on his shirt, which were attracting a horde of flies and causing him to swat incessantly.

After a while he said, "Me either."

"You either *what*?" 20

"I don't know if I'll have much of a future either."

"Why not? *You're* not an orphan."

"No," he said. "I'm a Negro."

I felt embarrassed. "Well, you could play football for a college team and then be a professional player." 25

"Why is it sports is the only thing white people see us being successful at? I don't want to play football," he said. "I wanna be a lawyer."

"That's fine with me," I said, a little annoyed. "I've just never heard of a Negro lawyer, that's all. You've got to hear of these things 30 before you can imagine them."

"Bullshit. You gotta imagine what's never been."

---

2 **go along with sb./sth.**: (here) *das Spiel mitmachen*   3 **crunch**: crush between your teeth   4 **lime**: *Limone*   **Kool-Aid**: US drink popular with children
9 **theme** (old-fashioned): composition, essay   17 **patch of sth.**: small area of sth.
18 **incessantly**: without interruption

I closed my eyes. "All right then, I'm imagining a Negro lawyer. You are a Negro Perry Mason. People are coming to you from all over the state, wrong-accused people, and you get at the truth at the very last minute by tricking the real criminal on the witness stand."

5 "Yeah," he said, "I bust their ass with the truth." When he laughed, his tongue was grass green from Kool-Aid.

I started calling him Zach the ass-busting lawyer. "Oh, look who's here, Zach the ass-busting lawyer," I'd say.

It was along about this point Rosaleen started asking me what did I
10 think I was doing – auditioning myself to get adopted by the calendar sisters? She said I was living in a dream world. "Dream world" became her favorite two words.

It was living in a dream world to pretend we had a regular life when there was a manhunt going on, to think we could stay here
15 forever, to believe I would find out anything worth knowing about my mother.

Every time I shot back, *What's wrong with living in a dream world?* And she'd say, *You have to wake up.*

One afternoon when I was alone in the honey house, June
20 wandered in looking for August. Or so she said. She crossed her arms over her chest. "So," she said, "you've been here – what? Two weeks now?"

How obvious can you get?

"Look, if you want us to leave, me and Rosaleen will be on our
25 way," I said. "I'll write my aunt, and she'll send us bus money."

She raised her eyebrows. "I thought you didn't remember your aunt's last name, and now you know her name *and* her address."

"Actually, I knew it all along," I said. "I was just hoping for a little time before we had to leave."

---

2 **Perry Mason**: successful lawyer in a popular television series (1957–66)
5 **bust sb.'s ass** (infml, AE): to beat sb.   10 **audition yourself**: *sich selbst etwas vorspielen*

It seemed like her face softened some when I said that, but it could've been wishful thinking on my part.

"Heavens to Betsy, what's this talk about you leaving?" said August, standing in the doorway. Neither one of us had seen her come in. She gave June a hard look. "Nobody wants you to leave, 5 Lily, till you're good and ready."

Standing beside August's desk, I fidgeted with a stack of papers. June cleared her throat. "Well, I need to get back and practice," she said, and breezed out the door.

August walked over and sat down in her desk chair. "Lily, you can 10 talk to me. You know that, don't you?"

When I didn't answer, she caught my hand and drew me to her, pulling me right down onto her lap. It was not mattress deep like Rosaleen's but thin and angular.

I wanted nothing more than to come clean with her. Go pull my 15 bag from underneath the cot and bring out my mother's things. I wanted to produce the black Mary picture and say, *This belonged to my mother, this exact same, identical picture you put on your honey jars. And it has Tiburon, South Carolina, written on the back, so I know she must've been here.* I wanted to hold up her photograph and say, *Have 20 you ever seen her? Take your time now. Think carefully.*

But I hadn't yet pressed my hand to the black Mary's heart in the parlor, and I was too afraid to say all this without having done at least that. I leaned against August's chest, pushing aside my secret wanting, too afraid she'd say, *No, I never saw this woman in my life.* 25 And that would be that. Not knowing anything at all was better.

I struggled to my feet. "I guess I'll go help in the kitchen." I crossed the yard without a glance back.

That night, when the darkness was weighed down with singing crickets and Rosaleen was snoring right along with them, I had 30 myself a good cry. I couldn't even say why. Just everything, I guess. Because I hated lying to August when she was so good to me.

---

3 **heavens to Betsy**: mild swear word   7 **fidget**: behave nervously
9 **breeze out**: walk out   15 **come clean with sb.**: explain a secret to sb.
29 **weigh down**: make heavy

Because Rosaleen was probably right about dream worlds. Because I was pretty sure the Virgin Mary was not back there on the peach farm standing in for me the way she'd stood in for Beatrix.

Neil came over most evenings and sat with June in the parlor while
5 the rest of us watched *The Fugitive* on television in the den. August said she wished the fugitive would go ahead and find the one-armed man and get it over with.

During commercials I pretended to go for water and instead crept down the hall, where I tried to make out what June and Neil were
10 saying.

"I'd like you to tell me why not," I heard Neil say one evening. And June, "Because I can't."

"That's not a reason."

"Well, it's the only one I've got."

15 "Look, I'm not gonna wait around forever," Neil said.

I was anticipating what June would say to that, when Neil came through the door without warning and caught me pressed against the wall listening to their most private sayings. He looked for a second like he might turn me over to June, but he left, banging the
20 front door behind him.

I hightailed it back to the den, but not before I heard the beginnings of a sob in June's throat.

One morning August sent Zach and me six miles out in the county to bring in the last of the supers to be harvested. Lord, it was hot,
25 plus we had at least ten gnats per square inch of air.

Zach drove the honey wagon as fast as it would go, which was about thirty miles an hour. The wind whipped my hair and flooded the truck with a weedy, new-mown smell.

---

5 **The Fugitive**: popular US television series (1963–7)
7 **get sth. over with** (infml): finish an unpleasant task
21 **hightail it** (infml, AE): leave quickly   22 **sob**: *Schluchzen*   25 **gnat**: *Stechmücke*

The roadsides were covered with fresh-picked cotton, blown from the trucks carrying it to the gin in Tiburon. Zach said the farmers had planted and harvested their cotton early this year because of the boll weevil. Scattered along the highway, it looked for all the world like snow, which made me wish for a blizzard to come 5 cool things down.

I went off into a daydream about Zach pulling the truck over because he couldn't see to drive for the snow and us having a snowball fight, blasting each other with soft white snow cotton. I imagined us building a snow cave, sleeping with our bodies twined 10 together to get warm, our arms and legs like black-and-white braids. This last thought shocked my system so bad I shivered. I stuck my hands under my arms, and my sweat was ice-water cold.

"You all right?" asked Zach.

"Yeah, why?" 15

"You're shaking over there."

"I'm fine. I do that sometimes."

I turned away and looked out the window, where there was nothing but fields and now and then a falling-down wooden barn or some old, abandoned colored house. "How much further?" I said in 20 a way that suggested the excursion could not be over too soon.

"You upset or something?"

I refused to answer him, glaring instead through the dirty windshield.

When we turned off the highway onto a beat-up dirt road, Zach 25 said we were on property belonging to Mr. Clayton Forrest, who kept Black Madonna Honey and beeswax candles in the waiting room of his law office so his customers could buy them. Part of Zach's job was going around to deliver fresh supplies of honey and candles to places that sold them on consignment. 30

"Mr. Forrest lets me poke around his law office," he said.

"Uh-huh."

"He tells me about the cases he's won."

2 **gin**: place where cotton is processed   4 **boll weevil**: insect that eats cotton plants
10–11 **twine sth. together**: bind sth. together   11 **braid** (AE): *Zopf*
25 **dirt road** (AE): road of hard earth   30 **sell sth. on consignment**: sell sth. for
sb. else

We hit a rut and bounced on the seat so hard our heads rammed into the truck roof, which for some reason flipped my mood upside down. I started to laugh like somebody was holding me down tickling my armpits. The more my head slammed against the truck,
5 the worse it got, till I was having one big, hilarious seizure. I laughed the way May cried.

At first Zach aimed for the ruts just to hear me, but then he got nervous because I couldn't seem to stop. He cleared his throat and slowed way down till we were bounce-free.

10 Finally it drained out of me, whatever it was. I remembered the pleasure of fainting that day during the Daughters of Mary meeting and thought now how much I would like to keel over right here in the truck. I envied turtles their shells, how they could disappear at will.

15 I was conscious of Zach's breathing, his shirt pulled across his chest, one arm draped on the steering wheel. The hard, dark look of it. The mystery of his skin.

It was foolish to think some things were beyond happening, even being attracted to Negroes. I'd honestly thought such a thing couldn't
20 happen, the way water could not run uphill or salt could not taste sweet. A law of nature. Maybe it was a simple matter of being attracted to what I couldn't have. Or maybe desire kicked in when it pleased without noticing the rules we lived and died by. *You gotta imagine what's never been*, Zach had said.

25 He stopped the honey wagon beside a cluster of twenty hives tucked in a thicket of trees, where the bees could have shade in the summer and shelter from the wind through the winter. Bees were more fragile than I ever imagined. If it wasn't mites ruining them, it was pesticides or terrible weather.

30 He climbed out and dragged a load of equipment off the back of the truck – helmets, extra supers, fresh brood frames, and the smoker, which he handed me to light. I moved through camphorweed

---

1 **rut**: deep track in the dirt road   **bounce**: move up and down
1–2 **ram into sth.**: hit sth.   4 **tickle**: *kitzeln*   5 **hilarious**: very funny
seizure: uncontrollable fit   13–14 **at will**: whenever you like   28 **mite**: small
insect   32 **camphorweed**: *Kamphergras*

and wild azalea, stepping over fire-ant mounds and swinging the smoker while he lifted the lids off the hives and peered inside looking for capped frames.

He moved like a person with a genuine love of bees. I could not believe how gentle and softhearted he could be. One of the frames he lifted out leaked honey the color of plums.

"It's purple!" I said.

"When the weather turns hot and the flowers dry up, the bees start sucking elderberry. It makes a purple honey. People will pay two dollars a jar for purple honey."

He dipped his finger into the comb and, lifting my veil, brought it close to my lips. I opened my mouth, let his finger slide in, sucking it clean. The sheerest smile brushed his lips, and heat rushed up my body. He bent toward me. I wanted him to lift back my veil and kiss me, and I knew he wanted to do it, too, by the way he fixed his eyes on mine. We stayed like that while bees swirled around our heads with a sound like sizzling bacon, a sound that no longer registered as danger. Danger, I realized, was a thing you got used to.

But instead of kissing me, he turned to the next hive and went right on with his work. The smoker had gone out. I followed behind him, and neither of us spoke. We stacked the filled supers onto the truck like the cat had our tongues, and neither of us said a word till we were back in the honey truck passing the city-limits sign.

TIBURON, POPULATION 6,502
Home of Willifred Marchant

"Who is Willifred Marchant?" I said, desperate to break the silence and get things back to normal.

"You mean you've never heard of Willifred Marchant?" he said. "She is only a world-famous writer who wrote three Pulitzer Prize books about the deciduous trees of South Carolina."

---

1 **fire ant**: a variety of stinging ants   9 **elderberry**: *Holunder*   22 **the cat has your tongue**: used to describe silent people   29 **Pulitzer Prize**: US prize awarded to outstanding writers   30 **deciduous tree**: *laubabwerfender Baum*

I giggled. "They didn't win any Pulitzer Prizes."

"You better shut your mouth, because in Tiburon, Willifred Marchant's books are way up there with the Bible. We have an official Willifred Marchant Day every year, and the schools hold tree-
5 planting ceremonies. She always comes wearing a big straw hat and carrying a basket of rose petals, which she tosses to the children."

"She does not," I said.

"Oh, yes. Miss Willie is very weird."

"Deciduous trees are an interesting topic, I guess. But I myself
10 would rather write about people."

"Oh, that's right, I forgot," he said. "You're planning on being a writer. You and Miss Willie."

"You act like you don't believe I can do it."

"I didn't say that."

15 "You implied it."

"What are you talking about? I did not."

I turned to concentrate on things beyond the window. The Masonic Lodge, Hot Buy Used Cars, the Firestone Tire store.

Zach braked at a stop sign next to the Dixie Cafe, which sat
20 practically in the front yard of the Tri-County Livestock Company, and for some reason this made me furious. What I wanted to know was how people ate breakfast, lunch, and dinner with the smell of cows – and worse – overwhelming their nose buds. I wanted to scream out the window, "Eat your damned breakfast grits somewhere
25 else, why don't you? There's cow shit in the air!" The way people lived their lives, settling for grits and cow shit, made me sick. My eyes stung all around the sockets.

Zach crossed the intersection. I could feel his eyes bore into the back of my head. "You mad at me?" he said.

30 I meant to say, *Yes, I most certainly am, because you think I will never amount to anything.* But what came out of my mouth was something else, and it was embarrassingly stupid. "I will never throw rose petals

---

8 **weird**: strange   23 **nose bud**: *Riechnerv*   28 **intersection**: place where two roads cross each other   **bore**: dig a hole

to anybody," I said, and then I broke down, the kind of crying where you're sucking air and making heaving sounds like a person drowning.

Zach pulled over on the side of the road, saying, "Holy moly. What's the matter?" He wrapped one arm around me and pulled me 5 across the seat to him.

I'd thought the whole thing was about my lost future, the one Mrs. Henry encouraged me to believe in by plying me with books and summer reading lists and big talk about scholarships to Columbia College, but sitting there close to Zach, I knew I was 10 crying because he had that one-side dimple I loved, because every time I looked at him I got a hot, funny feeling that circulated from my waist to my kneecaps, because I'd been going along being my normal girl self and the next thing I knew I'd passed through a membrane into a place of desperation. I was crying, I realized, for 15 Zach.

I laid my head on his shoulder and wondered how he could stand me. In one short morning I had exhibited insane laughter, hidden lust, pissy behavior, self-pity, and hysterical crying. If I'd been *trying* to show him my worst sides, I could not have done a better job than 20 this.

He gave me a squeeze and spoke into my hair. "It's gonna be all right. You're gonna be a fine writer one day." I saw him glance behind us, then across the road. "Now, you go back over to your side of the truck and wipe your face," he said, and handed me a floor rag that 25 smelled like gasoline.

When we got to the honey house, it was deserted except for Rosaleen, who was gathering up her clothes so she could move up to May's room. I'd been gone two slim hours, and our whole living arrangement had been overturned. 30

---

4 **holy moly**: mild swear word   8 **ply sb. with sth.**: keep giving sth. to sb.
19 **pissy** (infml, derog): sulky, annoying

"How come you get to sleep over there?" I asked her.

" 'Cause May gets scared at night by herself."

Rosaleen was going to sleep in the extra twin bed, get the bottom drawer of May's dresser for her stuff, and have the bathroom at her
5 fingertips.

"I can't believe you're leaving me over here by myself!" I cried. Zach grabbed the hand truck and wheeled it out as fast as he could to start unloading the supers from the honey wagon. I think he'd had enough female emotion for the time being.

10 "I'm not leaving you. I'm getting a mattress," she said, and dropped her toothbrush and the Red Rose snuff into her pocket.

I crossed my arms over my blouse that was still damp from all the crying I'd been doing. "Fine then, go on. I don't care."

"Lily, that cot is bad on my back. And if you ain't noticed, the legs
15 on it are all bent out of whack now. Another week and it's gonna collapse on the floor. You'll be fine without me."

My chest closed up. Fine without her. Was she out of her mind?

"I don't wanna wake up from the dream world," I said, and midsentence my voice cracked, and the words twisted and turned in
20 my mouth.

She sat on the cot, the cot I now hated with a passion because it had driven her to May's room. She pulled me down beside her. "I know you don't, but I'll be here when you do. I might sleep up there in May's room, but I'm not going anywhere."

25 She patted my knee like old times. She patted, and neither of us said anything. We could've been back in the policeman's car riding to jail for how I felt. Like I would not exist without her patting hand.

I followed Rosaleen as she carried her few things over to the pink house, intending to inspect her new room. We climbed the steps
30 onto the screen porch. August sat on the porch swing that was

---

15 **out of whack** (infml): not working well

suspended from two chains in the ceiling. She was rocking back and forth, having her orangeade break and reading her new book, which she'd gotten from the bookmobile. I turned my head to read the title. *Jane Eyre*.

May was on the other side of the porch running clothes through ⁵ the rubber rollers on the wringer washing machine. A brand-new pink Lady Kenmore, which they kept out on the porch because there was no room in the kitchen. In television commercials the woman who worked the Lady Kenmore wore an evening gown and seemed to be enjoying herself. May just looked hot and tired. She smiled as 10 Rosaleen went by with her things.

"Are you okay with Rosaleen moving over here?" August said, propping the book on her stomach. She took a sip of her drink, then ran her hand across the cold moisture on the glass and pressed her palm to the front of her neck. 15

"I guess so."

"May will sleep better with Rosaleen in there," she said. "Won't you, May?" I glanced over at May, but she didn't seem to hear over the washer.

Suddenly the last thing I wanted was to follow Rosaleen and 20 watch her tuck her clothes into May's dresser. I looked at August's book.

"What are you reading about?" I asked, thinking I was making casual conversation, but boy, was I wrong.

"It's about a girl whose mother died when she was little," she said. 25 Then she looked at me in a way that made my stomach tip over, the same way it'd tipped over when she'd told me about Beatrix.

"What happens to the girl?" I asked, trying to make my voice steady.

"I've only started the book," she said. "But right now she's just 30 feeling lost and sad."

---

4 **Jane Eyre**: novel by Charlotte Brontë about an orphan girl (1847)
6 r**ubber roller**: *Gummirolle*   **wringer washing machine**: machine for squeezing water out of clothes   7 **Kenmore**: US brand of household machines
9 **evening gown**: long woman's dress for special occasions

I turned and looked out toward the garden, where June and Neil were picking tomatoes. I stared at them while the crank on the washer squeaked. I could hear the clothes falling into the basin behind the rollers. *She knows,* I thought. *She knows who I am.*

5 I stretched out my arms like I was pushing back invisible walls of air and, looking down, caught sight of my shadow on the floor, this skinny girl with wild hair curling up in the humidity, with her arms flung out and her palms erect like she was trying to stop traffic in both directions. I wanted to bend down and kiss her, for how small 10 and determined she looked.

When I glanced back at August, she was still staring at me, like she expected me to say something.

"Well, I guess I'll go see Rosaleen's new bed," I said.

August picked up her book, and that was that. The moment 15 passed, and so did the feeling that she knew who I was. I mean, it didn't make sense: how could August Boatwright know anything about me?

It was around this time that June and Neil started a first-class fight out there in the tomato garden. June shouted something, and 20 he shouted back.

"Uh-oh," said August. She put down the book and stood up.

"Why can't you just let it be?" yelled June. "Why does it always come back to this? Get this through your head: I'm not getting married. Not yesterday, not today, not next year!"

25 "What are you scared of?" Neil said.

"For your information, I'm not scared of anything."

"Well, then, you're the most selfish bitch I ever met," he said, and started walking toward his car.

"Oh, Lord," said August under her breath.

30 "How dare you call me that!" said June. "You come back here. Don't you walk off when I'm talking to you!"

2 **crank**: *Kurbel*

Neil kept right on walking, didn't look over his shoulder once. Zach, I noticed, had stopped loading supers onto the hand truck and watched, shaking his head like he couldn't believe he was witnessing another scene where people's worst sides come out.

"If you leave now, don't plan on coming back!" she yelled. Neil ⁵ climbed into his car, and suddenly June came running with tomatoes in her hands. She reared back and threw one, *smat!* right into the windshield. The second one landed on the door handle.

"Don't you come back!" she yelled as Neil drove off. Trailing tomato juice. ₁₀

May sank down onto the floor, crying and looking so hurt inside I could almost see soft, red places up under her rib bones. August and I walked her out to her wall, and for the umpteenth time she wrote *June and Neil* on a scrap of paper and wedged it between the rocks. ₁₅

We spent the rest of the day working on the supers that Zach and I had hauled in. Stacked six high, they made a miniature skyline all through the honey house. August said it looked like Bee City in there.

We ran twelve extractor loads through the whole system – all the ₂₀ way from the uncapping knife to the bottling tank. August didn't like her honey to sit around waiting too long, because the flavor got lost. We had two days to finish it up, she said. Period. At least we didn't have to store the honey in a special hot room to keep it from crystallizing, because every room we had was a hot room. Sometimes ₂₅ Carolina heat turned out to be good for something.

Just when I thought we were done for the day and could go eat dinner and say our evening prayers with the beads, no, we were just beginning. August had us load up the empty supers and haul them out to the woods so the bees could come and do the big cleanup. ₃₀

---

7 **rear back**: move back   13 **for the umpteenth time**: *zum x-ten Mal*
21 **bottling tank**: tank containing processed honey

She would not store her supers for the winter until the bees had
sucked out the last remaining bits of honey from the combs. She said
that was because honey remnants attracted roaches. But really, I'm
sure it was because she loved throwing a little end-of-the-year party
5 for her bees, seeing them descend on the supers like they'd
discovered honey heaven.

The whole time we worked, I marveled at how mixed up people
got when it came to love. I myself, for instance. It seemed like I was
now thinking of Zach forty minutes out of every hour, Zach, who
10 was an impossibility. That's what I told myself five hundred times:
impossibility. I can tell you this much: the word is a great big log
thrown on the fires of love.

That night it felt strange to be in the honey house by myself. I missed
Rosaleen's snoring the way you'd miss the sound of ocean waves
15 after you've gotten used to sleeping with them. I didn't realize how it
had comforted me. Quietness has a strange, spongy hum that can
nearly break your eardrums.

I didn't know if it was the emptiness, the stifling heat, or the fact
it was only nine o'clock, but I couldn't settle into sleep despite how
20 tired I was. I peeled off my top and my underwear and lay on the
damp sheets. I liked the feel of nudeness. It was a smooth, oiled
feeling on the sheets, a set-free feeling.

I imagined then that I heard a car pull into the driveway.
I imagined it was Zach, and the thought of him moving in the night
25 just outside the honey house caused my breath to speed up.

I rose and slipped across the dark space to the wall mirror. Pearled
light poured through the open window behind me, molding to my
skin, giving me a true halo, not just around my head but across my
shoulders, along my ribs and thighs. I was the last person to deserve
30 a halo, but I studied the effect, cupping my hands under my breasts,

---

3 **remnant**: what is left over   7 **marvel at sth.**: be surprised by sth.   11 **log**: piece
of wood   16 **spongy**: with qualities of a sponge   17 **eardrum**: *Trommelfell*
30 **cup your hand**: curve your hand in a cup shape

studying my pinky-brown nipples, the thin curves of my waist,
every soft and glowing turn. It was the first time I'd felt like more
than a scraggly girl.

I closed my eyes, and the balloon full of craving finally burst
open in my chest, and when it did, wouldn't you know – one minute   5
I was dreaming of Zach and the next I was hungering for my mother,
imagining her calling my name, saying, *Lily, girl. You are my flower.*

When I turned to the window, there was no one there. Not that
I had expected there would be.

Two days later, after we had run ourselves into the ground harvesting   10
the rest of the honey, Zach showed up with the prettiest notebook –
green with rosebuds on the cover. He met me coming out of the pink
house. "This is for you," he said. "So you can get a head start on your
writing."

That's when I knew I would never find a better friend than   15
Zachary Taylor. I threw my arms around him and leaned into his
chest. He made a sound like *Whoa*, but after a second his arms
folded around me, and we stayed like that, in a true embrace. He
moved his hands up and down my back, till I was almost dizzy.

Finally he unwound my arms and said, "Lily, I like you better   20
than any girl I've ever known, but you have to understand, there are
people who would kill boys like me for even looking at girls like
you."

I couldn't restrain myself from touching his face, the place where
his dimple caved into his skin. "I'm sorry," I said.   25

"Yeah. Me, too," he said.

For days I carried the notebook everywhere. I wrote constantly.
A made-up story about Rosaleen losing eighty-five pounds, looking
so sleek nobody could pick her out of a police lineup. One about
August driving a honeymobile around, similar to the bookmobile,   30

---

3 **scraggly**: very thin and underdeveloped   4 **craving**: strong desire
10 **run yourself into the ground**: work so hard that you become extremely tired
13 **head-start**: advantage   16–17 **lean into sb./sth.**: bend towards sb./sth.
25 **cave into sth.**: *einsinken*   29 **sleek**: slim and attractive

only she had jars of honey to dispense instead of books. My favorite, though, was one about Zach becoming the ass-busting lawyer and getting his own television show like Perry Mason. I read it to him during lunch one day, and he listened better than a child at story
5   hour.

"Move over, Willifred Marchant" was all he said.

1 **dispense sth.**: distribute sth.

Honeybees depend not only on physical contact with the colony, but also require its social companionship and support. Isolate a honeybee from her sisters and she will soon die.

The Queen Must Die: And Other Affairs of Bees and Men

Chapter Eight

August tore the page for July from the wall calendar that hung by her desk in the honey house. I wanted to tell her that technically it was still July for five more days, but I figured she knew already. It was a simple case of her wanting July over with so she could start into August, her special month. Just like June was June's month and May belonged to May.

August had explained to me how when they were children and their special month came around, their mother excused them from house chores and let them eat all their favorite foods even if it wrecked their teeth and stay up a full hour later at night doing whatever their heart desired. August said her heart had desired to read books, so the whole month she got to prop on the sofa in the quiet of the living room reading after her sisters went to bed. To listen to August talk, it had been the highlight of her youth.

After hearing this, I'd spent a good amount of time trying to think up which month I would have liked to have been named for. I picked October, as it is a golden month with better-than-average weather, and my initials would be O.O. for October Owens, which would make an interesting monogram. I pictured myself eating three-tiered chocolate cake for breakfast throughout the entire month, staying up an hour after bedtime writing high-caliber stories and poems.

I looked over at August, who stood by her desk with the July calendar page in her hand. She wore her white dress with the lime
5 green scarf tied on her belt, just like she was wearing the first day I showed up. The scarf had no purpose hanging there other than adding a touch of flair. She hummed their song: *Place a beehive on my grave and let the honey soak through.* I was thinking what a good, fine mother she must've had.

10 "Come on, Lily," she said. "We've got all these jars of honey to paste labels on, and it's just me and you."

Zach was spending the day delivering honey to her selling places all over town and picking up money from the previous month's sales. "Honey money" was what Zach called it. Even though the big
15 honey flow was over, the bees were still out there sucking nectar, going about their business. (You could not stop a bee from working if you tried.) Zach said August's honey brought fifty cents a pound. I figured she must be dripping in honey money. I didn't see why she wasn't living in a hot pink mansion somewhere.

20 Waiting on August to open a box containing the new shipment of Black Madonna labels, I studied a piece of honeycomb. People don't realize how smart bees are, even smarter than dolphins. Bees know enough geometry to make row after row of perfect hexagons, angles so accurate you'd think they used rulers. They take plain flower
25 juice and turn it into something everyone in the world loves to pour on biscuits. And I have personally witnessed how it took a whole fifteen minutes for about fifty thousand bees to find those empty supers August had left out for them to clean up, passing along the discovery in some kind of advanced bee language. But the main
30 thing is they are hardworking to the point of killing themselves. Sometimes you want to say to them, *Relax, take some time off, you deserve it.*

---

20 **shipment**: *Lieferung*

As August reached down inside the box for the labels, I studied the return address: Holy Virgin Monastery Gift Shop, Post Office Box 45, St. Paul, Minnesota. Next she pulled a fat envelope from her desk drawer and poured out dozens of a different, smaller label with printed letters: BLACK MADONNA HONEY – Tiburon, South Carolina.   5

I was supposed to swipe the backs of both labels with a wet sponge and hand them off to August to position on the jars, but I paused a minute to take in the Black Madonna's picture, which I'd studied so many times glued onto my mother's little block of wood. I admired the fancy gold scarf draped over her head, how it was   10 decorated with red stars. Her eyes were mysterious and kind and her skin dark brown with a glow, darker than toast and looking a little like it had been buttered. It always caused a tiny jump start in my chest, me thinking that my own mother had stared at this same picture.   15

I hated to imagine where I might have ended up if I hadn't seen the Black Madonna's picture that day in the Frogmore Stew General Store and Restaurant. Probably sleeping on creek banks all over South Carolina. Drinking pond water with the cows. Peeing behind chinaberry bushes and wishing for the joy of toilet paper.   20

"I hope you don't take this the wrong way," I said. "But I never thought of the Virgin Mary being colored till I saw this picture."

"A dark-faced Mary is not as unusual as you think," August said. "There are hundreds of them over in Europe, places like France and Spain. The one we put on our honey is old as the hills. She's the   25 Black Madonna of Breznichar in Bohemia."

"How did you learn about all that?" I asked.

She rested her hands and smiled, like this had dredged up a sweet, long-lost memory. "I guess I would have to say it started with my mother's prayer cards. She used to collect them, the way good   30 Catholics did back then – you know, those cards with pictures of saints on them. She'd trade for them like little boys traded baseball

---

6 **swipe**: (here) *bestreichen*   8 **take sth. in**: fully understand sth.   13 **jump start**: *Starthilfe*   20 **chinaberry**: subtropical deciduous tree   28 **rest your hand**: keep your hand still   28–29 **dredge sth. up**: bring sth. forgotten back to life

cards." August let out a big laugh at that. "I bet she had a dozen Black Madonna cards. I used to love to play with her cards, especially the Black Madonnas. Then, when I went off to school, I read everything I could about them. That's how I found out about the
5 Black Madonna of Breznichar in Bohemia."

I tried to say Breznichar, but it didn't come out right. "Well, I can't say her name, but I *love* her picture." I swiped the back of the label and watched August fix it on the jar, then fasten the second label beneath it, as if she'd done this ten thousand times.

10 "What else do you love, Lily?"

No one had ever asked me this before. What did I love? Right off the bat I wanted to say I loved the picture of my mother, how she was leaning against the car with her hair looking just like mine, plus her gloves and her picture of the black Mary with the
15 unpronounceable name, but I had to swallow that back.

I said, "Well, I love Rosaleen, and I love writing stories and poems – just give me something to write and I will love it." After that, I really had to think.

I said, "This may be silly, but after school I love Coca-Cola with
20 salted peanuts poured in the bottle. And when I'm finished with it, I love turning up the bottle to see where it came from." Once I'd gotten a bottle from Massachusetts, which I kept as a tribute to how far something can go in life.

"And I love the color blue – the real bright blue like the hat May
25 had on at the Daughters of Mary meeting. And since coming here, I've learned to love bees and honey." I wanted to add, *And you, I love you*, but I felt too awkward.

"Did you know there are thirty-two names for love in one of the Eskimo languages?" August said. "And we just have this one. We are
30 so limited, you have to use the same word for loving Rosaleen as you do for loving a Coke with peanuts. Isn't that a shame we don't have more ways to say it?"

11–12 **right off the bat** (infml, AE): at once   22–23 **as tribute to sth.**: as proof of sth.

I nodded, wondering where was the limit of her knowing things. Probably one of those books she'd read after bedtime during the month of August had been about Eskimos.

"I guess we'll just have to invent more ways to say it," she said. Then she smiled. "Do you know I love peanuts in my Coke, too? And blue is my favorite color?"

You know that saying, "Birds of a feather flock together"? That's how I felt.

We were working on the jars of tupelo tree honey, which Zach and I had gathered out there on Clayton Forrest's land, plus a few jars of purple honey from the hive where the bees had struck it rich on elderberries. It was a nice color coordination the way the Bohemian Madonna's skin was set off by the golds in the honey. Unfortunately, the purple honey didn't do a whole lot for her.

"How come you put the Black Madonna on your honey?" I asked. I'd been curious about this from day one. Usually people got in a rut putting honey bears on them.

August grew still, holding a jar in her hand and looking into the distance like she'd gone in search of the answer and that finding it had been the bonus of the day. "I wish you could've seen the Daughters of Mary the first time they laid eyes on this label. You know why? Because when they looked at her, it occurred to them for the first time in their lives that what's divine can come in dark skin. You see, everybody needs a God who looks like them, Lily."

I only wished I'd been there when the Daughters of Mary had made this big discovery. I pictured them whooping it up in their glorious hats. Feathers flying.

Sometimes I would catch myself jiggling my foot till I thought it might fall off my leg bone – "jimmy-leg," Rosaleen called it – and looking down now, I noticed it was going at high speed. Usually it happened in the evenings when we did our prayers before Our Lady

---

7 **birds of a feather flock together**: *Gleich und Gleich gesellt sich gern.*
9 t**upelo tree**: type of tree   11–12 **strike it rich on sth.**: (here) to feast on sth.
16 **get in a rut**: get into a habit   26 **whoop it up** (infml, AE): have a lot of fun

of Chains. Like my feet wanted to get up and march around the room in a conga line.

"So how did you get the black Mary statue in the parlor?" I asked.

"I can't say, exactly. I only know she came into the family at some point. You remember the story about Obadiah taking the statue to the praise house, and how the slaves believed it was Mary who had come to be among them?"

I nodded. I remembered every detail. I'd seen it a hundred times in my mind since she'd first told it. Obadiah down on his knees in the mud, bent over the washed-up statue. The statue standing proud in the praise house, Our Lady's fist in the air and all the people coming up one at a time to touch her heart, hoping to find a little strength to go on.

"Well," August said, going right on with her pasting, "you know, she's really just the figurehead off an old ship, but the people needed comfort and rescue, so when they looked at it, they saw Mary, and so the spirit of Mary took it over. Really, her spirit is everywhere, Lily, just everywhere. Inside rocks and trees and even people, but sometimes it will get concentrated in certain places and just beam out at you in a special way."

I had never thought of it like that, and it gave me a shocked feeling, like maybe I had no idea what kind of world I was actually living in, and maybe the teachers at my school didn't know either, the way they talked about everything being nothing but carbon and oxygen and mineral, the dullest stuff you can imagine. I started thinking about the world loaded with disguised Marys sitting around all over the place and hidden red hearts tucked about that people could rub and touch, only we didn't recognize them.

August arranged the jars she'd labeled so far in a cardboard box and set it on the floor, then dragged out more jars. "I'm just trying to explain to you why the people took such care with Our Lady of Chains, passing her one generation to the next. The best we can

figure, sometime after the Civil War she came into the possession of
my grandmother's people.

"When I was younger than you, me and June and May – and
April, too, because she was still alive then – all of us would visit our
grandmother for the whole summer. We'd sit on the rug in the   5
parlor, and Big Mama – that's what we called her – would tell us the
story. Every time, when she finished, May would say, 'Big Mama, tell
it again,' and off she'd go, repeating the whole thing. I swear, if you
listen to my chest with a stethoscope, what you'd hear is that story
going on and on in my Big Mama's voice."   10

I was so caught up in what August was saying I had stopped
wetting labels. I was wishing I had a story like that one to live inside
me with so much loudness you could pick it up on a stethoscope,
and not the story I did have about ending my mother's life and sort
of ending my own at the same time.   15

"You can wet the labels and listen," August said, and smiled. "So,
after Big Mama died, Our Lady of Chains was passed to my mother.
She stayed in Mother's bedroom. My father hated her being in there.
He wanted to get rid of the statue, but Mother said, 'If she goes, I go.'
I think the statue was the reason Mother became a Catholic, so she   20
could kneel down before her and not feel like she was doing anything
peculiar. We would find her in there talking to Our Lady like they
were two neighbors having sweet iced tea. Mother would tease Our
Lady; she'd say, 'You know what? You should've had a girl instead.' "

August set down the jar she was working on, and there was a mix   25
of sorrow and amusement and longing across her face, and I thought,
She is missing her mother.

I stopped wetting the labels, not wanting to get ahead of her.
When she picked up the jar again, I said, "Did you grow up in this
house?" I wanted to know everything there was about her.   30

---

11 **be caught up in sth.**: be absorbed in sth.

She shook her head. "No, but my mother did. This is where I spent my summers," she said. "You see, the house belonged to my grandparents, and all this property around it. Big Mama kept bees, too, right out there in the same spot they're in today. Nobody around
5 here had ever seen a lady beekeeper till her. She liked to tell everybody that women made the best beekeepers 'cause they have a special ability built into them to love creatures that sting. 'It comes from years of loving children and husbands,' she'd say." August laughed, and so did I.

10 "Was your Big Mama the one who taught you to keep bees?" August took off her glasses and cleaned them on the scarf at her waist. "She taught me lots more about bees than just how to keep them. She used to tell me one tall bee tale after another."

I perked up. "Tell me one," I said.

15 August thumped her finger on her forehead like she was trying to tap one of them off some back shelf in her head. Then her eyes lit up, and she said, "Well, one time Big Mama told me she went out to the hives on Christmas Eve and heard the bees singing the words of the Christmas story right out of the gospel of Luke." August started
20 to sing then in a humming sort of way, " 'Mary brought forth her firstborn child and wrapped him in swaddling clothes and laid him in the manger.' "

I giggled. "Do you think that really happened?"

"Well, yes and no," she said. "Some things happen in a literal way,
25 Lily. And then other things, like this one, happen in a notliteral way, but they still happen. Do you know what I mean?"

I didn't have a clue. "Not really," I said.

"What I mean is that the bees weren't *really* singing the words from Luke, but still, if you have the right kind of ears, you can listen
30 to a hive and hear the Christmas story somewhere inside yourself. You can hear silent things on the other side of the everyday world that nobody else can. Big Mama had those kind of ears. Now, my

13 **tall tale**: unbelievable story   14 **perk up**: become interested
21 **swaddling clothes**: strips of cloth used in the past for wrapping a baby
22 **manger**: container that cows eat from

mother, she didn't really have that gift. I think it skipped a generation."

I was itching to know more about her mother. "I bet your mother kept bees, too," I said.

She seemed amused at that. "Goodness no, she wasn't interested at all. She left here as soon as she could and went to live with a cousin up in Richmond. Got a job in a hotel laundry. You remember the first day you got here, I told you I grew up in Richmond? Well, that's where my father was from. He was the first colored dentist in Richmond. He met my mother when she went to see him with a toothache."

I sat there a minute and thought about the odd ways of life. If it wasn't for a toothache, August wouldn't be here. Or May or June, or Black Madonna Honey, and I wouldn't be sitting here talking to her.

"I loved Richmond, but my heart was always right here," she said. "Growing up, I couldn't wait to get here and spend the summers, and when Big Mama died, she left all this property to me, June, and May. I've been here keeping bees nearly eighteen years now."

Sunlight gleamed against the honey-house window, flickering now and then with a shifting cloud. We sat in the yellowish quiet for a while and worked without talking. I was afraid I'd tire her out with all my questions. Finally I couldn't hold myself back. I said, "So what did you do in Virginia before you came here?"

She gave me a teasing look that seemed to say, *My goodness, you sure do wanna know a lot of things*, but then she dived right in, her hands not slowing down one bit pasting labels.

"I studied at a Negro teachers' college in Maryland. June did, too, but it was hard to get a job, since there weren't that many places for Negroes to teach. I ended up working nine years as a housekeeper. Eventually I got a job teaching history. It lasted six years, till we moved down here."

"What about June?"

---

3 **be itching to do sth**.: want very much to do sth.   19 **flicker**: move unsteadily

She laughed. "June – you wouldn't catch her keeping house for white people. She went to work at a colored funeral home, dressing the bodies and doing their hair."

That seemed like the perfect job for her. It would be easy for her to get along with dead people.

"May said June almost got married one time."

"That's right. About ten years ago."

"I was wondering – " I stopped, looking for a way to ask her.

"You were wondering if there was ever a time when I almost got married."

"Yeah," I said. "I guess I was."

"I decided against marrying altogether. There were enough restrictions in my life without someone expecting me to wait on him hand and foot. Not that I'm against marrying, Lily. I'm just against how it's set up."

I was thinking, *Well, it's not just marriage that's set up like that.* What about me waiting on T. Ray hand and foot, and we were just father and daughter? *Pour me some more tea, Lily. Polish my shoes, Lily. Go get the truck keys, Lily.* I sincerely hoped she didn't mean this sort of thing went on in a marriage.

"Weren't you ever in love?" I asked.

"Being in love and getting married, now, that's two different things. I was in love once, of course I was. Nobody should go through life without falling in love."

"But you didn't love him enough to marry him?"

She smiled at me. "I loved him enough," she said. "I just loved my freedom more."

We glued labels till we ran out of jars. Then, for the heck of it, I moistened the back of one more and pressed it onto my T-shirt, in the gully between my breasts.

August looked at the clock, announcing we'd done so good with our time we had a whole hour left before lunch.

"Come on," she said. "Let's do bee patrol."

---

2 **funeral home**: place where dead people are kept before being buried
12–13 **wait on sb. hand and foot**: be sb.'s servant while they do nothing
27 **for the heck of it** (infml): for no good reason

✲

Though I'd done bee patrol with Zach, I hadn't been back to the
hives with August since that first time. I pulled on long cotton pants
that used to be June's and August's white shirt, which needed the
sleeves rolled up about ten turns. Then I placed the jungle helmet on
my head, letting the veil fall down over my face.   5

We walked to the woods beside the pink house with her stories
still pulled soft around our shoulders. I could feel them touching me
in places, like an actual shawl.

"There is one thing I don't get," I said.

"What's that?"   10

"How come if your favorite color is blue, you painted your house
so pink?"

She laughed. "That was May's doing. She was with me the day
I went to the paint store to pick out the color. I had a nice tan color
in mind, but May latched on to this sample called Caribbean Pink.   15
She said it made her feel like dancing a Spanish flamenco. I thought,
'Well, this is the tackiest color I've ever seen, and we'll have half the
town talking about us, but if it can lift May's heart like that, I guess
she ought to live inside it.' "

"All this time I just figured you liked pink," I said.   20

She laughed again. "You know, some things don't matter that
much, Lily. Like the color of a house. How big is that in the overall
scheme of life? But lifting a person's heart – now, *that* matters. The
whole problem with people is –"

"They don't know what matters and what doesn't," I said, filling   25
in her sentence and feeling proud of myself for doing so.

"I was gonna say, The problem is they *know* what matters, but
they don't *choose* it. You know how hard that is, Lily? I love May, but
it was still so hard to *choose* Caribbean Pink. The hardest thing on
earth is choosing what matters."   30

14 **tan**: brownish-yellow   17 **tacky** (infml): cheap and tasteless

I couldn't locate a stray bee anywhere. The hives looked like an abandoned neighborhood, the air groggy with heat. You got the impression the bees were inside having a big siesta. Maybe all that excessive work had finally caught up with them.

5 "Where are they?" I said.

August placed her finger to her lips, signaling me to be quiet. She lifted off her helmet and laid the side of her face flat against the top of the hive box. "Come listen," she whispered.

I removed my hat, tucking it under my arm, and placed my face
10 next to hers so that we were practically nose to nose.

"You hear that?" she said.

A sound rushed up. A perfect hum, high-pitched and swollen, like someone had put the teakettle on and it had come to a boil. "They're cooling the hives down," she said, and her breath broke
15 over my face with the smell of spearmint. "That's the sound of one hundred thousand bee wings fanning the air."

She closed her eyes and soaked it in the way you imagine people at a fancy orchestra concert drinking up highbrow music. I hope it's not too backward to say that I felt like I had never heard anything on
20 my hi-fi back home that came out that good. You would have to hear it yourself to believe the perfect pitch, the harmony parts, how the volume rolled up and down. We had our ears pressed to a giant music box.

Then the whole side of my face started to vibrate as if the music
25 had rushed into my pores. I could see August's skin pulsating the tiniest bit. When we stood back up, my cheek prickled and itched.

"You were listening to bee air-conditioning," August said. "Most people don't have any idea about all the complicated life going on inside a hive. Bees have a secret life we don't know anything about."
30 I loved the idea of bees having a secret life, just like the one I was living.

---

1 **stray bee**: bee that has lost its hive   2 **groggy** (infml): tired, weak
18 **highbrow**: serious cultural entertainment   19 **backward**: old-fashioned
26 **prickle**: sting   **itch**: *jucken*

"What other secrets have they got?" I wanted to know.

"Well, for instance, every bee has its role to play."

She went through the whole thing. The nest builders were the group that drew the comb. I told her the way they created hexagons, they must be the ones who could do math in their heads, and she 5 smiled and said, yes, nest builders had true math aptitude.

Field bees were the ones with good navigation skills and tireless hearts, going out to gather nectar and pollen. There was a group called mortician bees whose pitiful job it was to rake the dead bees out of the hive and keep everything on the clean side. Nurse bees, 10 August said, had a gift for nurturing, and they fed all the baby bees. They were probably the self-sacrificing group, like the women at church socials who said, "No, you take the chicken breast. I'm just fine with the neck and gizzard, really." The only males were the drones who sat around waiting to mate with the queen. 15

"And of course," August said, "there's the queen and her attendants."

"She has attendants?"

"Oh, yes, like ladies-in-waiting. They feed her, bathe her, keep her warm or cool – whatever's needed. You can see them always 20 circled around her, fussing over her. I've even seen them caress her."

August returned her helmet to her head. "I guess I'd want comfort, too, if I did nothing but lay eggs all day long, week in and week out."

"That's all she does – lay eggs?" I wasn't sure what I expected, it 25 wasn't like she wore a crown and sat on a throne giving out royal orders.

"Egg laying is the main thing, Lily. She's the mother of every bee in the hive, and they all depend on her to keep it going. I don't care what their job is – they know the queen is their mother. She's the 30 mother of thousands."

The mother of thousands.

---

9 **mortician** (AE): undertaker   11 **nurture**: feed and care for offspring
14 **gizzard**: part of the stomach that digests the food   19 **lady-in-waiting**: woman
servant to a queen

I put on my helmet as August lifted the lid. The way the bees poured out, rushing up all of a sudden in spirals of chaos and noise, caused me to jump.

"Don't move an inch," said August. "Remember what I told you.
5 Don't be scared."

A bee flew straight at my forehead, collided with the net, and bumped against my skin.

"She's giving you a little warning," August said. "When they bump your forehead, they're saying, *I've got my eye on you, so you be*
10 *careful.* Send them love and everything will be fine."

I love you, I love you, I said in my head. *I LOVE YOU.* I tried to say it thirty-two ways.

August pulled out the brood frames not even wearing her gloves. While she worked, the bees spun around us, gathering strength till
15 they made soft wind on our faces. It reminded me of the way the bees had flown out of my bedroom walls, stranding me at the center of a bee whirlwind.

I watched the different shadows on the ground. The funnel of bees. Me, still as a fence post. August bent over the hive, inspecting
20 the frames, looking for wax buildup on the comb, the halfmoon shape of her helmet bouncing along.

The bees began to light on my shoulders the ways birds sit on telephone wires. They sat along my arms, speckled the bee veil so I could scarcely see through it. *I love you. I love you.* They covered my
25 body, filled the cuffs of my pants.

My breath came faster, and something coiled around my chest and squeezed tighter and tighter, until suddenly, like somebody had snapped off the panic switch, I felt myself go limp. My mind became unnaturally calm, as if part of me had lifted right up out of my body
30 and was sitting on a tree limb watching the spectacle from a safe distance. The other part of me danced with the bees. I wasn't moving

---

16 **strand sb.**: (here) get sb. in a position from which they can't escape
18 **funnel**: *Trichter* 22 **light on sth.**: touch down on sth. 23 **speckle sth.**: form little spots on sth. 25 **cuff**: *Umschlag* 28 **panic switch**: switch to call for help
limp: without energy

a lick, but in my mind I was spinning through the air with them. I had joined the bee conga line.

I sort of forgot where I was. With my eyes closed, I slowly raised my arms, weaving them through the bees, until finally I stood with them stretched out from my sides in a dreamy place I'd never been 5 before. My neck rolled back and my mouth opened. I was floating somewhere, somewhere that didn't rub too close against life. Like I'd chewed the bark from a toothache tree and it had made me dizzy.

Lost in the bees, I felt dropped into a field of enchanted clover that made me immune to everything, as if August had doused me 10 with the bee smoker and quieted me down to the point I could do nothing but raise my arms and sway back and forth.

Then, without warning, all the immunity wore off, and I felt the hollow, spooned-out space between my navel and breastbone begin to ache. The motherless place. I could see my mother in the closet, 15 the stuck window, the suitcase on the floor. I heard the shouting, then the explosion. I almost doubled over. I lowered my arms, but I didn't open my eyes. How could I live the whole rest of my life knowing these things? What could I ever do that would be good enough to make them go away? How come we couldn't go back and 20 fix the bad things we did?

Later my mind would remember the plagues God had been fond of sending early in his career, the ones designed to make the pharaoh change his mind and let Moses take the people out of Egypt. *Let my people go*, Moses said. I'd seen the plague of locusts at the movies, the 25 sky filled with hordes of insects looking like kamikaze planes. Back in my room on the peach farm, when the bees had first come out at night, I had imagined they were sent as a special plague for T. Ray. God saying, *Let my daughter go*, and maybe that's exactly what they'd been, a plague that released me. 30

But here, now, surrounded by stinging bees on all sides and the motherless place throbbing away, I knew that these bees were not a

---

1 **not a lick** (old-fashioned, AE): not at all   8 **bark**: outer covering of a tree
9 **enchanted**: *verzaubert*   10 **douse sb. with sth.**: cover sb. all over with sth.
14 s**pooned out**: (here) empty   17 **double over**: bend your body forward

plague at all. It felt like the queen's attendants were out here in a frenzy of love, caressing me in a thousand places. *Look who's here, it's Lily. She is so weary and lost. Come on, bee sisters.* I was the stamen in the middle of a twirling flower. The center of all their comforting.

5   "Lily … Lily." My name came across the blue distances.

"Lily!"

I opened my eyes. August stared through her spectacles. The bees had shaken the pollen dust off their feet and were starting to settle back into the hive. I could see tiny grains of it drifting in the air.

10   "Are you okay?" August said.

I nodded. Was I? I had no idea.

"You know, don't you, that the two of us need to have a good talk. And this time not about me. About you."

I wished I could do like the bees, just bump her forehead with a 15 warning, tap it with my finger. *I got my eye on you. Be careful. Don't go any further.*

"I suppose," I answered.

"What about right now?"

"Not right now."

20   "But, Lily –"

"I'm starved," I said. "I think I'll go on back to the house and see if lunch is ready."

I didn't wait for her to speak. Walking to the pink house, I could almost see the end of the line. I touched the place on my shirt where 25 I'd stuck the black Mary. She was starting to come unglued.

The whole house smelled like fried okra. Rosaleen was setting the table in the kitchen while May dipped down in the grease and brought up the golden brown kernels. I didn't know what had brought on the okra, since it was usually bologna sandwiches and 30 more bologna sandwiches.

---

2 **frenzy**: state of great activity and excitement   3 **stamen**: male part that produces pollen   4 **twirl**: move round and round   24 **end of the line**: point at which sth. can no longer continue in the same way   26 **okra**: green vegetable popular in the southern USA   28 **kernel**: inner part of a plant

May had not had a crying jag since June performed her tomato-throwing fit, and we were all holding our breath. After going this long, I worried that even something as simple as burned okra might send her over the edge.

I said I was hungry, and Rosaleen said to hold my wild horses. 5
Her lower lip was plumped out with Red Rose snuff. The smell followed her around the kitchen like it was on a leash, a combination of allspice, fresh earth, and rotten leaves. Between the okra and the snuff I could not get a decent breath. Rosaleen walked across the back porch, leaned out the door, and spit a tiny jet stream across the 10
hydrangeas.

Nobody could spit like Rosaleen. I'd had fantasies of her winning a hundred dollars in a spitting contest and the two of us going to a nice motel in Atlanta and ordering room service with the prize money. It had always been my fond wish to stay in a motel, but at 15
that moment if you had told me I could've had my choice of luxury motels with heated pools and television sets right in the room, I would've turned it down flat for the pink house.

There had been a few times, though, just after I woke up, when I thought about my old house, and I would miss it for a second or 20
two before I remembered kneeling on the kitchen floor with grits digging into my kneecaps or trying to step around a great big pile of T. Ray's nasty mood but usually landing right in it. I would remember him tearing into me, shouting *Jesus H. Christ, Jesus H. Christ!* The worst slap across the face I ever got was when I interrupted him to 25
ask just what did the H. stand for anyway? One quick walk down memory lane and the oldhome feeling would blow right over. I would take the pink house any day.

Zach shuffled into the kitchen behind August.

"My, my. Okra and pork chops for lunch. What's this about?" 30
August asked May.

---

1 **jag**: fit   5 **hold your wild horses**: be patient   7 **leash** (AE): rope to guide a dog
8 **allspice** (n): spice from a tropical tree   14 **room service**: arrangement in a hotel
to have food delivered to your room   18 **turn sth. down**: reject sth.
flat (adv): without hesitating   27 **blow right over**: come to a quick end

May sidled over to her and said in a low voice, "It has been five days since I've been to the wall," and I could see how proud of this fact she was, how she wanted to believe her days of hysterical crying were behind her, how this okra lunch was a celebration.

5 August smiled at her. "Five days, really? Well, that deserves a feast," she said. And May, she beamed.

Zach plopped down in a chair.

"Did you finish delivering the honey?" August asked him.

"Everywhere but Mr. Clayton's law office," he said. He was
10 fidgeting with everything in sight. First the place mat, then a loose thread on his shirt. Like he was bursting to say something.

August looked him over. "You got something on your mind?"

"You won't believe what people downtown are saying," he said. "They're saying Jack Palance is coming to Tiburon this weekend and
15 bringing a colored woman with him."

We all stopped what we were doing and looked at each other.

"Who's Jack Palance?" Rosaleen said. Even though we hadn't started lunch yet, she had bitten into a piece of pork chop and was chewing and talking with her mouth open. I tried to catch her eye,
20 pointing to my closed mouth, hoping she'd get the message.

"He's a movie star," said Zach.

June snorted. "Well, how dumb is *that*? What would a movie star be doing in Tiburon?"

Zach shrugged. "They say his sister lives here, and he's coming to
25 visit and intends to take this colored woman to the movie theater this Friday. Not to the balcony, but downstairs in the white section."

August turned to May. "Why don't you go out to the garden and pick some fresh tomatoes to go with our lunch?" she said, then waited till May was out the door. I could tell she was afraid Jack
30 Palance trying to integrate the movie theater might ruin May's okra

---

10 **place mat**: piece of cloth on a table on which a plate is put
14 **Jack Palance**: American actor   26 **balcony**: upstairs seats in a theatre
30 **integrate sth.**: (here) stop the segregation practices of sth.

feast. "Are people stirred up about this?" she asked Zach. Her eyes
looked serious.

"Yes, ma'am," he said. "In Garret's Hardware there were white
men talking about standing guard outside the theater."

"Lord, here we go," said Rosaleen.   5

June made a *pffff* sound with her lips while August shook her
head, and it washed over me for the first time in my life just how
much importance the world had ascribed to skin pigment, how
lately it seemed that skin pigment was the sun and everything else in
the universe was the orbiting planets. Ever since school let out this 10
summer, it had been nothing but skin pigment every livelong day.
I was sick of it.

In Sylvan we'd had a rumor at the first of the summer about a
busload of people from New York City showing up to integrate the
city pool. Talk about a panic. We had a citywide emergency on our   15
hands, as there is no greater affliction for the southern mind than
people up north coming down to fix our way of life. After that was
the whole mess with the men at the Esso station. It seemed to me it
would have been better if God had deleted skin pigment altogether.

As May came back into the kitchen, August said, "Let's enjoy our   20
meal," which meant Jack Palance was not a lunch topic.

May plopped down three big tomatoes, and while she and
Rosaleen sliced them up, August went to the den and put a Nat King
Cole record on the player – a machine so old the records would not
even drop automatic fashion. She was crazy about Nat King Cole,   25
and she returned, with the volume up, frowning in that way people
do when they bite into something and it tastes so delicious they
appear to be in pain over it. June turned up her nose. She only cared
for Beethoven and that whole group. She went and turned the sound
down. "I can't think," she said.   30

---

1 **stir sb. up**: excite sb., make sb. feel strong emotions   7 **wash over sb.**: catch sb.'s
attention, make sb. realize sth.   8 **ascribe sth. to sth.**: attribute sth. to sth.
10 l**et out** (AE): stop   16 **affliction**: reason for suffering   19 **delete sth.**: wipe sth.
out   25 **Nat King Cole**: African-American singer (1919–65)

August said, "You know what? You think too much. It would do you a world of good to stop thinking and just go with your feelings once in a blue moon."

June said she would take her lunch in her room, thank you. 5 I guess that was just as well, because I was looking at the tomatoes May and Rosaleen were slicing and rehearsing in my head how I would say, *So will you have some tomatoes, June? Don't you love tomatoes?* Now at least I would be saved from that.

We ate till we were tired out from eating, which is the way people 10 in South Carolina eat at family reunions. Zach pushed back from the table, saying he was heading to Clayton Forrest's office to leave a dozen jars of honey.

"Can I go?" I asked.

August knocked over her sweet tea, a thing so unlike her. You did 15 not associate spills with August. With May, for sure, but not August. Tea ran across the table and onto the floor. I thought this might set May off, the tragedy of a spilled drink. But she only got up, humming "Oh! Susanna" without real urgency, and grabbed a towel.

"I don't know, Lily," August said.

20 "Please." All I really wanted was some time with Zach and to expand my world by visiting the office of a real-life lawyer.

"Well, all right," she said.

The office was situated one block off Main Street, where Rosaleen and I had paraded into town that Sunday more than three weeks 25 ago. It didn't look like my idea of a law office. The whole operation was really a large house, white with black shutters and a wraparound porch with big rocking chairs, which must have been for people to collapse into with relief after they'd won their cases. A sign on the lawn said CLAYTON FORREST, ATTORNEY AT LAW.

---

26 **wraparound** (adj): circling the whole house   29 **attorney at law** (AE): *Anwalt*

His secretary was a white lady who looked about eighty years old. She sat at a desk in the reception area, putting on fire-red lipstick. Her hair was permed into tight curls that had a faint blue cast.

"Hi, Miss Lacy," Zach said. "I brought more honey."

She worked the lipstick back into the tube, looking mildly   5 annoyed. "More honey," she said, shaking her head. She let out an overdone sigh and reached into a drawer. "The money for the last batch is in here." She dropped an envelope onto the desk.

She looked me over. "You're new."

"I'm Lily," I said.   10

"She's staying with August," Zach explained.

"You're staying in her *house*?" she said.

I wanted to tell her that her lipstick was bleeding into the wrinkles around her lips. "Yes, ma'am, I'm staying there."

"Well, I'll be," she said. She gathered her pocketbook and stood   15 up. "I've got an appointment at the dentist. Put the jars over there on the table."

I pictured her whispering the news to all the people in the waiting room who were about to get their cavities drilled. This white girl, Lily, is staying with the colored Boatwright sisters. Now, doesn't that   20 seem strange to you?

As she left, Mr. Forrest came out of his office. The first thing I noticed was his red suspenders. I'd never seen a thin person wear suspenders, and it was a nice look, the way it matched his red bow tie. He had sandy hair, and bushy eyebrows that curled toward his   25 blue eyes, and smile crinkles in his face that signaled a good person. So good that apparently he couldn't bring himself to get rid of Miss Lacy.

He looked at me. "And who would this pretty young lady be?"

"Lily uh –" I could not remember what last name I was currently   30 using. I think it was because he'd referred to me as pretty, which had

---

3 **perm hair**: make permanent curls in hair   **cast**: shadow of a colour
8 **batch**: (here) shipment   15 **I'll be** (infml, AE): I'll be darned! used to show that
you are surprised   19 **cavity**: hollow space in a tooth   23 **suspenders** (AE):
straps of leather or elastic to hold up trousers   26 **crinkle**: thin fold in the skin

been a shock to my system. "Just Lily." I stood there looking gawky, with one foot tucked behind the other. "I'm staying with August till I go live with my aunt in Virginia." Him being a lawyer, I worried he might ask me to take a lie-detector test.

5   "How nice. August is a good friend of mine," he said. "I hope you're enjoying your stay?"

    "Yes, sir. Very much."

    "What case are you working on?" asked Zach, stuffing the envelope of honey money into his pocket and setting the box of jars
10 on the side table by the window. It had a framed honey for sale sign on it.

    "Run-of-the-mill stuff. Deeds, wills. I got something for you, though. Come on back to the office and I'll show you."

    "I'll just wait out here and arrange the honey," I said, hating to
15 intrude but mostly feeling uncommonly awkward around him.

    "You sure? You're welcome to come, too."

    "I'm sure. I like it out here."

    They disappeared down a hallway. I heard a door close. A car horn on the street. The blast of the window air conditioner that
20 dripped water into a dog bowl on the floor. I stacked the jars in a pyramid. Seven on bottom, four in the middle, and one on top, but it looked misshapen, so I took it apart and settled for plain rows.

    I went over and inspected the pictures that covered one whole wall. First was a diploma from the University of South Carolina and
25 then another one from Duke University. Next was a picture of Mr. Forrest on a boat, wearing sunglasses and holding a fish about my size. After that, Mr. Forrest shaking hands with Bobby Kennedy. Last, Mr. Forrest and a small blond-headed girl, standing in the ocean. She was jumping over a wave. The spray made a blue fan
30 behind her, a peacock tail of water, and he was helping her, lifting her up and over it with his hand, smiling down on her. I bet he knew her favorite color, what she ate for afternoon snacks, everything she loved.

---

1 **gawky**: awkward   12 **run-of-the-mill** (adj): ordinary, everyday   **deed**: legal document concerning property

I went and sat on one of the two red sofas in the room. Williams. My made-up last name finally came to me. I counted the plants in the room. Four. The floorboards from the desk to the front door. Fifteen. Closing my eyes, I pictured the ocean stretched out the color of fresh-polished silver, the white froth on it, light scattering 5 everywhere. I saw myself jumping a wave.

T. Ray held my hand, pulling me up and over. I had to concentrate so hard to make this happen.

Thirty-two names for love.

Was it unthinkable he could speak one of them to me, even the 10 one reserved for lesser things like peanuts in your Coke? Was it so out of the question that T. Ray knew I loved the color blue? What if he was home missing me, saying, *Why oh why didn't I love her better?*

Miss Lacy's telephone sat right there on her desk. I picked up the receiver and dialed 0 for operator. "I am making a collect call," I told 15 her, and gave her the number. Almost faster than I would've believed, I heard the phone in my house ringing. I stared down the hallway at the closed door and counted the rings. Three, four, five, six.

"Hello." His voice caused my stomach to pitch into my throat. I was unprepared for the way it buckled my knees. I had to sit down 20 in Miss Lacy's chair spraddle-legged.

"I have a collect call from Lily Owens," the operator said. "Will you accept the charge?"

"You're goddamn right I'll accept it," he said. Then, without waiting for me to say P-turkey, he launched right in. "Lily, where the 25 hell are you?"

I had to hold the phone from my eardrum for fear of him rupturing it. "T. Ray, I'm sorry I had to leave, but –"

"You tell me where you are right now, do you hear me? Do you have any idea the trouble you're in? Busting Rosaleen out of the 30 hospital – holy shit, what were you thinking?"

"I was only –"

5 **froth**: mass of small bubbles on a liquid   15 **operator**: person working for a telephone company   **collect call**: phone call charged to the person who receives it   19 **pitch**: (here) move   20 **buckle**: (here) shake   21 **spraddle-legged**: with legs wide apart   24–25 … **to say P-turkey**: at once   28 **rupture sth.**: burst or break sth.   30 **bust sb. out**: help sb. escape

"I'll tell you what you were. You were a goddamn fool who went looking for trouble and found it. Because of you I can't walk down the street in Sylvan without people staring at me. I've had to stop everything and search for you all over creation, and meanwhile the
5 peaches have gone to hell."

"Well, quit yelling, all right? I said I was sorry."

"Your sorry ain't worth a shitload of peaches, Lily. I swear to God –"

"I called because I was just wondering something."

10 "Where are you? Answer me."

I squeezed the arm of the chair till my knuckles hurt. "I was wondering, do you know what my favorite color is?"

"Jesus Christ. What are you talking about? You tell me where you are."

15 "I said, do you know what my favorite color is?"

"I know one thing, and that's I'm gonna find you, Lily, and when I do, I'm gonna tear your behind to pieces –"

I lowered the receiver back to the cradle and sat on the sofa again. I sat in the brightness of the afternoon and watched the hem of light
20 under the venetian blinds. I told myself, *Don't you cry. Don't you dare cry. So what if he doesn't know the color you love best? So what?*

Zach returned holding a big brown book that looked half moldy with age. "Look what Mr. Clayton gave me," he said, and honestly, you would have thought it was a six-pound baby he'd birthed by the
25 proud look of him.

He turned it over so I could read the binding. *South Carolina Legal Reports 1889.* Zach rubbed his hand across the front, and little flecks of it fell off onto the floor. "I'm starting my law library."

"That's nice," I said.

Mr. Forrest stepped closer, staring at me with such intensity I thought I must need to wipe my nose.

"Zach says you're from Spartanburg County, that your parents both died?"

"Yes, sir." One thing I didn't want was to get on the witness stand   5
right here in his office and have him fire lawyer questions at me. An hour from now Rosaleen and I could be packing for prison.

"What brings you —"

"I really do need to get back." I put my hand low on my stomach. "I'm having a little female trouble." I tried to look very female and   10
mysterious, slightly troubled by internal things they could not imagine and did not want to. It had been my experience for nearly a year that uttering the words "female trouble" could get me into places I wanted to go and out of places I didn't.

"Oh," said Zach. "Well, let's go."   15

"Nice to meet you, Mr. Forrest," I said. Clutching my abdomen. A small wince. Walking slowly to the door.

"Believe me, Lily," he said, calling after me, "the pleasure was all mine."

Have you ever written a letter you knew you could never mail but   20
you needed to write it anyway? Back in my room at the honey house, I wrote a letter to T. Ray, during which I broke the points off three pencils, and the words … well, they looked like they'd been laid on the paper with branding irons.

17 **wince**: expression on the face to express pain   24 **branding iron**: heated iron used to burn signs on animals

Dear T. Ray,

I am sick to death of you yelling at me. I am not deaf. I am only stupid for calling you up.

If you were being tortured by Martians and the only thing that could save you was telling them my favorite color, you would die on the spot. What was
5 *I thinking? All I had to do was remember the Father's Day card I made for you when I was nine and still hoping for love. Do you remember it, well of course you don't. I do, because I nearly killed myself working on it. I never told you I was up half the night with a dictionary looking up words to go with the letters in Daddy. I got the idea, not that you are interested, from Mrs.*
10 *Poole who had us do this in Sunday school with the word Joy. J – Jesus; O – Others; Y – Yourself. This is the correct order for life, she said, and if you follow it, you will have JOY, JOY, JOY. Well, I tried that, putting myself last left and right, and I am still waiting for Joy to show up. So the exercise was good for nothing except for giving me the idea for your card. I thought if I*
15 *spelled out the meaning of Daddy to you, it would help you along. I was trying to say, here, try these things, I will so appreciate it. I used words like DELIGHTFUL, DETERMINED TO BE KIND.*

I expected it to get propped on your dresser, and the next day I find it on the telephone table where you have peeled a peach on top of it, and the
20 *skin and pit are stuck to the paper. I have always wanted to say to you that was DESPICABLE.*

D – DESPICABLE
A – ANGRY
D – DUD OF A FATHER
25 *D – DISAPPPOINTMENT*
Y – YOKE AROUND MY NECK

Writing this is not the Jesus–Others–Yourself philosophy of life, but it brings me J–O–Y to finally say these things to your face.

Love, Lily

30 *P. S. I do not for one half second believe my mother left me.*

---

20 **pit** (AE): stone   26 **yoke**: (here) heavy burden

I read the letter back, then tore it into tiny pieces. I felt relief to get all that out of my system, but I had lied about it bringing me joy. I almost wanted to write another letter that I would not send and say I'm sorry.

That night, when the pink house was sound asleep, I came creeping in, needing the bathroom. I never worried about finding my way through the house, as August left a trail of night-lights on from the kitchen to the bathroom.

I had come barefoot, collecting dew on the soles of my feet. Sitting on the toilet, trying to pee very quietly, I could see crepe myrtle petals stuck to my toes. Over my head, Rosaleen's snores sifted through the ceiling. It is always a relief to empty your bladder. Better than sex, that's what Rosaleen said. As good as it felt, though, I sincerely hoped she was wrong.

I headed toward the kitchen, but then something made me turn around; your guess is as good as mine. I walked in the opposite direction to the parlor. Stepping inside, I heard a sigh so deep and satisfying that for a moment I didn't realize it had come from my own lungs.

The candle in the red glass beside the Mary statue still burned, looking like a tiny red heart in a cave of darkness, pulsing out light to the world. August kept it going night and day. It reminded me of the eternal flame they'd put on John F. Kennedy's grave that will never go out no matter what.

Our Lady of Chains looked so different late at night, her face older and darker, her fist bigger than I remembered. I wondered about all the places she'd traveled out there on the waters of the world, all the sad things that had been whispered to her, the things she'd endured.

Sometimes, after we'd done our prayers with the beads, I could not remember how to cross myself right, getting it mixed up like you would expect any Baptist-raised person to do. Whenever that happened, I just put my hand over my heart like we did in school for the Pledge of Allegiance. I felt one was as good as another, and that's what happened now – my hand just went automatically to my heart and stayed there.

I told her, *Fix me, please fix me. Help me know what to do. Forgive me. Is my mother all right up there with God? Don't let them find us. If they find us, don't let them take me back. If they find us, keep Rosaleen from being killed. Let June love me. Let T. Ray love me. Help me stop lying. Make the world better. Take the meanness out of people's hearts.*

I moved closer, so now I could see the heart on her chest. In my mind I heard the bees fanning their wings down in the dark music box. I saw August and me with our ears against the hive. I remembered her voice the first time she told the story of Our Lady of Chains. *Send them rescue, send them consolation, send them freedom.*

I reached out and traced black Mary's heart with my finger. I stood with the petals on my toes and pressed my palm flat and hard against her heart.

I live in a hive of darkness, and you are my mother, I told her. You are the mother of thousands.

The whole fabric of honey bee society depends on communication – on an innate ability to send and receive messages, to encode and decode information.

The Honey Bee

Chapter Nine

July 28 was a day for the record books. I look back on it and what comes to me are people going over Niagara Falls in barrels. Ever since I'd heard about that, I'd tried to imagine people crouched inside, bobbing along peacefully like a rubber duck in a child's bathtub, and suddenly the water turning choppy and the barrel starting to thrash around while a roar grows in the distance. I knew they were in there saying, *Shitbucket*, what *was I thinking?*

At eight o'clock in the morning it hit 94, with the ambitious plan of reaching 103 before noon. I woke up with August shaking my shoulder, saying it was gonna be a scorcher, get up, we had to water the bees.

I climbed into the honey wagon with my hair uncombed, with May handing me buttered toast and orange juice through the window and Rosaleen sticking in thermoses of water, both of them practically running alongside the truck while August rolled out of the driveway. I felt like the Red Cross springing to action to save the bee queendom.

2 **barrel**: *Fass*   5 **choppy**: rough, moving violently   10 **scorcher**: very hot day

In the back of the truck August had gallons of sugar water already made up. "When it gets over a hundred," she said, "the flowers dry up and there's no food for the bees. They stay in the hives fanning themselves. Sometimes they just roast."

5 I felt like we might roast alive ourselves. You could not touch the door handle for fear of a third-degree burn. Sweat ran between my breasts and sopped my underwear band. August turned on the radio for the weather, but what we heard was how *Ranger* 7 had finally been launched to the moon in a place called the Sea of Clouds, how 10 police were looking for the bodies of those three civil rights workers in Mississippi, and the terrible things happening in Vietnam. It ended with a story about what was happening "closer to home," how black people from Tiburon, Florence, and Orangeburg were marching today all the way to Columbia asking the governor to 15 enforce the Civil Rights Act.

August turned it off. Enough was enough. You cannot fix the whole world.

"I've already watered the hives around the house," she said. "Zach is taking care of the hives on the east side of the county. So you and 20 I've got the west side."

Rescuing bees took us the entire morning. Driving back into remote corners of the woods where there were barely roads, we would come upon twenty-five beehives up on slats like a little lost city tucked back in there. We lifted the covers and filled the feeders 25 with sugar water. Earlier we'd spooned dry sugar into our pockets, and now, just as a bonus, we sprinkled it on the feeding rims.

I managed to get stung on my wrist while replacing a lid onto a hive box. August scraped out the stinger.

"I was sending them love," I said, feeling betrayed.

30 August said, "Hot weather makes the bees out of sorts, I don't care how much love you send them." She pulled a small bottle of olive oil and bee pollen from her free pocket and rubbed my skin –

---

7 **sop sth.**: make sth. wet   10 **three civil rights workers**: reference to the murders of three civil rights workers   24 **feeder**: cf. p. 306   30 **out of sorts**: sick or upset

her patented remedy. It was something I'd hoped never to test out. "Count yourself initiated," she said. "You can't be a true beekeeper without getting stung."

A true beekeeper. The words caused a fullness in me, and right at that moment an explosion of blackbirds lifted off the ground in a 5 clearing a short distance away and filled up the whole sky. I said to myself, *Will wonders never cease?* I would add that to my list of careers. A writer, an English teacher, *and* a beekeeper.

"Do you think I could keep bees one day?" I asked.

August said, "Didn't you tell me this past week one of the things 10 you loved was bees and honey? Now, if that's so, you'll be a fine beekeeper. Actually, you can be bad at something, Lily, but if you love doing it, that will be enough."

The sting shot pain all the way to my elbow, causing me to marvel at how much punishment a minuscule creature can inflict. I'm 15 prideful enough to say I didn't complain. After you get stung, you can't get unstung no matter how much you whine about it. I just dived back into the riptide of saving bees.

When we had watered all the hives of Tiburon and sprinkled enough sugar to cause a human being to gain fifty pounds, we drove 20 home hot, hungry, and nearly drowned in our own sweat.

Pulling into the driveway, we found Rosaleen and May sipping sweet tea on the back porch. May said she'd left our lunches in the refrigerator, cold pork-chop sandwiches and slaw. While we ate, we heard June upstairs in her room playing the cello like something had 25 died.

We scarfed down every morsel without talking, then pushed back from the table. We were wondering how to get our tired selves to a standing position when we heard squealing and laughing, the kind you're apt to hear at a school recess. August and I dragged 30

---

15 **inflict sth.**: cause to feel sth. unpleasant   18 **riptide**: *Strudel*
24 **slaw** (AE): salad of raw vegetables   27 **scarf sth. down** (AE): eat sth. quickly
morsel: small piece   29 **squeal**: long, high sound

ourselves to the porch to see. And there were May and Rosaleen
running through the water sprinkler, barefoot and fully clothed.
They had gone berserk.

Rosaleen's muumuu was sopped and plastered to her body, and
5 May was catching water in the bowl of her dress skirt and tossing it
up across her face. Sunlight hit the hair sheen on her braids and lit
them up.

"Well, isn't this the living end?" August said.

When we got out there, Rosaleen picked up the sprinkler and
10 aimed it at us. "You come over here and you gonna get wet," she
said, and *splat*! we were hit full in the chest with ice-cold water.

Rosaleen turned the sprinkler head down and filled May's dress.
"You come over here and you gonna get wet," May said, echoing
Rosaleen, and she came after us, pitching the contents of her skirt
15 across our backs.

I can tell you this much: neither one of us protested that loudly.
In the end we stood there and let ourselves be drenched by two
crazy black women.

All four of us turned into water nymphs and danced around the
20 cool spray, just the way it must have been when Indians danced
circles around blazing fires. Squirrels and Carolina wrens hopped as
close as they dared and drank from the puddles, and you could
almost see the blades of brown grass lift themselves up and turn
green.

25 Then the porch door banged, and here came June with her
dander up. I must have been drunk with water and air and dancing,
because I picked up the sprinkler and said, "You come over here and
you're gonna get wet." Then I hosed her.

She began to holler. "Damn it to hell!" I knew this was going
30 down the wrong path, but I couldn't stop. I was seeing myself as the
fire department and June as the raging inferno.

---

3 **go berserk**: become angry and violent   4 **muumuu**: long, loose dress
6 **sheen**: shiny appearance   14 **pitch sth.**: throw sth.   21 **wren**: small bird
25–26 **with your dander up**: very angry   28 **hose sb.**: direct the water hose on sb.
29 **holler**: shout, yell

She yanked the sprinkler out of my hands and turned the spray on me. Some of the water rushed up my nose and burned. I yanked at the sprinkler, and each of us held on to one side of it while it blasted away at our stomachs and chins. We went to our knees, wrestling for it, the geyser weaving between us, her eyes staring at 5 me, close and bright with beads of water on her eyelashes. I heard May start to hum "Oh! Susanna." I laughed to let her know it was all right, but I wouldn't let go. I would not let June Boatwright win.

Rosaleen said, "They say if you aim the hose on two locked dogs, they'll turn loose, but I guess that ain't always so." 10

August laughed, and I saw the softening come around June's eyes, how she was trying not to laugh, but it was like the Dutch boy pulling his finger out of the dike – the minute she softened her eyes, the whole thing collapsed. I could almost see her smack her forehead, thinking, *I am wrestling with a fourteen-year-old girl over a garden* 15 *sprinkler. This is ridiculous.*

She let go and sprawled back on the grass in convulsions of laughter. I plopped down next to her and laughed, too. We could not stop. I wasn't exactly sure of everything we were laughing about – I was just glad we were doing it together. 20

When we got up, June said, "Lord, I feel woozy, like somebody has pulled the plugs in my feet and drained me out."

Rosaleen, May, and August had returned to the business of being water nymphs. I looked back down at the ground where our bodies had lain side by side, the wet grasses pressed down, perfect 25 depressions in the earth. I stepped over them with the utmost care, and, seeing how careful I was, June stepped over them, too, and then, to my shock, she hugged me. June Boatwright hugged me while our clothes made sweet, squishy sounds up and down our bodies. 30

9 **locked**: unable to separate   17 **convulsion**: shaking of the body
21 **woozy** (infml): dizzy   29 **squishy**: cf. squish p. 85

If the heat goes over 104 degrees in South Carolina, you have to go to bed. It is practically the law. Some people might see it as shiftless behavior, but really, when we're lying down from the heat, we're giving our minds time to browse around for new ideas, wondering at
5 the true aim of life, and generally letting things pop into our heads that need to. In the sixth grade there was a boy in my class who had a steel plate in his skull and was always complaining how test answers could never get through to him. Our teacher would say, "Give me a break."

10 In a way, though, the boy was right. Every human being on the face of the earth has a steel plate in his head, but if you lie down now and then and get still as you can, it will slide open like elevator doors, letting in all the secret thoughts that have been standing around so patiently, pushing the button for a ride to the top. The real
15 troubles in life happen when those hidden doors stay closed for too long. But that's just my opinion.

August, May, June, and Rosaleen were supposedly over in the pink house in their rooms lying under the fans with the lights out. In the honey house I reclined on my cot and told myself I could think
20 about anything I wanted, except my mother, so naturally she was the only thing that wanted on the elevator.

I could feel things unraveling around me. All the fraying edges of the dream world. Pull one wrong thread and I would be standing in wreckage to my elbows. Ever since I'd called T. Ray, I'd wanted so
25 badly to tell Rosaleen about it. To say, *If you've been wondering whether my leaving has caused T. Ray to examine his heart, or change his ways, don't waste your time.* But I couldn't bring myself to admit to her that I'd cared enough to call him.

What was wrong with me that I was living here as if I had nothing
30 to hide? I lay on the cot and stared at the glaring square of window,

2 **shiftless**: lazy   4 **browse**: look around without a fixed aim
9 **give me a break** (infml): used to express that sth. is hard to believe
22 **unravel**: become clearer   **fraying edges**: unconnected parts

exhausted. It takes so much energy to keep things at bay. *Let me on, my mother was saying. Let me on the damn elevator.*

Well, fine. I pulled out my bag and examined my mother's picture. I wondered what it had been like to be inside her, just a curl of flesh swimming in her darkness, the quiet things that had passed between us.

The wanting-her was still in me, but it wasn't nearly so fierce and raging as before. Pulling on her gloves, I noticed how tight they fit all of a sudden. By the time I was sixteen, they would feel like baby gloves on my hands. I would be Alice in Wonderland after she ate the cake and grew twice her size. My palms would split the seams of the gloves, and I would never wear them again.

I peeled the gloves from my sweaty hands and felt a wave of jitteriness, the old saw-edged guilt, the necklace of lies I could not stop wearing, the fear of being cast out of the pink house.

"No," I breathed. The word took a long time to work its way to my throat. A scared whisper. No, I will not think about this. I will not feel this. I will not let this ruin the way things are. *No.*

I decided that lying down from the heat was a hick idea. I gave up and walked to the pink house for something cold to drink. If I ever managed to get to heaven after everything I'd done, I hoped I would get just a few minutes for a private conference with God. *I wanted to say, Look, I know you meant well creating the world and all, but how could you let it get away from you like this? How come you couldn't stick with your original idea of paradise?* People's lives were a mess.

When I came into the kitchen, May was sitting on the floor with her legs straight out and a box of graham crackers in her lap. That would be about right – me and May the only two who couldn't lie peaceful on the bed for five minutes.

---

1 **keep sth. at bay**: keep sth. away from you   14 **jitteriness**: nervousness
saw-edged: rough and biting   19 **hick** (infml, AE): stupid, unrefined

"I saw a roach," she said, reaching into a bag of marshmallows that I hadn't noticed was there. She pulled one out and pinched off little pieces of it. Crazy May.

I opened the refrigerator and stood there staring at the contents
5 like I was waiting for the grape-juice bottle to jump in my hand and say, Here, *drink me.* I could not seem to register what May was doing. Sometimes things of magnitude settle over you with excruciating slowness. Say you break your ankle and don't feel it hurting till you've walked another block.

10 I had nearly finished a glass of juice before I let myself look at the little highway of broken graham crackers and marshmallow bits that May was constructing across the floor, how it started at the sink and angled toward the door, thick with golden crumbs and smudges of sticky white.

15 "The roaches will follow this out the door," May said. "It works every time."

I don't know how long I stared at the line on the floor, at May's face turned toward mine, eager for me to say something, but I couldn't think what to say. The room filled with the steady whir of
20 the refrigerator motor. I felt a strange, thick feeling inside. A memory. I stood there waiting, letting it come. ... *Your mother was a lunatic when it came to bugs,* T. Ray had said. *She used to make trails of graham cracker crumbs and marshmallows to lure roaches outside.*

I looked again at May. *My mother couldn't have learned the roach*
25 *trick from May,* I thought. *Could she?*

Ever since I'd set foot in the pink house, some part of me had kept believing that my mother had been here. No, not believing it so much as daydreaming it and running it through a maze of wishful thinking. But now that the actual possibility seemed to be right in
30 front of me, it seemed so far-fetched, crazy. It couldn't be, I thought again.

2–3 **pinch sth. off**: remove sth. by pressing your fingers together and pulling
7 **excruciating**: extremely painful   13 **smudge**: dirty spot   28 **maze**: labyrinth

I walked over and sat down at the table. Shadows from late afternoon pushed into the room. They were peach tinted, fading in and out, and the kitchen was completely silent. Even the refrigerator hum had died away. May had turned back to her work. She seemed oblivious to me sitting there.　　　　　　　　　　　　　　　　　　5

My mother could have learned it from a book, maybe from her mother. How did I know that households everywhere didn't use this particular roach-ridding method? I stood up and walked over to May. I felt a trembly feeling at the back of my knees. I put my hand on her shoulder. *Okay*, I thought, *here goes.* I said, "May, did you ever　10 know a Deborah? Deborah Fontanel? A white woman from Virginia? It would have been a long time ago."

There wasn't a trace of cunning in May, and you could depend on her not to overthink her answers. She didn't look up, didn't pause, just said, "Oh, yes, Deborah Fontanel. She stayed out there in the　15 honey house. She was the sweetest thing."

And there it was. There it all was.

For a moment I felt light-headed. I had to reach for the countertop to steady myself. Down on the floor the trail of crumbs and marshmallows looked half alive.　　　　　　　　　　　　　　　20

I had a million more questions, but May had started humming "Oh! Susanna." She set down the box of crackers and got up slowly, starting to sniffle. Something about Deborah Fontanel had set her off.

"I think I'll go out to the wall for a little while," she said. And　25 that's how she left me, standing in the kitchen, hot and breathless, the world tilted under me.

Walking to the honey house, I concentrated on my feet touching down on the hard-caked dirt in the driveway, the exposed tree roots, fresh-watered grass, how the earth felt beneath me, solid, alive,　30 ancient, right there every time my foot came down. There and there and there, always there. The things a mother should be.

27 **tilted**: (here) at an uneven angle

Oh, yes, Deborah Fontanel. She stayed out there in the honey house. She was the sweetest thing.

In the honey house I sat on the cot with my knees drawn up, hugging them with my arms and making a shelf for the side of my
5 face to rest on. I looked at the floor and the walls with brandnew eyes. My mother had walked about in this room. A real person. Not somebody I made up but a living, breathing person.

The last thing I expected was to fall asleep, but when there's a blow to the system, all the body wants to do is go to sleep and dream
10 on it.

I woke an hour or so later in the velvety space where you don't yet remember what you've dreamed. Then suddenly the whole thing washed back to me.

I am constructing a spiraling trail of honey across a room that seems to
15 *be in the honey house one minute and the next in my bedroom back in Sylvan. I start it at a door I've never seen before and end it at the foot of my bed. Then I sit on the mattress and wait. The door opens. In walks my mother. She follows the honey, making twists and turns across the room until she gets to my bed. She is smiling, so pretty, but then I see she is not a*
20 *normal person. She has roach legs protruding through her clothes, sticking through the cage of her ribs, down her torso, six of them, three on each side.*

I couldn't imagine who sat in my head making this stuff up. The air was now dusky rose and cool enough for a sheet. I pulled it
25 around my legs. My stomach felt icky, like I might throw up.

If I told you right now that I never wondered about that dream, never closed my eyes and pictured her with roach legs, never wondered why she came to me like that, with her worst nature exposed, I would be up to my old habit of lying. A roach is a creature
30 no one can love, but you cannot kill it. It will go on and on and on. Just try to get rid of it.

13 **wash back**: cf. wash over (p. 156)   25 **icky** (infml, AE): unpleasant

The next few days I was a case of nerves. I jumped out of my skin if somebody so much as dropped a nickel on the floor. At the dinner table I poked at my food and stared into space like I was in a trance. Sometimes the picture of my mother with roach legs would leap into my head, and I would have to swallow a spoonful of honey for my   5
stomach. I was so antsy I couldn't sit through five minutes of *American Bandstand* on television, when ordinarily I was glued to Dick Clark's every word.

I walked around and around the house, pausing here and there to picture my mother in the various rooms. Sitting with her skirt spread   10
over the piano bench. Kneeling beside Our Lady. Studying the recipe collection that May clipped from magazines and kept taped on the refrigerator. I would stare at these visions with my eyes glazed over, only to look up and see August, or June, or Rosaleen watching me. They clucked their tongues and felt my face for fever.   15

They said, "What's wrong? What's got into you?" I shook my head. "Nothing," I lied. "Nothing."

In truth I felt as if my life was stranded out on the high dive, about to leap into unknown waters. *Dangerous* waters. I only wanted to postpone the plunge awhile, to feel my mother's closeness in the   20
house, to pretend I wasn't afraid of the story that had brought her here or that she might go and surprise me the way she had in the dream, turning up six-legged and ugly.

I wanted to march up to August and ask why my mother had been here, but fear stopped me. I wanted to know, and I didn't want   25
to know. I was all hung up in limbo.

Late Friday afternoon, after we had finished cleaning the last of the supers and storing them away, Zach went out to take a look under

---

1 **case of nerves**: extremely nervous   **jump out of your skin**: react violently to a shock   6 **antsy** (infml, AE): unable to keep still   7 **American Bandstand**: US TV programme for teenagers presented by Dick Clark   18 **stranded out**: cf. strand sb. (p. 151)   **high dive**: *10-Meter Brett*   20 **plunge**: deep fall   26 **in limbo**: in a situation of indecision

the hood of the honey wagon. It was still acting funny and overheating, in spite of Neil having worked on it.

I wandered back to my room and sat on my cot. Heat radiated from the window. I considered getting up to turn on the fan but only
5 sat there staring through the panes at the milky-blue sky, a sad, ragged feeling catching hold inside. I could hear music coming from the truck radio, Sam Cooke singing "Another Saturday Night," then May calling across the yard to Rosaleen, something about getting the sheets off the clothesline. And I was struck all at once how life was
10 out there going through its regular courses, and I was suspended, waiting, caught in a terrible crevice between living my life and not living it. I couldn't go on biding time like there was no end of it, no end to this summer. I felt tears spring up. I would have to come clean. Whatever happened … well, it would just happen.
15 I went over to the sink and washed my face.

Taking a deep breath, I stuffed my mother's black Mary picture and her photograph into my pocket and started toward the pink house to find August.

I thought we would sit down on the end of her bed, or out in the
20 lawn chairs if the mosquitoes weren't bad. I imagined August would say, *What's on your mind, Lily? Are we finally gonna have our talk?* I would pull out the wooden picture and tell her every last thing, and then she would explain about my mother.

If only that had happened, instead of what did.

25 As I strode toward the house, Zach called to me from the truck. "Wanna ride to town with me? I've gotta get a new radiator hose before the store closes."

"I'm going to talk to August," I said.

---

6 **ragged** (infml): weary   10 **suspended**: (here) still and passive
26 **radiator**: (here) *Kühler*

He slammed down the hood and smeared his hands front and
back on his pants. "August is with Sugar-Girl in the parlor. She
showed up crying. Something about Otis using their life savings to
buy a secondhand fishing boat."

"But I've got something really important to talk to her about."   5

"You'll have to get in line," he said. "Come on, we'll be back
before Sugar-Girl leaves."

I hesitated, then gave in. "All right."

The auto-parts store sat two doors down from the movie theater.
As Zach pulled into a parking space in front, I saw them – five or six   10
white men standing by the ticket booth. They milled around, casting
quick glances up and down the sidewalk, like they were waiting for
someone, all of them so nicely dressed, wearing ties with clips on
them like store clerks and bank tellers. One man held what looked
like the handle from a shovel.   15

Zach turned off the honey wagon and stared at them through the
windshield. A dog, an old beagle with an age-white face, wandered
out of the auto-parts store and began to sniff at something on the
sidewalk. Zach drummed his fingers on the steering wheel and
sighed. And I suddenly realized: it was Friday, and they were out   20
here waiting for Jack Palance and the colored woman.

We sat there a minute not speaking, the sounds in the truck
magnified. The squeak in a spring under the seat. The tapping of
Zach's fingers. The sharp way I was breathing.

Then one of the men yelled, causing me to jump and bang my   25
knee against the glove compartment. He gazed across the street and
shouted, "What are you staring at over there?"

Zach and I both turned and looked through the back window.
Three teenaged colored boys stood on the sidewalk, drinking R.C.
Colas out of the bottle and glaring over at the men.   30

"Let's come back another time," I said.

"It'll be okay," Zach said. "You wait here."

---

11 **mill around**: move around without going anywhere in particular
29–30 **R.C. Cola**: Royal Crown Cola

No, it won't be okay, I thought.

As he slid out of the honey wagon, I heard the boys call Zach's name. They crossed the street and came over to the honey wagon. Glancing through the window at me, they gave Zach a few playful
5 shoves. One of them waved his hand in front of his face like he'd bitten into a Mexican pepper. "Who you got in there?" he said.

I looked at them, tried to smile, but my mind was on the men, who I could see were watching us.

The boys saw it, too, and one of them – who I would later find
10 out was named Jackson – said real loud, "You gotta be dumb as dirt to believe Jack Palance is coming to Tiburon," and all of them laughed. Even Zach.

The man holding the shovel handle walked right up to the truck bumper and stared at the boys with that same half smile, half sneer I
15 had seen on T. Ray's face a thousand times, the sort of look conjured from power without benefit of love, and he yelled, "What did you say, boy?"

The murmuring noise on the street fell away. The beagle dropped his ears and slunk off under a parked car. I saw Jackson bite down,
20 causing a tiny ripple across his jaw. I saw him raise his R.C. Cola bottle over his head. And throw it.

I closed my eyes as it flew out of his hand. When I opened them again, there was glass sprayed across the sidewalk. The man with the shovel handle had dropped it and had his hand over his nose. Blood
25 seeped through his fingers.

He turned back to the other men. "That nigger busted open my nose," he said, sounding more surprised than anything. He looked around, confused for a moment, then headed into a nearby store, dripping blood all the way.

30 Zach and the boys stood by the truck door in a little knot, stuck to the pavement, while the rest of the men walked over and formed

14 **sneer**: unpleasant smile

a half circle around them, hemming them in against the truck.
"Which one of you threw that bottle?" one man said.

The boys didn't open their mouths.

"Bunch of cowards," another man said. This one had picked up
the shovel handle from the sidewalk and was jabbing it in the air in   5
the boys' direction every time they moved. "Just tell us which one of
you it was, and you other three can go," he said.

Nothing.

People had started coming out of the stores, gathering in clumps.
I stared at the back of Zach's head. I felt like my heart had a little   10
ledge on it and I was standing there leaning as far out as I could,
waiting to see what Zach would do. I knew that being a snitch was
considered the lowest sort of person, but I wanted him to point his
finger and say, *The one over there. He did it.* That way he could climb
back into the honey truck and we would be on our way.   15

Come on, Zach.

He turned his head and looked at me from the corner of his eye.
Then he shrugged his shoulder slightly, and I knew it was over and
done. He would never open his mouth. He was trying to say to me,
I'm sorry, but these are my friends.   20

He chose to stand there and be one of them.

I watched the policeman put Zach and the other three boys in his
car. Driving away, he turned on his siren and red light, which seemed
unnecessary, but I guess he didn't want to disappoint the audience
on the sidewalk.   25

I sat in the truck like I had frozen and the world had frozen
around me. The crowd faded away, and all the cars downtown went
home one by one. People closed up their stores. I stared through the

---

1 **hem sb. in**: surround sb. so that they can't escape   12 **snitch**: *Petzer*

windshield as if I was watching the test pattern that came on television at midnight.

After the shock wore off some, I tried to think what to do, how to get home. Zach had taken the keys, or I might've tried driving
5 myself, even though I didn't know gears from brakes. There wasn't a store open now to ask to use a phone, and when I spotted a pay phone down the street, I realized I didn't have a dime. I got out of the truck and walked.

When I got to the pink house a half hour later, I saw August,
10 June, Rosaleen, Neil, and Clayton Forrest gathered in the long shadows near the hydrangeas. The murmur of their voices floated up into the dying light. I heard Zach's name. I heard Mr. Forrest say the word "jail." I guessed that Zach had called him with his one phone call, and here he was, breaking the news.

15 Neil stood next to June, which told me they hadn't really meant all that *don't you come back* and *you selfish bitch* that they'd hurled at each other. I walked toward them, unnoticed. Someone down the road was burning grass clippings. The whole sky smelled sour green, and stray pieces of ash flicked over my head.

20 Coming up behind them, I said, "August?"

She pulled me to her. "Thank goodness. Here you are. I was about to come looking for you."

I told them what had happened as we walked back to the house. August's arm was around my waist like she was afraid I'd keel over
25 again in a blind faint, but really, I had never been more present. The blue in the shadows, the shape of them against the house, how they looked like certain unkind animals – a crocodile, a grizzly bear – the smell of Alka-Seltzer circulating over Clayton Forrest's head, the white part in his hair, the weight of our caring strapped around our
30 ankles. We could hardly walk for it.

We sat in the ladder-back chairs around the kitchen table, except for Rosaleen, who poured glasses of tea and set a plate of pimiento-

25 **blind**: (here) uncontrollable

cheese sandwiches on the table, as if anybody could eat. Rosaleen's
hair was done up in perfect cornrow plaits, which I guessed May had
done for her after supper.

"Now, what about bail?" August said.

Clayton cleared his throat. "Judge Monroe is out of town on   5
vacation, so nobody is getting out before next Wednesday, it looks
like."

Neil stood up and walked over to the window. His hair was cut in
a neat square at the back. I tried to concentrate on it to keep from
breaking down. Next Wednesday was five days from now. *Five days.*   10

"Well, is he all right?" asked June. "He wasn't hurt, was he?"

"They only let me see him for a minute," said Clayton. "But he
seemed all right."

Outside, the night sky was moving over us. I was aware of it,
aware of the way Clayton had said *he seemed all right*, as if we all   15
understood he wasn't but would pretend otherwise.

August closed her eyes, used her fingers to smooth out the skin
on her forehead. I saw a shiny film across her eyes – the beginning of
tears. Looking at her eyes, I could see a fire inside them. It was a
hearth fire you could depend on, you could draw up to and get   20
warm by if you were cold, or cook something on that would feed the
emptiness in you. I felt like we were all adrift in the world, and all
we had was the wet fire in August's eyes. But it was enough.

Rosaleen looked at me, and I could read her thoughts. *Just because
you broke me out of jail, don't get any bright ideas about Zach.* I   25
understood how people became career criminals. The first crime was
the hardest. After that you're thinking, *What's one more?* A few more
years in the slammer. Big deal.

"What are you gonna do about this?" said Rosaleen, standing
beside Clayton, looking down at him. Her breasts sat on her   30
stomach, and her fists were planted in her hips. She looked like she

---

2 **cornrow plait**: African hairstyle   4 **bail**: *Kaution*   28 **slammer** (infml): prison

wanted us all to fill our lips with snuff and go directly to the Tiburon jail and spit on people's shoes.

It was plain Rosaleen had fire in her, too. Not hearth fire, like August, but fire that burns the house down, if necessary, to clean up
5 the mess inside it. Rosaleen reminded me of the statue of Our Lady in the parlor, and I thought, *If August is the red heart on Mary's chest, Rosaleen is the fist.*

"I'll do my best to get him out," said Clayton, "but I'm afraid he's got to stay in there a little while."

10 I reached into my pocket and felt the black Mary picture, remembering the things I'd planned to say to August about my mother. But how could I do that now, with this terrible thing happening to Zach? Everything I wanted to say would have to wait, and I'd go back to the same suspended animation I'd been in before.

15 "I don't see why May needs to know about this," June said. "It will do her in. You know how she loves that boy."

Every one of us turned to look at August. "You're right," she said. "It would be too much for May."

"Where is she?" I asked.

20 "In her bed, asleep," Rosaleen said. "She was worn out."

I remembered I had seen her in the afternoon, out by the wall, pulling a load of stones in the wagon. Building onto her wall. As if she sensed a new addition was called for.

The jail in Tiburon did not have curtains like the one in Sylvan. It
25 was concrete-block gray, with metal windows and poor lighting. I told myself it was an act of stupidity to go inside. I was a fugitive from justice, and here I was breezing into a jail where there were probably policemen trained to recognize me. But August had asked if I wanted to come with her to visit Zach. How was I going to say
30 anything but yes to that?

14 **suspended animation**: feeling that you can't do anything because you are waiting for sth. to happen

The policeman inside had a crew cut and was very tall, taller than
Neil, and Neil was Wilt Chamberlain size. He didn't seem especially
glad to see us. "Are you his mother?" he asked August.

I looked at his name tag. Eddie Hazelwurst.

"I'm his godmother," August said, standing very erect, like she
was having her height measured. "And this is a friend of the family."

His eyes passed over me. The only thing he seemed suspicious
about was how a girl as white as me could be a friend of the family.
He picked up a brown clipboard from a desk and popped the
fastener up and down while he tried to decide what to do with us.
"All right, you can have five minutes," he said.

He opened a door into a corridor that led to a single row of four
jail cells, each of them holding a black boy. The smell of sweating
bodies and sour urinals almost overpowered me. I wanted to bring
my fingers up to pinch my nose, but I knew that would be the worst
insult. They couldn't help that they smelled.

They sat on benchlike cots hooked along the wall, staring at us as
we passed. One boy was throwing a button against the wall, playing
some kind of game. He stopped when we came by.

Mr. Hazelwurst led us to the last cell. "Zach Taylor, you got
visitors," he said, then glanced at his watch.

When Zach stepped toward us, I wondered if he'd been
handcuffed, fingerprinted, photographed, pushed around. I wanted
so much to reach through the bars and touch him, to press my
fingers against his skin, because it seemed only by touch that I could
be sure all this was actually happening.

When it was apparent Mr. Hazelwurst wasn't leaving, August
began to speak. She spoke about one of the hives she kept over on
the Haney farm, how it had up and swarmed. "You know the one,"
she said. "The one that had trouble with mites."

---

1 **crew cut**: very short haircut   2 **Wilt Chamberlain** (1936–1999): very tall US
basketball player

She went into minute detail about the way she'd searched high and low, into the dusk hours, combing the woods out past the watermelon fields, finally finding the bees in a magnolia sapling, the whole swarm hanging there like a black balloon caught in the
5 branches. "I used the funnel to drop them in a swarm box," she said, "then I hived them again."

I think she was trying to put it in Zach's mind that she would never rest till he was back home with us. Zach listened with his eyes watery brown. He seemed relieved to keep the conversation on the
10 level of bee swarms.

I'd worked on lines I wanted to say to him, too, but in the moment I couldn't remember them. I stood by while August asked him questions – how was he doing, what did he need?

I watched him, filled with tenderness and ache, wondering what
15 it was that connected us. Was it the wounded places down inside people that sought each other out, that bred a kind of love between them?

When Mr. Hazelwurst said, "Time's up, let's go," Zach cast his eyes in my direction. A vein stuck out right above his temple. I
20 watched it quiver, the blood pulsing through it. I wanted to say something helpful, to tell him we were more alike than he knew, but it seemed ridiculous to say that. I wanted to reach through the bars and touch the vein with the blood rushing through it. But I didn't do that either.

25 "Are you writing in your notebook?" he asked, his face and voice suddenly, oddly, desperate.

I looked at him and nodded. In the next cell, the boy – Jackson – made a noise, a kind of catcall, that caused the moment to seem silly and cheap. Zach shot him an angry look.

30 "Come on, you've had your five minutes," the policeman said. August placed her hand on my back, nudging me to leave. Zach

3 **sapling**: young tree   28 **catcall**: whistle or shout of a sexual nature

seemed as if he wanted to ask me something. He opened his mouth, then closed it.

"I'll write this all down for you," I said. "I'll put it in a story." I don't know if that's what he wanted to ask me, but it's something everybody wants – for someone to see the hurt done to them and set 5 it down like it matters.

We went around not bothering to smile, even in front of May. When she was in the room, we didn't talk about Zach, but we didn't act like the world was fine and rosy either. June resorted to her cello, the way she always did when sorrow came along. And walking to the 10 honey house one morning, August stopped and stared at the tire ruts in the driveway left by Zach's car. The way she stood there, I thought she might start to cry.

Everything I did felt heavy and difficult – drying the dishes, kneeling for evening prayers, even pulling down the sheets to get 15 into bed.

On the second day of the month of August, after the supper dishes were washed up, and the Hail Marys had been done, August said, No more moping tonight, we're going to watch Ed Sullivan. And that's what we were doing when the phone rang. To this day 20 August and June wonder how our lives would have been different if one of them had answered the phone instead of May.

I remember that August made a move to answer it, but May was closest to the door. "I'll get it," she said. No one thought a thing about it. We fixed our eyes on the television, on Mr. Sullivan, who 25 introduced a circus act involving monkeys that rode tiny scooters across a high wire.

19 **mope**: pity yourself   **Ed Sulllivan** (1902–74): US TV presenter

When May stepped back into the room a few minutes later, her eyes zigzagged from face to face. "That was Zach's mother," she said. "Why didn't you tell me about him getting put in jail?"

5 She looked so normal standing there. For a moment none of us moved. We watched her like we were waiting for the roof to cave in. But May just stood there, calm as she could be.

I started thinking maybe some sort of miracle had taken place and she'd somehow gotten cured.

"You all right?" said August, easing to her feet. May didn't answer.

10 "May?" June said.

I even smiled over at Rosaleen and nodded, as if to say, *Can you believe how well she's taking this?*

August, though, turned off the television and studied May, frowning.

15 May's head was angled to the side, and her eyes were fixed on a cross-stitched picture of a birdhouse that hung on the wall. It struck me all of a sudden that her eyes weren't actually seeing the picture. They had glazed completely over.

August went over to May. "Answer me. Are you all right?" In the

20 silence I heard May's breathing grow loud and a little ragged. She took several steps backward, until she came to the wall. Then she slid down onto the floor without making a sound. I'm not sure when it sank in that May had gone off to some unreachable place inside herself. Even August and June didn't realize it right away. They called

25 her name like she'd only lost her hearing.

Rosaleen bent over May and spoke in a loud voice, trying to get through to her. "Zach is gonna be all right. You don't need to worry any. Mr. Forrest is getting him out of jail on Wednesday." May stared straight ahead like Rosaleen wasn't even there.

30 "What's happened to her?" June asked, and I could hear a note of panic in her voice. "I've never seen her like this."

18 **glaze over**: become expressionless   20 **ragged**: (here) irregular

May was here but not here. Her hands lay limp in her lap, palms up. No sobbing into her dress skirt. No rocking back and forth. No pulling at her hair braids. She was so quiet, so different.

I turned my face to the ceiling, I just couldn't watch.

August went to the kitchen and came back with a dish towel   5
filled with ice. She pulled May's head to her so it rested against her shoulder for a minute, and then she lifted her sister's face and pressed the towel to May's forehead and temples and along her neck. She kept on doing this for several minutes, then put the cloth down and tapped May's cheeks with her hands.   10

May blinked a time or two and looked at August. She looked at all of us, huddled above her, as if she were returning from a long trip.

"You feel better?" said August.

May nodded. "I'll be okay." Her words came out in an odd   15
monotone.

"Well, I'm glad to see you can talk," said June. "Come on, let's get you in the bathtub."

August and June pulled May to her feet.

"I'm going to the wall," May said.   20

June shook her head. "It's getting dark."

"Just for a little while," May said. She moved into the kitchen, with all of us following after her. She opened a cabinet drawer, took out a flashlight, her tablet, a stub of a pencil, and walked onto the porch. I pictured her writing it down – *Zach in jail* – and pushing it   25
into a crevice in the wall.

I felt somebody should personally thank every rock out there for the human misery it had absorbed. We should kiss them one by one and say, *We are sorry, but something strong and lasting had to do this for May, and you are the chosen ones. God bless your rock hearts.*   30

"I'll go with you," said August.

24 **tablet**: *Schreibunterlage*

May spoke over her shoulder. "No, please, August, just me."

August started to protest. "But –"

"Just me," said May, turning to face us. "Just me."

We watched her go down the porch steps and move into the
trees. In life there are things you can't get over no matter how hard
you try, and that sight is one of them. May walking into the trees
with the little circle of light bobbing in front of her, then swallowed
up by the dark.

A bee's life is but short. During spring and summer – the most strenuous periods of foraging – a worker bee, as a rule, does not live more than four or five weeks … Threatened by all kinds of dangers during their foraging flights, many workers die before they have reached even that age.

The Dancing Bees

Chapter Ten

I sat in the kitchen with August, June, and Rosaleen while the night spread out around the house. May had been gone a whole five minutes when August got up and began to pace. She walked out to the porch and back and then stared out toward the wall.

After twenty minutes she said, "That's it. Let's go get her."   5

She got the flashlight from the truck and struck out for the wall, while June, Rosaleen, and I hurried to keep pace. A night bird was singing from a tree branch, just singing its heart out, urgent and feverish, like it was put there to sing the moon up to the top of the sky.   10

"Ma-a-a-a-y," called August. June called, too, then Rosaleen and me. We went along shouting her name, but no sound came back. Just the night bird singing up the moon.

After we walked from one end of the wailing wall to the other, we went back and walked it again, like this time we were going to get it 15 right. Walk slower, look closer, call louder. This time May would be there kneeling with the flashlight batteries burned out. We would think, *My goodness, how did we miss her here the first time?*

---

strenuous: demanding great effort   **forage**: look for food
3 **pace**: walk around nervously   7 **keep pace**: walk at the same speed

That didn't happen, though, so we walked into the woods behind the wall, calling her name louder and louder till I could hear the hoarseness creeping into our throats, but not one of us would say, *Something is terribly wrong.*

5   Despite the night, the heat had lingered on bad as ever, and I could smell the hot dampness of our bodies as we combed the woods with a spot of light four inches across. Finally August said, "June, you go to the house and call the police. Tell them we need help to find our sister. When you hang up, you kneel before Our
10 Lady and beg her to watch over May, then you come back. We're going to walk toward the river."

June took off running. We could hear her crashing through the brush as we turned toward the back of the property where the river flowed. August's legs moved faster and faster. Rosaleen struggled to
15 keep up, gulping for air.

When we reached the river, we stood there a moment. I'd been in Tiburon long enough for the full moon to fade away and grow back full again. It hung over the river, sliding in and out of clouds. I stared at a tree on the opposite bank, where the roots were exposed and
20 twisted, and felt a metallic-dry taste rise from the back of my throat and slide over my tongue.

I reached for August's hand, but she had turned right and was moving along the bank, calling May's name.

"Ma-a-a-ay."

25 Rosaleen and I moved behind her in our clumsy knot, so close we must have seemed to the night creatures like one big organism with six legs. I was surprised when the prayer we said after dinner each night, the one with the beads, started up of its own accord and recited itself in the back reaches of my head. I could hear each word
30 plainly. *Hail Mary, full of grace, the Lord is with thee. Blessed art thou among women, and blessed is the fruit of thy womb, Jesus. Holy Mary,*

---

3 **hoarseness**: roughness of sound   30 **art thou**: (old use) are you
31 **thy** (old use): your   **womb** [wuːm]: part of the female body where a foetus
develops

mother of God, pray for us sinners, now and at the hour of our death. Amen.

It wasn't till August said, "Good, Lily, we should all pray," that I realized I'd been repeating it out loud. I couldn't tell if I was saying it as a prayer or muttering it as a way to push down the fear. August 5 said the words with me, and then Rosaleen did, too. We walked along the river with the words streaming behind us like ribbons in the night.

When June came back, she was holding another flashlight she'd dug up somewhere at the house. The puddle of light wobbled as she 10 came through the woods.

"Over here," called August, aiming her flashlight up through the trees. We waited for June to reach the riverbank.

"The police are on their way," she said.

The police are coming. I looked at Rosaleen, at the ends of her 15 mouth turned down. The police hadn't recognized me the day I'd visited the jail; I hoped they didn't get lucky with Rosaleen.

June shouted May's name and plowed up the riverbank into the dark, followed by Rosaleen, but August moved slowly now, carefully. I stayed close behind her, saying Hail Marys to myself, faster and 20 faster.

Suddenly August stopped in her tracks. I stopped, too. And I didn't hear the night bird singing anymore.

I watched August, not taking my eyes off her. She stood tense and alert, staring down at the bank. At something I could not see. "June," 25 she called in a strange, whispery voice, but June and Rosaleen had pushed farther up the riverbank and didn't hear. Only I heard.

The air felt thick and charged, too thick to breathe. I stepped over beside August, letting my elbow touch her arm, needing the weight of her next to me; and there was May's flashlight, shut off and sitting 30 on the wet ground.

25 **alert** [ə'lɜːt]: very attentive

It seems odd to me now how we went on standing there another minute, me waiting for August to say something, but she didn't speak, just stood, soaking up that last moment. A wind rose up, raking its sound along the tree branches, hitting our faces like an
5 oven blast, like the sudden breezes of hell. August looked at me, then moved her flashlight beam out to the water.

The light swept across the surface, making a spatter of inkgold splotches before it stopped, abruptly. May lay in the river, just beneath the surface. Her eyes were wide open and unblinking, and
10 the skirt of her dress fanned out and swayed in the current.

I heard a noise come from August's lips, a soft moan.

I clutched frantically at August's arm, but she pulled free of me, threw down her flashlight, and waded into the river.

I splashed in after her. Water surged around my legs, causing me
15 to fall once on the slippery bottom. I grabbed for August's skirt, just missing. I came up sputtering.

When I reached her, August was staring down at her baby sister. "June," she shouted. "*June!*"

May lay in two feet of water with a huge river stone on top of her
20 chest. It weighted her body, holding it on the bottom. Looking at her, I thought, *She will get up now. August will roll away the stone, and May will come up for air, and we will go back to the house and get her dry.* I wanted to reach down and touch her, shake her shoulder a little. She couldn't have died out here in the river. That would be
25 impossible.

The only parts of her not submerged were her hands. They floated, her palms little ragged cups bobbing on the surface, the water weaving in and out of her fingers. Even now that's the picture that will wake me up in the night, not May's eyes, open and staring,
30 or the stone resting on her like a grave slab. Her hands.

---

3 **soak sth. up**: absorb sth.   4 **rake sth.**: (here) carry sth. loudly
8 **splotch**: spot, area   14 **surge**: move quickly upwards
20 **weight sth.**: keep sth. in its place   26 **submerged**: (here) under water
30 **slab**: thick piece of stone

June came thrashing into the water. When she reached May, she stood beside August, panting, her arms dangling beside her body. *"Oh, May,"* she whispered and looked away, squeezing her eyes closed.

Glancing toward the bank, I saw Rosaleen standing ankle deep in the river, her whole body shaking.

August knelt down in the water and shoved the stone off May's chest. Grabbing May by the shoulders, she pulled her up. Her body made an awful sucking sound as it broke the surface. Her head rolled back, and I saw that her mouth was partially open and her teeth were rimmed with mud. River reeds clung to her hair braids. I looked away. I knew then. *May was dead.*

August knew, too, but she put her ear to May's chest, listening. After a minute, though, she drew back and pulled May's head to *her* breast, and it almost seemed like she wanted May to listen now for *her* heart.

"We've lost her," August said.

I started to shiver. I could hear my teeth in my mouth, crashing against each other. August and June scooped their arms under May's body and struggled to carry her to the bank. She was saturated, bulging. I grabbed her ankles and tried to steady them. The river, it seemed, had carried away her shoes.

When they laid her down on the bank, water gushed from her mouth and nostrils. I thought, *This is the way Our Lady came washing up on the river near Charleston.* I thought, *Look at her fingers, her hands. They are so precious.*

I imagined how May had rolled the rock from the bank out into the river, then lay down, pulling it on top of her. She had held it tight, like a baby, and waited for her lungs to fill. I wondered if she had flailed and jerked toward the surface at the last second, or did she go without fighting, embracing the rock, letting it soak up all the

---

11 **reed**: water plant   20 **saturated**: completely wet   21 **bulging**: swollen
23 **gush**: stream out   30 **flail**: move your arms and legs around
jerk: move quickly

pain she felt? I wondered about the creatures that had swum by while she died.

June and August, sopping wet, stooped on either side of her, while mosquitoes sang in our ears and the river went on about its
5 business, coiling off into the darkness. I was sure they'd pictured May's last moments, too, but I did not see horror on their faces now, just a heartbroken acceptance. This had been the thing they'd been waiting for half their lives without even realizing it.

August tried to close May's eyes with her fingers, but they would
10 only stay half shut. "It's just like April," June said.

"Hold the flashlight on May for me," August said to her. The words came out quiet and steady. I could barely hear them over the bamming of my heart.

By the small beam of light, August plucked out the tiny green
15 leaves stuck in the plaits in May's hair and tucked each one into her pocket.

August and June scraped off every piece of river debris there was from May's skin and clothes, and Rosaleen, poor Rosaleen, who I realized had lost her new best friend, stood, not making a sound,
20 but with her chin shaking so awful I wanted to reach up and hold it for her.

Then a sound I will never forget whooshed out of May's mouth – a long, bubbling sigh, and we all looked at each other, confused, with a second of actual hope, as if the miracle of miracles was about
25 to take place after all, but it was only a pocket of swallowed air that had suddenly been released. It swept across my face, smelling like the river, like a piece of old wood that had gone moldy.

I looked down at May's face and felt a wave of nausea. Stumbling off into the trees, I bent over and vomited.

30 Afterward, as I wiped my mouth on the hem of my shirt, I heard a sound break through the darkness, a cry so piercing it made the

---

5 **coil off**: move in the shape of a spiral   13 **bam**: beat fast
17 **debris** [dəˈbriː]: pieces of rubbish   22 **whoosh out**: move out with watery
sound   28 **nausea** [ˈnɔːziə]: sickness

bottom of my heart drop. Looking back, I saw August framed in the light of June's flashlight, the sound coming from deep in her throat. When it faded away, she dropped her head straight down onto May's soggy chest.

I reached for the limb of a small cedar and held tight, as though 5
everything I had was about to slip from my hands.

"So you're an orphan?" the policeman said. It was that tall, crewcut Eddie Hazelwurst who'd escorted August and me in to see Zach in jail.

Rosaleen and I sat in the rocking chairs in the parlor, while he 10
stood before us holding a small notebook, ready to capture every word. The other policeman was outside searching around the wailing wall, for what I couldn't imagine.

My chair rocked so fast I was in danger of being pitched out of it. Rosaleen's, however, remained motionless – her face closed down. 15

When we'd first gotten back to the house after finding May, August had met both policemen and then sent me and Rosaleen upstairs. "Go on up there and get dried off," she'd said to me.

I'd peeled off my shoes and rubbed myself with a towel while we stood at the upstairs window. We'd watched the men from the 20
ambulance bring May back from the woods on a stretcher, then listened as the two policemen asked August and June all sorts of questions. Their voices had floated up the stairwell. *Yes, she's been depressed lately. Well, actually, she was depressed on and off all the time. She had a condition. She couldn't seem to distinguish other people's* 25
suffering from her own. No, we didn't find a note. An autopsy? All right, we understand.

Mr. Hazelwurst had wanted to talk to everyone, so here we were. I'd told him exactly what happened from the time May answered the telephone to the moment we found her in the river. Then he started 30

---

4 **soggy**: wet   25 **condition**: illness

with the personal questions. Wasn't I that girl who came to the jail last week to see one of the colored boys? What was I doing staying here? Who was Rosaleen?

I explained everything about my mother dying when I was small,
5 my father going to his Maker earlier this summer after a tractor accident, which was the story I was sticking with. Rosaleen, I said, was my nanny.

"I guess you could say I'm an orphan," I told him. "But I've got family in Virginia. It was my father's dying wish for me to go live
10 with my aunt Bernie. She's expecting me and Rosaleen both. She'll be sending us bus fare or driving down here and picking us up herself. She keeps saying, 'Lily, I can't wait for you to get here.' I tell her, 'Just so we're there before school starts.' I'll be a sophomore, which I cannot believe."

15 He narrowed his eyes like he was trying to follow all this. I was breaking every rule of successful lying. *Do not talk so much*, I told myself, but I couldn't seem to stop.

"I am so happy about going to live with her up there. She is real nice. You wouldn't believe all the stuff she has sent me over the
20 years. Especially costume jewelry and teddy bears. One bear after another."

I was only glad August and June were not present to hear this. They had left to follow the ambulance in the honey wagon, wanting to see May's body delivered safe and sound to wherever it was going.
25 It was bad enough Rosaleen was in the room. I was afraid she was going to give us away, say something like *Actually we came here right after Lily broke me out of jail*. But she sat drawn into herself, a complete mute.

"Now, what was your last name again?" he said.

30 "Williams," I said. I had told him this twice already, so I had to wonder what kind of educational requirements they had for policemen in Tiburon. It looked like the same ones as Sylvan.

---

13 **sophomore** [ˈsɒːfəmɔːr]: second year student

He drew up even taller. "Well, what I don't understand is, if you're going to live with your aunt in Virginia, what are you doing here?"

Here is the translation: *I am completely confused what a white girl like you is doing staying in a colored house.*   5

I took a breath. "Well, see, my aunt Bernie had to have an operation. It was female trouble. So Rosaleen over there said, 'Why don't me and you stay with my friend August Boatwright in Tiburon till Aunt Bernie gets on her feet again?' It was no sense in us going up there while she was in the hospital."   10

He was actually writing this down. Why? I wanted to yell at him, *This is not about me and Rosaleen and Aunt Bernie's operation. This is about May. She is dead, or haven't you noticed?*

I should've been in my room right then crying my eyeballs out, and here I was having the stupidest conversation of my life.   15

"Didn't you have any white people back in Spartanburg you could stay with?"

Translation: *Anything would be better than you staying in a colored house.*

"No, sir, not really. I didn't have that many friends. For some   20 reason I didn't fit in that well with the crowd. I think it was because I made such good grades. One lady at church said I could stay there till Aunt Bernie got well, but then she got shingles, and there went that."

Lord God, somebody stop me.   25

He looked at Rosaleen. "So how did you know August?"

I held my breath, aware that my rocking chair had come to a standstill.

"She's my husband's first cousin," Rosaleen said. "Me and her kept up after my husband left me. August was the only one of his   30 family who knew what a sorry jackass he was." She cut her eyes at

23 **shingles**: *Gürtelrose*   31 **jackass** (infml, AE): fool

me as if to say, *See? You aren't the only one who can concoct lies at the drop of a hat.*

He flipped his notebook shut and, crooking his finger at me, motioned me to follow him to the door. After he stepped outside, he
5 said, "Take my advice and call your aunt and tell her to come on and get you, even if she isn't a hundred percent well. These are colored people here. You understand what I'm saying?"

I wrinkled up my forehead. "No, sir, I'm afraid I don't."

"I'm just saying it's not natural, that you shouldn't be … well,
10 lowering yourself."

"Oh."

"I'm gonna come back soon, and I better not find you still here. Okay?" He smiled and put his gigantic hand on my head like we were two white people with a secret understanding.

15 "Okay."

I closed the door behind him. Whatever glue had kept me together throughout all that cracked then. I walked back into the parlor, already starting to sob. Rosaleen put her arm around me, and I saw tears coming down her face, too.

20 We walked up the stairs to the room she'd shared with May. Rosaleen pulled down the sheets on her bed. "Go on, get in," she told me.

"But where will you sleep?"

"Right over here," she answered, pulling back the covers on May's
25 bed, the pink-and-brown afghan May had crocheted with popcorn stitches. Rosaleen climbed in and pushed her face into the creases of the pillow. I knew she was smelling for May's scent.

You'd think I would have dreamed about May, but when I fell asleep, it was Zach who came. I can't even tell you what was
30 happening in the dream. I woke up, my breath panting a little, and I knew it had been about him. He seemed close and real, like I could sit up and touch my fingertips to his cheek. Then I remembered

---

1 **concoct lies**: invent lies   1–2 **at the drop of a hat**: very quickly
3 **crook your finger**: bend your finger   4 **motion sb. to do sth.**: indicate to sb.
what you want them to do   25 **crochet** [krouˈʃeɪ]: *häkeln*
25–26 **popcorn stitch**: particular style of crocheting

where he was, and an unbearable heaviness came over me. I pictured
his cot with his shoes sitting under it, how he was probably lying
awake this very moment watching the ceiling, listening to the other
boys breathe.

Across the room a rustling noise startled me, and I had one of   5
those strange moments where you don't know quite where you are.
Only half awake, I'd thought I was in the honey house, but it came
to me now that the sound was Rosaleen turning over in bed. And
then, then I remembered May. I remembered her in the river.

I had to get up, slip into the bathroom, and throw water on my   10
face. I was standing there with the night-light casting its small
brightness when I looked down and saw the claw-footed tub wearing
the red socks May had put on its porcelain feet. I smiled then; I
couldn't help it. It was the side of May I never wanted to forget.

I closed my eyes, and all the best pictures of her came to me. I   15
saw her corkscrew braids glistening in the sprinkler, her fingers
arranging the graham-cracker crumbs, working so hard on behalf of
a single roach's life. And that hat she wore the day she danced the
conga line with the Daughters of Mary. Mostly, though, I saw the
blaze of love and anguish that had come so often into her face.   20

In the end it had burned her up.

After the autopsy, after the police made her suicide official, after the
funeral home had fixed May up as pretty as they could, she came
home to the pink house. First thing Wednesday morning, August 5,
a black hearse pulled up in the driveway, and four men in dark suits   25
lifted out May's casket and brought it right into the parlor. When I
asked August why May was coming through the front door in her
coffin, she said, "We're going to sit with her till she's buried."

I hadn't expected this, as all the people I knew in Sylvan had their
dead loved ones go straight from the funeral home to the graveyard.   30

---

25 **hearse** [hɜːs]: vehicle that carries a coffin   26 **casket** (AE): coffin

August said, "We sit with her so we can tell her good-bye. It's called a vigil. Sometimes people have a hard time letting death sink in, they can't say good-bye. A vigil helps us do that."

If the dead person is right there in your living room, it would
5 certainly make things sink in better. It was strange to think about a dead person in the house, but if it helped us say good-bye better, then okay, I could see the point of it.

"It helps May, too," August said.

"Helps May?"

10 "You know we all have a spirit, Lily, and when we die, it goes back to God, but nobody really knows how long that takes. Maybe it takes a split second, and maybe it takes a week or two. Anyway, when we sit with May, we're saying, 'It's okay, May, we know this is your home, but you can go now. It'll be all right.'"

15 August had them roll the coffin, which sat on its own table with wheels, in front of Our Lady of Chains and then open it up. After the funeral home men drove away, August and Rosaleen walked up to the coffin and stared down at May, but I hung back. I was walking around, inspecting myself in the various mirrors, when June came
20 down with her cello and began to play. She played "Oh! Susanna," which made all of us smile. There is nothing like a small joke at a vigil to help you relax. I walked up to the coffin and stood between August and Rosaleen.

It was the same old May, except her skin was pulled tight across
25 her face bones. The lamplight spilling into the coffin gave her a kind of glow. They had her wearing a royal blue dress I had never seen, with pearl buttons and a boat-neck collar, and her blue hat. She looked like any second she would pop open her eyes and grin at us.

This was the woman who'd taught my mother everything there
30 was to know about getting rid of roaches in a nice way. I counted on my fingers the days since May had told me about my mother staying here. Six. It seemed like six months. I still wanted so badly to tell

---

2–3 **sink in**: if sth. sinks in you begin to understand it
27 **boat-neck collar**: collar with a rim tapering out to the shoulders

August what I knew. I guess I could've told Rosaleen, but it was really August I wanted to tell. She was the only one who knew what any of it meant.

Standing at the coffin, looking up at August, I had a powerful urge to tell her right then. Just blurt it out. *I'm not Lily Williams, I'm* 5 *Lily Owens, and it was my mother who stayed here. May told me.* And then it would all come out. Whatever terrible things might happen, would. When I peered up at her, though, she was brushing tears off her face, looking for a handkerchief in her pocket, and I knew it would be selfish to pour this into her cup when it was already to the 10 brim with grief for May.

June played with her eyes closed, as if May's spirit getting into heaven depended solely on her. You have never heard such music, how it made us believe death was nothing but a doorway.

August and Rosaleen finally sat down, but once I was up at the 15 coffin, I found I couldn't leave. May's arms were crossed over her chest, wings folded in on themselves, a pose I did not find flattering. I reached in and held her hand. It was waxy-cool, but I didn't care. *I hope you will be happier in heaven, I told her. I hope you will not need any kind of wall up there. And if you see Mary, Our Lady, tell her we know* 20 *Jesus is the main one down here, but we're doing our best to keep her memory going.* For some reason I felt exactly like May's spirit was hovering in a corner of the ceiling hearing every word, even though I wasn't speaking out loud.

And I wish you would look up my mother, I said. Tell her you saw me, 25 *that I'm at least away from T. Ray for the time being. Say this to her: "Lily would appreciate a sign letting her know that you love her. It doesn't have to be anything big, but please send something."*

I let out a long breath, still holding her dead hand, thinking how big her fingers felt in mine. *So I guess this is good-bye*, I told her. A 30

---

14 **doorway**: opening into a building, where the door is   25 **look sb. up**: visit sb.

shudder went through me, a burning along my eyelashes. Tears fell off my cheeks and spotted her dress.

Before I left her, though, I rearranged her a little. I folded her hands together and tucked them under her chin like she was
5 thinking seriously about the future.

At ten o'clock that morning, while June was playing more songs for May, and Rosaleen was poking around in the kitchen, I sat on the back-porch steps with my notebook, trying to write everything down, but really I was watching for August. She had gone out to the
10 wailing wall. I pictured her out there working her pain into the spaces around the stones.

By the time I spotted her coming back, I'd stopped writing and was doodling in the margins. She paused halfway across the yard and stared toward the driveway, shielding her eyes from the sun.
15 "Look who's here!" she yelled, breaking into a run.

I had never seen August run before, and I could not believe how quickly she crossed the grass with her loping strides, her long legs stretched out under her skirt. "It's Zach!" she shouted at me, and I dropped my notebook and flew down the steps.
20 I heard Rosaleen behind me in the kitchen shouting to June that Zach was here, heard June's music stop in the middle of a note. When I got to the driveway, he was climbing out of Clayton's car. August wrapped him up in her arms. Clayton stared at the ground and smiled.
25 When August turned Zach loose, I saw how much skinnier he looked. He stood there watching me. I couldn't read the expression on his face. I walked up to him, wishing I knew the right thing to say. A breeze tossed a piece of my hair across my face, and he reached out and brushed it away. Then he pulled me hard against his chest
30 and held me for a few moments.

---

13 **doodle**: draw random things   **margin**: *Rand*   17 **loping strides**: long steps

"Are you all right?" June said, rushing up and cupping his jaw in her hand. "We've been worried sick."

"I'm fine *now*," Zach said. But something I couldn't put my finger on had evaporated from his face.

Clayton said, "The girl who sells tickets at the theater – well,   5
apparently she saw the whole thing. It took her long enough, but she finally told the police which one of the boys threw the bottle. So they dropped the charges against Zach."

"Oh, *thank God*," said August, and every one of us seemed to breathe out all at once.   10

"We just wanted to come by and say how sorry we are about May," Clayton said. He embraced August, then June. When he turned to me, he placed his hands on my shoulders, not an embrace, but close. "Lily, how nice to see you again," he said, then looked at Rosaleen, who was hanging back by the car. "You, too, Rosaleen."   15
August took Rosaleen's hand and pulled her over, then went on holding it, the way she used to hold May's sometimes, and it struck me that she loved Rosaleen. That she would like to change Rosaleen's name to July and bring her into their sisterhood.

"I couldn't believe it when Mr. Forrest told me about May," said   20
Zach.

Walking back to the house so Clayton and Zach could take their turns beside the casket, I was thinking, *I wish I'd rolled my hair. I wish I'd done it in one of those new, beehive hairdos.*

We all gathered around May. Clayton bowed his head, but Zach   25
stared into her face.

We stood there and stood there. Rosaleen made a little humming sound, I think out of awkwardness, but eventually she stopped.

I looked over at Zach, and the tears were pouring down his cheeks.   30

---

24 **hairdo** (infml): hairstyle

"I'm sorry," he said. "It was all my fault. If I'd turned in the one¹ who threw the bottle, I wouldn't have gotten arrested and none of this would've happened."

I had thought maybe he would never find out it was his arrest
5 that sent May to the river. But that had been too much to hope for.

"Who told you?" I said.

He waved his hand like it didn't matter. "My mother heard it from Otis. She didn't want to tell me, but she knew I'd hear it from somewhere, sooner or later." He wiped his face. "I just wish I'd –"

10 August reached over and touched Zach's arm. She said, "Well, now, I guess I could say if I'd told May from the beginning about you getting arrested, instead of keeping it from her, none of this would've happened. Or if I'd stopped May from going out to the wall that night, none of this would've happened. What if I hadn't waited so
15 long before going out there and getting her –" She looked down at May's body. "It was May who did it, Zach."

I was afraid, though, the blame would find a way to stick to them. That's how blame was.

"I could use your help right now to drape the hives," August said to
20 Zach as they started to leave. "You remember like we did when Esther died?" Looking over at me, she said, "Esther was a Daughter of Mary who died last year."

"Sure, I can stay and help," said Zach.

"You wanna come, Lily?" August asked.

25 "Yes, ma'am." Draping the hives – I had no idea what that was, but you couldn't have paid me fifty dollars to miss it.

After Clayton said good-bye, we fastened on our hats and veils and went out to the hives, bearing armloads of black crepe material cut in giant squares. August showed us how to drape a square over

---

1 **turn sb. in**: hand sb. over to the police

each hive box, securing it with a brick and making sure we left the bees' entrance door open.

I watched how August stood a moment before each hive with her fingers knitted together under her chin. *Exactly what are we doing this for?* I wanted to know, but it seemed like a holy ritual I shouldn't interrupt.

When we had all the hives covered, we stood under the pines and gazed at them, this little town of black buildings. A city of mourning. Even the humming turned gloomy under the black drapes, low and long like foghorns must sound going across the sea at night.

August pulled off her hat and walked to the lawn chairs in the backyard with me and Zach tagging behind her. We sat with the sun behind us, staring out toward the wailing wall.

"A long time ago beekeepers always covered their hives when someone in their family died," said August.

"How come?" I asked.

"Covering the hives was supposed to keep the bees from leaving. You see, the last thing they wanted was their bees swarming off when a death took place. Having bees around was supposed to ensure that the dead person would live again."

My eyes grew wide. "Really?"

"Tell her about Aristaeus," Zach said.

"Oh, yes, Aristaeus. Every beekeeper should know that story." She smiled at me in a way that made me feel I was about to get Part Two of the beekeeper's induction, Part One being the sting. "Aristaeus was the first keeper of bees. One day all his bees died, punishment by the gods for something bad that Aristaeus had done. The gods told him to sacrifice a bull to show he was sorry, and then return to the carcass in nine days and look inside it. Well, Aristaeus did just what they said, and when he came back, he saw a swarm of bees fly out of the dead bull. His own bees, reborn. He took them home to his hives, and after that people believed that bees had power over

25 **induction**: introduction into a profession

death. The kings in Greece made their tombs in the shape of beehives for that very reason."

Zach sat with his elbows on his knees staring at the circle of grass, still fat and emerald green from our dance in the sprinkler. "When a
5 bee flies, a soul will rise," he said.

I gave him a blank look.

"It's an old saying," August said. "It means a person's soul will be reborn into the next life if bees are around."

"Is that in the Bible?" I said.

10 August laughed. "No, but back when the Christians hid from the Romans down in the catacombs, they used to scratch pictures of bees on the walls. To remind each other that when they died they'd be resurrected."

I shoved my hands under my thighs and sat up, trying to picture
15 catacombs, whatever they were. "Do you think putting black cloths over the hives will help May get to heaven?" I asked.

"Goodness no," August said. "Putting black cloths on the hives is for us. I do it to remind us that life gives way into death, and then death turns around and gives way into life."

20 I leaned back in my chair, gazing at the sky, how endless it was, the way it fit down over the world like the lid of a hive. I wished more than anything we could bury May in a beehive tomb. That I could, myself, lie down in one and be reborn.

When the Daughters of Mary showed up, they were loaded down
25 with food. The last time I'd seen them, Queenie and her daughter, Violet, had on the smallest hats in the group, and this time they'd left them off completely. I think it was because Queenie hated to cover the whiteness of her hair, which she was proud to have, and Violet, who had to be forty at least, couldn't bring herself to wear a hat if her

mother wasn't wearing one. If Queenie went into the kitchen and stuck her head in the oven, Violet would go stick hers in, too.

Lunelle, Mabelee, Cressie, and Sugar-Girl each wore a black hat, not as spectacular as the previous ones, except for Lunelle's, which had both a red veil and a red feather. They took off the hats and   5
lined them up on the piano as soon as they came in, so that you wanted to say, *What's the use?*

They got under way slicing ham, laying out fried chicken, shaking paprika on the deviled eggs. We had green beans, turnips, macaroni and cheese, caramel cake – all kinds of funeral foods. We ate standing   10
in the kitchen holding paper plates, saying how much May would have liked everything.

When we were so full that what we needed was a nap, we went to the parlor and sat with May. The Daughters passed around a wooden bowl full of something they called manna. A salted mixture of   15
sunflower, sesame, pumpkin, and pomegranate seeds drizzled with honey and baked to perfection. They ate it by the handfuls, saying they wouldn't dream of sitting with the dead without eating seeds. Seeds kept the living from despair, they explained.

Mabelee said, "She looks so good – doesn't she look good?"   20

Queenie snorted. "If she looks that good, maybe we ought to put her on display in the drive-by window at the funeral home."

"Oh, *Queenie!*" cried Mabelee.

Cressie noticed Rosaleen and me sitting there in the dark and said, "The funeral home in town has a drive-by window. It used to   25
be a bank."

"Nowadays they put the open casket right up in the window where we used to drive through and get our checks cashed," said Queenie. "People can drive through and pay their respects without having to get out. They even send the guest book out in the drawer   30
for you to sign."

"You ain't serious," said Rosaleen.

9 **deviled**: (of food) hot, spicy   16 **pomegranate** ['pɒmɪɡrænɪt]: *Granatapfel*

"Oh, yeah," Queenie said. "We're serious."

They might've been speaking the truth, but they didn't look serious. They were falling on each other laughing, and there was May, dead.

5   Lunelle said, "I drove in there one time to see Mrs. Lamar after she passed, since I used to work for her way back when. The woman who sat in the window beside her casket used to be the bank teller there, and when I drove off, she said, 'You have a nice day now.' "

I turned to August, who was wiping her eyes from tears of hilarity.
10   I said, "You won't let them put May in the bank window, will you?"

"Honey, don't worry about it," said Sugar-Girl. "The drive-by window is at the white people's funeral home. They're the only ones with enough money to fix up something that ridiculous."

They all broke down again with hysterics, and I could not help
15   laughing, too, partly with relief that people would not be joyriding through the funeral home to see May and partly because you could not help laughing at the sight of all the Daughters laughing.

But I will tell you this secret thing, which not one of them saw, not even August, the thing that brought me the most cause for
20   gladness. It was how Sugar-Girl said what she did, like I was truly one of them. Not one person in the room said, *Sugar-Girl*, really, *talking about white people like that and we have a white person present.* They didn't even think of me being different.

Up until then I'd thought that white people and colored people
25   getting along was the big aim, but after that I decided everybody being colorless together was a better plan. I thought of that policeman, Eddie Hazelwurst, saying I'd lowered myself to be in this house of colored women, and for the very life of me I couldn't understand how it had turned out this way, how colored women had
30   become the lowest ones on the totem pole. You only had to look at them to see how special they were, like hidden royalty among us. Eddie Hazelwurst. What a shitbucket.

9 **hilarity**: feeling of enjoyment   15 **joyride**: (here) drive for pleasure

I felt so warm inside toward them I thought to myself that if I should die, I would be glad to go on display in the bank window and give the Daughters of Mary a good laugh.

On the second morning of the vigil, long before the Daughters arrived, even before June came downstairs, August found May's 5 suicide note caught beneath the roots of a live oak, not ten yards from the spot she'd died. The woods had buried it under freshsprouted leaves, the kind that shoot up overnight.

Rosaleen was making banana cream pie in honor of May, and I was sitting at the table working on my cereal and trying to find 10 something decent on the transistor radio when August burst into the kitchen holding the note with two hands, like the words might fall off if she wasn't real careful.

She yelled up the stairs, "June, come down here. I found a note from May." 15

August spread it out on the table and stood over it with her hands pressed together. I turned off the plastic radio and stared at the crinkle-stiff paper, how the words were faded from being outside.

June's bare feet slapped the stairs, and she broke into the room. "Oh, God, August. What does it say?" 20

"It's so … May," August said, and she lifted up the note and read it to us.

Dear August and June,
I'm sorry to leave you like this. I hate you being sad, but think how 25
happy I'll be with April, Mama, Papa, and Big Mama. Picture us up there
together, and that will help some. I'm tired of carrying around the weight
of the world. I'm just going to lay it down now. It's my time to die, and it's
your time to live. Don't mess it up.
Love, May 30

18 **crinkle-stiff**: stiff but not smooth

August laid the note down and turned to June. She opened her arms wide, and June walked into them. They clung to each other – big sister to little sister, bosom to bosom, their chins wrapped around each other's necks.

5 They stayed that way long enough for me to wonder – should Rosaleen and I leave the room? – but finally they unwound themselves, and we all sat with the smell of banana cream pie.

June said, "Do you think it was really her time to die?"

"I don't know," said August. "Maybe it was. But one thing May
10 was right about is that it's our time to live. It's her dying wish that we do that, June, so we need to see to it. All right?"

"What do you mean?" said June.

We watched August walk over to the window, put her hands on the countertop, and gaze out at the sky. It was aquamarine and shiny
15 as taffeta. You had the feeling she was making a big decision.

"August, what?"

When August turned back, her jaw was set. "I'm going to say something to you, June." She walked over and stood in front of her. "You've been halfway living your life for too long. May was saying
20 that when it's time to die, go ahead and die, and when it's time to live, live. Don't sort-of-maybe live, but live like you're going all out, like you're not afraid."

"I don't know what you're talking about," June said.

"I'm saying marry Neil."

25 "What?"

"Ever since Melvin Edwards backed out of your wedding all those years back, you've been afraid of love, refusing to take a chance. Like May said, it's your time to live. Don't mess it up." June's mouth sat open in a wide circle, and not a word crossed her lips.

30 Suddenly the air was coated with the smell of burning. Rosaleen flung open the oven and yanked out the pie to find every last meringue tip scorched.

---

15 **taffeta**: stiff shiny cloth made from silk, used especially for dresses
30 **be coated with**: full of

"We'll eat it like that," said August. "A little burn taste never hurt anybody."

※

Every day for four days straight we kept the vigil. August had May's note with her at all times, tucked in her pocket or slipped under her belt if she had on a no-pocket dress. I watched June, how she seemed 5 quieter since August had lowered the boom on her about Neil. Not exactly sulking. Contemplating is more like it. I would catch her sitting beside the coffin leaning her forehead against it, and you could tell she was doing more than saying good-bye to May. She was trying to find her own answers to things.

One afternoon August and Zach and I went out to the hives and took off the black cloths. August said we couldn't leave them on too 10 long, since the bees had memorized everything about their hive and a change like that could make them disoriented. They might not find their way home again, she said. *Tell me about it*, I thought.

The Daughters of Mary showed up each day just before lunch and sat in the parlor with May through the afternoon, telling stories 15 about her. We cried a good bit also, but I could tell we were starting to feel better about saying good-bye. I only hoped May was feeling all right about it, too.

Neil stayed at the house nearly as much as the Daughters, and seemed downright confused by the way June stared into his face. 20 She could barely play the cello, because it meant turning loose of his hand. To tell the truth, the rest of us spent nearly as much time watching June and Neil as we did seeing May into the next life.

---

6 **lower the boom on sb.**: make it easier for sb.   7 **sulk**: *schmollen*

On the afternoon that the funeral home came to pick up May for the burial, bees buzzed around the front-window screens. As the coffin was loaded into the hearse, bee hum swelled and blended into the late-afternoon colors. Yellow-gold. Red. Tinges of brown.

5   I could still hear them humming at the graveside, even though we were miles away in a colored cemetery with crumbled markers and weeds. The sound carried on the breezes while we huddled together and watched them lower May's coffin into the ground. August passed around a paper bag full of manna, and we scooped up 10 handfuls and threw the seeds into the hole with the coffin, and my ears were filled with nothing but bee hum.

That night, in my bed, when I closed my eyes, bee hum ran through my body. Ran through the whole earth. It was the oldest sound there was. Souls flying away.

---

4 **tinge**: small amount of a colour   6 **marker** : tombstone

It takes honeybee workers ten million foraging trips to gather enough nectar to make one pound of honey.
Bees of the World

Chapter Eleven

After May's burial August shut down honey making, honey selling, even bee patrol. She and June took the meals that Rosaleen cooked to their rooms. I barely saw August except in the mornings when she crossed the yard headed toward the woods. She would wave at me, and if I ran over and asked where she was going, could 5 I come, too, she would smile and say not today, that she was still doing her mourning. Sometimes she would stay out in the woods past lunch.

I had to fight an impulse to say, *But I need to talk to you.* Life was so funny. I'd spent over a month here dillydallying around, refusing 10 to tell August about my mother when I could have done it so easy, and now that I really needed to tell her, I couldn't. You just don't interrupt somebody's mourning with your own problems.

I helped Rosaleen some in the kitchen, but mostly I was free to lie around and write in my notebook. I wrote so many things from my 15 heart that I used up all the pages.

It surprised me no end how much I missed our ordinary, routine life – the simple act of pouring wax into a candle mold or repairing

10 **dillydally around** (infml): waste time

a broken hive box. Kneeling between August and June for evening prayers to Our Lady.

I walked in the woods in the afternoon when I was sure August wasn't out there. I would pick out a tree and say, *If a bird lands in that*
5 *tree before I count to ten, that is my mother sending her sign of love.* When I got to seven, I would start counting real slow, dragging it out. I would get to fifty sometimes, and no bird.

I studied my map of South Carolina at night when everyone was asleep, trying to figure where me and Rosaleen might head next. I
10 had always wanted to see the rainbow-colored houses of Charleston, how they had real horse and buggies on the street, but as appealing as all that was, it nearly crushed me to think of leaving. And even if another cantaloupe truck miraculously appeared and drove us down there, Rosaleen and I would have to get jobs somewhere, rent a place
15 to stay, and hope nobody asked any questions.

Sometimes I didn't even feel like getting out of bed. I took to wearing my days-of-the-week panties out of order. It could be Monday and I'd have on underwear saying Thursday. I just didn't care.

20 The only time I saw June was when Neil came over, which was every single day. She would come out wearing hoop earrings, and off they'd go, taking long rides in his car, which, she said, did her a world of good. The wind rearranged her thoughts, and the countryside made her see all the life still left out there waiting to be
25 lived. Neil would get behind the wheel, and June would slide over on the front seat so she was practically under the wheel with him. Honestly, I worried for their safety.

Zach showed up a few times just to visit and found me in the lawn chair with my legs tucked under me, reading back over my

21 **hoop earring**: large earring in the shape of a circle

notebook. Sometimes when I saw him my stomach went through a
series of sudden drops and lurches.

"You are one-third friend, one-third brother, one-third bee
partner, and one-third boyfriend," I told him. He explained to me I
had one too many thirds in the equation, which, of course, I knew,   5
as I am bad in math but not *that* bad. We stared at each other as I
tried to figure out which third would get deleted.

I said, "If I was a Negro girl –"

He placed his fingers across my lips so I tasted his saltiness. "We
can't think of changing our skin," he said. "Change the world – that's   10
how we gotta think."

All he could talk about was going to law school and busting ass.
He didn't say *white* ass, and I was thankful for that, but I believe
that's what he meant.

There was a place inside him now that hadn't been there before.   15
Heated, charged, angry. Coming into his presence was like stepping
up to a gas heater, to a row of blue fire burning in the dark, wet
curve of his eyes.

His conversations were all about the race riots in New Jersey,
policemen taking their nightsticks to Negro boys who threw rocks,   20
about Molotov cocktails, sit-ins, righteous causes, Malcolm X, and
the Afro-American Unity group giving the Ku Klux Klan a taste of
their own medicine.

I wanted to say to Zach, *Remember when we ate May's Kool-Aid ice
under the pine trees? Remember when you sang "Blueberry Hill"?*   25
Remember?

After nonstop mourning all week, just when I thought we would go
on forever in our private, grieving worlds and never again eat another
meal together or work side by side in the honey house, I found
Rosaleen in the kitchen laying the table for four, using the Sunday-   30

---

2 **drops and lurches**: downward and forward movements   16 **charged**: aggressive,
tense   20 **nightstick** (AE): stick that policemen carry as a weapon

china plates with pink flowers and lacy scallops around the edge. I broke out with happiness because life seemed headed back to normal.

Rosaleen put a beeswax candle on the table, and I believe that
5 was the first candlelit meal of my entire life. Here was the menu: smothered chicken, rice and gravy, butter beans, sliced tomatoes, biscuits, and *candlelight*.

We had barely started in when Rosaleen said to June, "So are you gonna marry Neil or not?"

10 August and I both stopped chewing and sat up.

"That's for me to know and you to find out," June answered.

"And how are we supposed to find out, if you won't tell us?"said Rosaleen.

When we'd finished the food, August produced four bottles of
15 ice-cold Coca-Cola from the refrigerator, along with four little packages of salted peanuts. We watched her pop the tops off the Cokes.

"What the heck is *this*?" said June.

"It's Lily's and my favorite dessert," August told her, smiling over
20 at me. "We like to pour our peanuts straight into the bottle, but you can eat yours separately if you prefer."

"I think I prefer mine separate," said June, rolling her eyes.

"I wanted to make a cobbler," Rosaleen told June, "but August said it was gonna be Cokes and peanuts." She said "Cokes and
25 peanuts" the way you might say "snot and boogers."

August laughed. "They don't know a delicacy when they see one, do they, Lily?"

"No, ma'am," I said, shaking the peanuts into my bottle, where they caused a little reaction of foam, then floated on the brown
30 liquid. I drank and munched with the glory of salt and sweet in my mouth at the same time, all the while looking toward the window, at birds flying home to their nests and moonlight just starting to pour

---

1 **lacy**: like lace   **scallop**: small decorative curve   25 **snot**: *Nasenschleim*
booger (AE): *getrockneter Nasenschleim*

down on the midlands of South Carolina, this place where I was
tucked away with three women whose faces shone with candle glow.

When we had drained the Cokes, we went to the parlor to say
our Hail Marys together for the first time since May had died.

I knelt on the rug by June, while Rosaleen, as usual, helped ₅
herself to the rocker. August stood beside Our Lady and folded May's
suicide letter so it resembled a tiny paper airplane. She wedged it
into a deep crevice that ran down the side of Our Lady's neck. Then
she patted black Mary's shoulder and let out a long sigh that made
the airless room feel alive again. And said, "Well, that's that." ₁₀

I'd been staying up in May's room with Rosaleen ever since May
died, but when Rosaleen and I started to climb the stairs that night,
on impulse I said, "You know what? I think I'll move back into the
honey house." I found out I'd missed having a room to myself.

Rosaleen put her hands on her waist. "Good Lord, all that fuss ₁₅
you made about me moving out and leaving you, now here you are
wanting to leave me."

Actually, she didn't care one bit that I wanted to move out; she
just couldn't pass up a chance to give me a hard time. "Come on, I'll
help you carry your stuff over there," she said. ₂₀

"You mean, *now*?"

"No time like the present," she told me.

I guess she'd missed having a room to herself, too.

After Rosaleen left, I looked around my old room in the honey
house – it was so quiet. All I could think was how this time tomorrow ₂₅
the truth would be out, how everything would change.

I got my mother's photograph and the black Mary picture from
my bag, ready to show August. I slid them under my pillow, but
when I turned out the light, fear filled up my hard, narrow bed. It

15–16 **make a fuss about sth.**: complain about sth. more than necessary

told me all the ways life could go wrong. It had me in a girls' prison camp in the Florida Everglades. Why the Everglades, I don't know, except I've always thought that would be the worst place to be in prison. Think of all the alligators and snakes, not to mention heat
5 worse than we had here, and people had been known to fry not just eggs but bacon and sausage on South Carolina sidewalks. I could not imagine breathing in Florida. I would be down there suffocating and never see August again.

It was fear all night long. I would've given anything to be back in
10 May's room, listening to Rosaleen snore.

The next morning I slept late, considering the on-and-off night I'd had, plus I'd been falling into lazy habits without the honey house to keep me industrious. The smell of fresh-baked cake wafted all the way from the pink house to my cot, curled into my nostrils, and
15 woke me up.

When I got to the kitchen, there were August, June, and Rosaleen, dusted with flour, baking these small one-layer cakes the size of honey buns. They were singing while they worked, singing like the Supremes, like the Marvelettes, like the Crystals wiggling their butts
20 to "Da Doo Ron Ron."

"What are y'all doing?" I said, grinning from the doorway. They stopped singing and giggled, giving each other little shoves and nudges.

"Well, look who's up," said Rosaleen.

25 June had on lavender pedal pushers with daisy buttons up the sides, the likes of which I'd never seen before. She said, "We're baking cakes for Mary Day. It's about time you got over here and helped us. Didn't August tell you this was Mary Day?"

I glanced at August. "No, ma'am, she didn't."

---

11 **on-and-off**: irregular over a period of time   13 **waft**: move in the air
19 **Supremes, Marvelettes, Crystals**: US girl groups
20 **Da Doo Ron Ron**: refrain of a pop song   25 **pedal pushers**: trousers reaching to the calves

August, who was wearing one of May's aprons, the one with ruffles trailing over the shoulders, wiped her hands across the front and said, "I guess I forgot to mention it. We've been celebrating Mary Day around here every August for fifteen years. Come on and get your breakfast, and then you can help us. We've got so much to do I   5
don't know whether we're gonna make it."

I filled a bowl with Rice Krispies and milk, trying to think over the snap-crackle conversation it was having with itself. How was I supposed to have a life-altering talk with August with all *this* going on?   10

"A thousand years ago women were doing this exact same thing," said August. "Baking cakes for Mary on her feast day."

June looked at my blank face. "Today is the Feast of the Assumption. August fifteenth. Don't tell me you never heard of that."

Oh, sure, the Feast of the Assumption–Brother Gerald preached   15
on that every other Sunday. Of course I'd never heard of it. I shook my head. "We didn't really allow Mary at our church except at Christmas."

August smiled and dunked a wooden drizzle into the vat of honey, which sat on the counter by the toaster oven. While she spun   20
honey across the tops of a fresh pan of cakes, she explained to me in detail how the Assumption was nothing less than Mary rising up to heaven. Mary died and woke up, and the angels carried her up there in swirling clouds.

"May is the one who started calling it Mary Day," said June. "It's   25
not just about the Assumption, though," August said, shoveling the cakes onto the wire racks. "It's a special remembrance for our own Lady of Chains. We reenact her story. Plus we give thanks for the honey crop. The Daughters of Mary come. It's our favorite two days of the year."   30

"You do this for two days?"

---

2 **ruffle**: *Krause*   8 **snap-crackle**: consisting of repeated sharp sounds
19 **drizzle**: *Rührstock*   **vat**: large container for liquids

"We start this evening and finish tomorrow afternoon," said August. "Hurry up with your cereal, because you've got to make streamers and garlands, hang the Christmas lights, put out the candleholders, wash the wagon, and get out the chains."

5 I was thinking, *Whoa, back up*. Wash the wagon? Hang Christmas lights? Get out the chains? The *chains*?

The knock on the back door came as I was putting my bowl in the sink. "If this isn't the best-smelling house in Tiburon, I'll be a monkey's uncle," said Neil, stepping inside.

10 "Well, I guess you're saved from that special relationship then," June said.

She offered him a honey cake, but he shook his head, which was a dead giveaway right there that he had something on his mind. Neil did not refuse food. Ever. He stood in the middle of the floor, 15 shuffling from one foot to the other.

"What are you doing here?" June asked.

He cleared his throat, rubbed his sideburns. "I – I came over here hoping for a word with you."

This sounded so stiff coming out of his mouth that June narrowed 20 her eyes and studied him a second. "Are you all right?"

"I'm fine." He put his hands in his pockets. Took them out. "I just want a word with you."

She stood there waiting. "Well, I'm listening," she said.

"I thought we could take a drive."

25 She looked around the kitchen. "If you haven't noticed, I'm up to my ears in work, Neil."

"I can see that, but –"

"Look, just tell me what it is," June said, starting to get into one of her huffs. "What is so all-fired important?"

30 I glanced at August, who had her lips screwed over to the side, trying to look busy. Rosaleen, on the other hand, had stopped all semblance of work and looked from June to Neil. Back to June.

---

3 **streamer**: long piece of coloured paper used as decoration
garland: *Girlande*   8–9 **I'll be a monkey's uncle**: expression of surprise
17 **sideburns**: *Koteletten*   29 **huff** (infml): bad mood   30 **screw over**: twist out of shape

"Hell," he said, "I came over here planning to ask you, for the hundredth time, to marry me."

I dropped my spoon in the sink. August laid down the honey drizzle. June opened her mouth and closed it without anything coming out. Everyone just stood there.   5

Come on. Don't mess up your time to live.

The house creaked, like old houses do. Neil glanced at the door. I felt my shirt dampen all under my arms. I had the sensation I used to get in fifth grade when the teacher would write some nonsense word on the blackboard, like "pnteahel," and we had two minutes to   10
unscramble it and find the word "elephant" before she dinged her bell. I used to break out in a sweat trying to beat the clock. I had that feeling now, like Neil was going to walk out the door before June could unscramble the answer in her heart.

Rosaleen said, "Well, don't just stand there with your mouth   15
open, June. Say something."

June stared at Neil, and I could see the struggle in her face. The surrender she had to make inside. Not just to Neil but to life. Finally she let out a long, sighing breath. "All right," she said. "Let's get married."   20

Rosaleen slapped her thigh and burst out with a whoop, while August broke into the biggest smile I believe I'd ever seen on her face. Me, I just looked from one person to another, trying to take it in.

Neil walked over and kissed June right on the mouth. I didn't   25
think they were ever going to come up for air.

When they did, Neil said, "We're going to the jewelry store this minute and pick out a ring before you change your mind."

June cast a look back at August. "Well, I hate to leave them with all this work," she said, but I could tell she didn't mind a bit.   30

"Go on," August said.

---

11 **unscramble sth.**: put sth. in the right order   11–12 **ding the bell**: ring the bell
21 **whoop**: cry of joy

When they'd left, August, Rosaleen, and I sat down and ate honey cake while it was still hot, talking over what had just happened. We had all these chores facing us, but some things you have to sit and mull over before you can go on. We said, "Did you see the look on
5 Neil's face?" … "Can you believe that kiss?" Mostly we just stared at each other, saying "June's getting *married*!"

Getting ready for Mary Day was nonstop work. First August got me started on the streamers. I cut packages of thick blue-and-white crepe paper into strips till I had rubbed blisters on both thumbs. I
10 formed little twists in the edges with my fingers to give them a curled effect, then dragged the stepladder into the yard and hung them from the myrtle trees.

I clear-cut the gladiolus bed and made a six-foot garland by wiring the blossoms to a piece of string, which I thought I never
15 would get right. When I asked August what I was supposed to do with it, she said, "Drape it around the wagon." Well, of course. Why didn't I think of that?

Next I rummaged around in the hall closet for the Christmas lights, which she had me wind around the bushes by the backporch
20 steps, not to mention all the extension cords I had to rig.

As I worked, Zach pushed the lawn mower, shirtless. I set up the card tables beside the myrtle trees so the streamers would drift over and tickle our faces while we ate. I tried not to look at him, his tight skin sparkling with sweat, his dogtag hanging from the chain around
25 his neck, his shorts slung low on his hips, the little tuft of hair starting under his navel.

He hoed up a big infestation of cabbage weeds, without even being asked to. He swung the hoe with a blaze of angry grunts, while I sat on the steps and dug candle wax out of two dozen glass holders.

---

4 **mull over sth.**: think about sth.   13 **clear-cut** (v): cut off everything
18 **rummage**: search for sth.   20 **extension cord**: *Verlängerungskabel*
25 **tuft of sth.**: small amount of sth.   27 **hoe up**: *aushacken* **infestation**:
Wucherung   28 **grunt**: pig noise

I refilled them with fresh candles and set them all around on the grass, under the trees, mostly in the little holes of earth where the cabbage weeds had grown.

Up on the back porch August cranked the ice cream churn. Beside her feet sat a coil of chains. I stared at it. "What's that for?"   5

"You'll see," she said.

At 6:00 p.m. I was exhausted from Mary Day goings-on, and the real part hadn't even started. I got the last thing on my list done and was headed to the honey house to get dressed, when June and Neil pulled into the driveway.   10

June waltzed up with her hand stuck out so I could admire her ring. I looked it over, and I have to say Neil had outdone himself. It wasn't that big, really, it was just so pretty. The diamond was tucked inside a scalloped silver setting.

"That's the most beautiful ring I've ever seen," I said.   15

She kept her hand stretched out, turning it this way and that, letting the diamond catch the light. "I think May would have loved it, too," she said.

The first carload of the Daughters drove up then, and June sauntered toward them with her hand outstretched.   20

Inside the honey house I lifted up my pillow to be sure my mother's photograph and her black Mary picture were still underneath like I'd left them. Feast Day or not, tonight *had* to be the night I got the truth from August. The thought set off a nervous quiver through me. I sat down on the cot and felt things building   25
inside – pushing against my chest.

Heading back to the pink house, wearing clean shorts and a top, my hair all combed, I stopped to behold everything. August, June, Rosaleen, Zach, Neil, Otis, and all the Daughters of Mary stood around on the mowed grass beside the card tables, their laughter   30

4 **churn**: ice cream machine   20 **saunter**: walk confidently and relaxed
25 **quiver**: slight shaking

low and vibrating. Piles of food. Blue-and-white streamers rippling in the breezes. The Christmas lights glowed in spirals of color around the porch, and all the candles were lit, even though the sun was still working its way down. Every molecule of air gave off red fire.

5   I said to myself, *I love this place with my whole heart.*

The Daughters fussed over me – how good I smelled, how exceptional my hair was when it was combed. Lunelle said, "Would you like me to make you a hat, Lily?"

"Really? You'd make me a hat?" Where I would wear a Lunelle-
10   created hat was a mystery, but I wanted one all the same. At the least, I could get buried in it one day.

"Of course I'll make you a hat. I'll make you a hat you won't believe. What color would you like?"

August, who was listening in, said, "Blue," and winked at me.
15   First we ate. By now I'd learned eating was a high priority with the Daughters. When we finished, the redness had seeped from the day and night was arranging herself around us. Cooling things down, staining and dyeing the evening purple and blue-black. Rosaleen brought out the platter of honey cakes and set them on one of the
20   tables.

August motioned us to stand around the table in a circle. The Mary Day program was under way.

"These are Mary's honey cakes. Cakes for the Queen of Heaven," August said.

25   She took one of them in her hand and, pinching off a piece, held it before Mabelee, who stood next to her in the circle. August said, "This is the body of the Blessed Mother." Mabelee closed her eyes and opened her mouth, and August laid the cake on her tongue.

After Mabelee had swallowed, she did the same thing August had
30   done – snipped off a piece and gave it to the next person in the circle, who happened to be Neil. Mabelee, who could not have measured five feet tall in spike heels, practically needed a stepladder

18 **dye sth.**: change the colour of sth.   30 **snip sth. off**: (here) pinch sth. off
32 **spike heels**: shoes with high heels

to get up to his mouth. Neil crouched down and opened wide. "This
is the body of the Mother," Mabelee said, and popped it in.

I did not know one thing, really, about the Catholic Church, but
somehow I felt sure the pope would have keeled over if he'd seen
this. Not Brother Gerald, though. He wouldn't have wasted time   5
fainting, just gotten busy arranging the exorcism.

Me, I had never seen grown-ups feed each other, and I watched
with the feeling I might burst out crying. I don't know what got to
me about it, but for some reason that circle of feeding made me feel
better about the world.   10

As life would have it, the one who fed me turned out to be June.
Opening my mouth, closing my eyes, and waiting for the body of
the Mother, I heard June's whisper brush my ear – "I'm sorry for
being hard on you when you first got here" – and then the sweetness
of honey cake spread through my mouth.   15

I wished it could have been Zach standing next to me so I could
lay the cake on his tongue. I would have said, *I hope this softens you
toward the world. I hope it brings you a tender feeling.* Instead I got to
give the pinch of cake to Cressie, who ate it with her eyes closed.

After we were all fed, Zach and Neil went to the parlor and   20
returned carrying Our Lady of Chains. Otis followed after them,
lugging the pile of chain. They stood her upright in the red wagon.
August leaned over to me. "We're going to reenact the story of Our
Lady of Chains. We're taking her over to the honey house and
chaining her in there for the night."   25

I thought, *Our Lady is spending the night in the honey house. With
me.*

As August pulled the wagon slowly across the yard, Zach and
Neil braced Our Lady with their hands. If I do say so, the flower
garland around the wagon set the whole thing off.   30

19 **pinch of sth.**: small quantity of sth.   22 **lug sth.**: carry sth. heavy   29 **brace
sb./sth.**: (here) hold sb./sth. in a steady position   30 **set sth. off**: make sth. look
perfect

June carried her cello, while the Daughters trailed the wagon single file, carrying burning candles. They sang, "Mary, star of the sea, Mary, brightest moon, Mary, comb of honey."

Rosaleen and I brought up the rear, toting candles, too, trying to
5 hum along, since we didn't know the words. I cupped one hand around the flame of my candle to be sure it didn't blow out.

At the door of the honey house, Neil and Zach lifted the statue out of the wagon and carried her inside. Sugar-Girl nudged Otis with her elbow, and he stepped up and helped them get her situated
10 between the extractor and the baffle tank.

"All right," August said. "Now we'll start the last part of our service. Why don't you stand in a semicircle right here around Our Lady."

June played us a gloomy-sounding song on the cello while August
15 retold black Mary's story start to finish. When she got to the part about the slaves touching Our Lady's heart and how she filled them with fearlessness and plans of escape, June turned up the volume.

"Our Lady became so powerful," said August, "that the master was forced to put her under house arrest, to chain her in the carriage
20 house. She was cast down and bound up."

"The blessed, blessed Mother," mumbled Violet.

Neil and Otis took the chains and started wrapping them around Our Lady. The way Otis tossed the chain around in the candlelight, I was sure it would be a miracle if he didn't kill somebody.

25 August went on. "But each time the master chained Mary in the carriage house, she would break the chains and return to her people."

August paused. She went around the circle and looked at us one by one, letting her eyes settle on each face like she wasn't in any kind
30 of rush.

Then she lifted her voice. "What is bound will be unbound. What is cast down will be lifted up. This is the promise of Our Lady."

---

4 **tote sth.**: carry sth.   20 **cast sth. down**: throw sth. to the ground

"Amen," said Otis.

June began to play again, this time a more joyful tune, thank goodness. I gazed at Mary, wrapped head to toe in rusted chain. Outside, heat lightning pulsed across the sky.

They all seemed to be sunk in their meditating, or whatever it 5 was they were doing. Everyone's eyes were closed, except Zach's. He stared right at me.

I glanced at poor, shackled Mary. I couldn't bear seeing her like that. "It is only a reenactment," August had said. "To help us remember. Remembering is everything." Still, the whole idea 10 wrapped me in sadness. I hated remembering.

I turned and walked out of the honey house, into the warm hush of night.

Zach caught up with me as I reached the tomato garden. He took my hand, and we kept walking, stepping over May's wall, walking into 15 the woods without speaking. The cicadas were going crazy, filling the air with their strange brand of singing. Twice I walked into a spider's web, feeling the fine, transparent threads across my face, and I liked them there. A veil spun from the night.

I wanted the river. Its wildness. I wanted to strip naked and let 20 the water lick my skin. Suck river stones the way I'd done that night Rosaleen and I'd slept by the creek. Even May's death had not ruined the river for me. The river had done its best, I was sure, to give her a peaceful ride out of this life. You could die in a river, but maybe you could get reborn in it, too, like the beehive tombs August had told 25 me about.

Beneath the trees, moonlight trailed down. I steered us toward the water.

Water can be so shiny in the dark. We stood on the bank and watched the moving pockets of light, letting the water sounds swell 30

---

8 **shackle sb.**: tie sb. in chains

up around us. We were still holding hands, and I felt his fingers tighten around mine.

"There was a pond near where I used to live," I said. "Sometimes I would go there to wade in the water. One day the boys from the
5 next farm were there fishing. They had all these little fish they'd caught fastened onto a stringer. They held me down on the bank and hooked it around my neck, making it too small to pull over my head. I was shouting, 'Let me up, get that off me,' but they laughed and said, 'What's the matter, don't you like your fish necklace?' "

10 "Goddamn boys," Zach said.

"A few of the fish were already dead, but most of them flapped around with their eyes staring at me, looking scared. I realized if I swam out into the water up to my neck, they could breathe. I got as far as my knees, but then I turned back. I was too afraid to go any
15 further. I think that was the worst part. I could've helped them, but I didn't."

"You couldn't have stayed out there in the pond forever," Zach said.

"But I could've stayed a long time. All I did was beg them to undo
20 the stringer. *Begged*. They said to shut up, I was their fish holder, so I sat there till all the fish died against my chest. I dreamed about them for a year. Sometimes I would be hooked on the chain along with them."

"I know that feeling," he said.

25 I looked as far into his eyes as I could see. "Getting arrested –" I didn't know how to put it.

"What about it?" he said.

"It changed you, didn't it?"

He stared at the water. "Sometimes, Lily, I'm so angry I wanna kill
30 something."

6 **stringer**: rope or wire to hold things   7 **hook sth.**: hang sth.

"Those boys who made me wear the fish – they were angry like that, too. Angry at the world, and it made them mean. You have to promise me, Zach, you won't be like them."

"I don't want to," he said.

"Me either."   5

He bent his face close to mine and kissed me. At first it was like moth wings brushing my lips, then his mouth opening on mine. I gave way against him. He kissed me gently, but at the same time hungrily, and I liked how he tasted, the scent of his skin, the way his lips opened and closed, opened and closed. I was floating on a river   10 of light. Escorted by fish. Jeweled with fish. And even with so much beautiful aching inside my body, with life throbbing beneath my skin and the rushing ways of love taking over, even with all of that, I could feel the fish dying against my heart.

When the kiss was over, he looked at me with burning in his face.   15 "Nobody will believe how hard I'm gonna study this year. That jail cell is gonna make me earn grades higher than I ever got. And when this year is over, nothing can keep me from leaving here and going to college."

"I know you'll do it," I said. "You will." And it wasn't just words.   20 I'm good at sizing up people, and I knew for a fact he would make himself into a lawyer. Changes were coming, even to South Carolina – you could practically smell them in the air – and Zach would help bring them. He would be one of those drum majors for freedom that Martin Luther King talked about. That's how I liked to think of Zach   25 now. A drum major.

He faced me, and shifting around on his feet, he said, "I want you to know that I –" He stopped and looked up into the treetops.

I stepped nearer to him. "You want me to know what?"

"That I – I care about you. I think about you all the time."

---

21 **size sb. up**: judge sb.   24 **drum major**: leader of a marching band

It crossed my mind to say there were things he didn't know about me, that he might not care so much if he knew them, but I smiled and said, "I care about you, too."

"We can't be together now, Lily, but one day, after I've gone away and become somebody, I'm gonna find you, and we'll be together then."

"You promise?"

"I promise." He lifted the chain with his dogtag from around his neck and lowered it over my head. "So you won't forget, okay?"

The silver rectangle dropped down under my shirt, where it dangled cold and certain between my breasts. Zachary Lincoln Taylor, resting there, along my heart.

Wading in up to my neck.

If the queen were smarter, she would probably be hopelessly neurotic. As is, she is shy and skittish, possibly because she never leaves the hive, but spends her days confined in darkness, a kind of eternal night, perpetually in labor. … Her true role is less that of a queen than mother of the hive, a title often accorded to her. And yet, this is something of a mockery because of her lack of maternal instincts or the ability to care for her young.

The Queen Must Die: And Other Affairs of Bees and Men

Chapter Twelve

I waited for August in her room. Waiting was a thing I'd had tons of experience doing. Waiting for the girls at school to invite me somewhere. For T. Ray to change his ways. For the police to show up and drag us off to the Everglades prison. For my mother to send a sign of love. 5

Zach and I had hung around outside till the Daughters of Mary finished in the honey house. We'd helped them clean up the mess in the yard, me stacking plates and cups and Zach folding up card tables. Queenie had smiled and said, "How come you two left before we finished?" 10

"It got too long," said Zach.

"So that's what it was," she teased, and Cressie giggled.

When Zach left, I slipped back into the honey house and retrieved my mother's photograph and her black Mary picture from underneath my pillow. Clutching them in my hands, I glided past the Daughters 15 as they finished up the dishes in the kitchen. They called to me, "Where're you going, Lily?"

---

skittish: easily excited   **be confined**: be kept in a small space   **labor**: *Wehen*
13–14 **retrieve sth.**: find sth.

I hated to be rude, but I found I couldn't answer, couldn't speak a word of idle talk. I wanted to know about my mother. I didn't care about anything else.

I marched straight into August's room, a room filled with the
5 smell of beeswax. I switched on a lamp and sat on the cedar chest at the end of her bed, where I folded and unfolded my hands eight or ten times. They were cool, damp, with a mind of their own. All they wanted to do was fidget and pop knuckles. I stuck them under my thighs.

10 The only other time I'd been in August's room was the time I'd fainted during the Daughters of Mary meeting and wakened in her bed. I must have been too muddled then to see it, because it all seemed new to me. You could've wandered around in this room for hours and had a field day looking at her stuff.

15 For starters, everything was blue. Bedspread, curtains, rug, chair cushion, lamps. Don't get the idea it was boring, though. She had ten different shades of it. Sky blue, lake blue, sailor blue, aqua blue – you name a blue. I had the feeling of scuba diving through the ocean.

20 On her dressing table, where less interesting people would've put a jewelry box or a picture frame, August had a fish aquarium turned upside down with a giant piece of honeycomb inside it. Honey had oozed out and formed puddles on the tray underneath.

On her bedside tables were beeswax candles, melted down into
25 brass holders. I wondered if they could be the ones I'd personally created. It gave me a little thrill to think so, how I had helped to light August's room when it was dark.

I walked over and inspected the books arranged neatly on her bookshelf. The *Advanced Language of Beekeeping, Apiary Science, Bee*
30 *Pollination, Bulfinch's Age of Fable, The Myths of Greece, The Cultivation of Honey, Bee Legends Around the World, Mary Through the Ages.* I pulled the last one off the shelf and opened it across my lap,

2 **idle talk**: conversation that is not serious   8 **pop knuckles**: make a noise with your knuckles by pulling your fingers   12 **muddled**: confused   14 **have a field day**: have a lot of fun (as with children let out of class to do sport events)
18 **scuba diving**: swimming under water with a tube for breathing   23 **ooze out**: flow out slowly

thumbing through the pictures. Sometimes Mary was brunette and brown-eyed, other times blond and blue-eyed, but gorgeous every time. She looked like a Miss America contestant. A Miss Mississippi. You can usually count on the girls from Mississippi to win. I couldn't help wishing to see Mary in a swimsuit and heels – before her 5 pregnancy, of course.

The big shock, though, was all the pictures of Mary being presented with a lily by the angel Gabriel. In every one, where he showed up to tell her she was going to have the baby of babies, even though she wasn't married yet, he had a big white *lily* for her. As if 10 this was the consolation prize for the gossip she was in for. I closed the book and put it back on the shelf.

A breeze moved through the room from the open window. I walked to it and stared out at the dark fringe of trees by the edge of the woods, a half moon wedged like a gold coin into a slot, about to 15 drop through the sky with a clink. Voices filtered through the screen. Women voices. They rose in chirps and melted away. The Daughters were leaving. I twisted my hair with my fingers, walked around the throw rug in circles, the way a dog will do before it settles onto the floor. 20

I thought about prison movies in which they're about to electrocute some prisoner – wrongly convicted, of course – the camera going back and forth between the poor man sweating in his cell block and the clock creeping toward twelve.

I sat down on the cedar chest again. 25

Footsteps landed on the floorboards in the hallway, precise, unhurried steps. August steps. I sat up straighter, taller, my heart starting to beat so I could hear it in my ears. When she stepped into the room, she said, "I thought I might find you here."

I had a desire to bolt past her through the door, dive out the 30 window. *You don't have to do this*, I told myself, but the wanting rose up. I had to know.

---

3 **contestant** [kən'testənt]: person taking part in a contest   16 **clink**: metallic sound   17 **chirp**: bird sound

"Remember when …" I said. My voice came out barely a whisper.
I cleared my throat. "Remember when you said we should have a
talk?"

She closed the door. A sound so final. *No turning back*, it said. *This
5 is it*, it said.

"I remember it very well."

I laid out the photograph of my mother on the cedar chest.

August walked over and picked up the picture. "You are the
spitting image of her."

10 She turned her eyes on me, her big, flickering eyes with the
copper fire inside them. I wished I could look out at the world
through them just one time.

"It's my mother," I said.

"I know, honey. Your mother was Deborah Fontanel Owens." I
15 looked at her and blinked. She stepped toward me, and the yellow
lamplight glazed her glasses so I could no longer make out her eyes.
I shifted my position so I could see them better.

She dragged the chair from her dressing table over to the cedar
chest and sat down facing me. "I'm so glad we're finally going to talk
20 this out."

I could feel her knee barely touching mine. A full minute passed
without either of us saying a word. She held the picture, and I knew
she was waiting for me to break the silence.

"You knew she was my mother all along," I said, uncertain
25 whether I felt anger, or betrayal, or just plain surprise.

She placed her hand on mine and brushed her thumb back and
forth across my skin. "The first day you showed up, I took one look
at you and all I could see was Deborah when she was your age. I
knew Deborah had a daughter, but I thought no, you couldn't be; it
30 was too much to believe that Deborah's daughter would turn up in
my parlor. Then you said your name was Lily, and right that minute
I knew who you were."

8–9 **be the spitting image of sb.**: look exactly like sb. else   15 **blink**: *blinzeln*

Probably I should have expected this. I felt tears gather in the back of my throat, and I didn't even know why. "But – but – you never said a word. How come you didn't tell me?"

"Because you weren't ready to know about her. I didn't want to risk you running away again. I wanted you to have a chance to get yourself on solid ground, get your heart bolstered up first. There's a fullness of time for things, Lily. You have to know when to prod and when to be quiet, when to let things take their course. That's what I've been trying to do."

It grew so quiet. How could I be mad at her? I had done the same thing. Held back what I knew, and my reasons were not the least bit noble like hers.

"May told me," I said.

"May told you what?"

"I saw her making a trail of graham crackers and marshmallows for the roaches to follow. My father told me once that my mother used to do the same thing. I figured she'd learned it from May. So I asked her, 'Did you ever know a Deborah Fontanel?' and she said yes she did, that Deborah had stayed in the honey house."

August shook her head. "Goodness, there's so much to tell. You remember how I told you I worked as a housekeeper back in Richmond, before I got my teaching job? Well, that was in your mother's house."

My mother's house. It seemed odd to think of her with a roof over her head. A person who lay on a bed, ate food at a table, took baths in a tub.

"You knew her when she was little?"

"I used to take care of her," August said. "I ironed her dresses and packed her school lunch in a paper bag. She loved peanut butter. That's all she wanted. Peanut butter Monday through Friday."

I let out my breath, realizing I'd been holding it. "What else did she love?"

---

6 **bolster sth. up**: make sth. stronger   7 **prod**: push

"She loved her dolls. She would hold little tea parties for them in the garden, and I would make these teeny-tiny sandwiches for their plates." She paused, like she was remembering. "What she didn't like was schoolwork. I had to stay after her all the time about it.

5   Chase her around calling out spelling words. One time she climbed a tree, hiding up there so she wouldn't have to memorize a poem by Robert Frost. I found her and climbed up there with the book and wouldn't let her come down till she could say the whole thing by heart."

10   Closing my eyes, I saw my mother perched beside August on a tree limb going through each line of "Stopping by Woods on a Snowy Evening," which I myself had had to learn for English. I let my head drop, closed my eyes.

"Lily, before we talk any more about your mother, I want you to

15   tell me how you came to be here. All right?"

I opened my eyes and nodded.

"You said your father was dead."

I glanced down at her hand still on mine, afraid she might move it. "I made that up," I said. "He's not really dead." *He just deserves to*

20   *be dead.*

"Terrence Ray," she said.

"You know my father, too?"

"No, I never met him, only heard about him from Deborah."

"I call him T. Ray."

25   "Not Daddy?"

"He's not the Daddy type."

"What do you mean?"

"He yells all the time."

"At you?"

30   "At everything in the world. But that's not the reason I left."

"Then what was it, Lily?"

---

2 **teeny-tiny** (infml, AE): very small   7 **Robert Frost**: American poet (1874–1963)
11–12 **Stopping by Woods on a Snowy Evening**: popular poem by Robert Frost

"T. Ray … he told me my mother …" The tears rushed up, and my words came out in high-pitched sounds I didn't recognize. "He said she left me, that she left both of us and ran away." A wall of glass broke in my chest, a wall I didn't even know was there.

August slid up to the edge of her chair and opened her arms, the way she'd opened them to June that day they'd found May's suicide letter. I leaned into them, felt them close around me. One thing is beautiful beyond my words to say it: August holding you.

I was pressed so close to her I felt her heart like a small throbbing pressure against my chest. Her hands rubbed my back. She didn't say, *Come on now, stop your crying, everything's going to be okay,* which is the automatic thing people say when they want you to shut up. She said, "It hurts, I know it does. Let it out. Just let it out."

So I did. With my mouth pressed against her dress, it seemed like I drew up my whole lifeload of pain and hurled it into her breast, heaved it with the force of my mouth, and she didn't flinch.

She was wet with my crying. Up around her collar the cotton of her dress was plastered to her skin. I could see her darkness shining through the wet places. She was like a sponge, absorbing what I couldn't hold anymore.

Her hands felt warm on my back, and every time I paused to sniff and gasp for a little air, I heard her breathing. Steady and even. In and out. As my crying wound down, I let myself be rocked in her breathing.

Finally I pulled back and looked at her, dazed by the force of what had erupted. She ran her finger along the slope of my nose and smiled a sad kind of smile.

"I'm sorry," I said.

"Don't be sorry," she said.

She went to her dresser and pulled a white handkerchief from the top drawer. It was folded, ironed, with "A.B." monogrammed on the front in silvery threads. She dabbed softly at my face.

---

16 **flinch**: draw back   23 **wind** (wound [waʊnd]) **down**: become weaker
25 **dazed**: unable to think clearly, especially after a shock

"I want you to know," I said, "I didn't believe T. Ray when he told me that. I know she never would've left me like that. I wanted to find out about her and prove how wrong he was."

I watched her move her hand up under her glasses and pinch the
5 place between her eyes. "And that's what made you leave?"

I nodded. "Plus, Rosaleen and I got in trouble downtown, and I knew if I didn't leave, T. Ray was gonna half kill me, and I was tired of being half killed."

"What sort of trouble?"
10 I wished I didn't have to go on. I looked at the floor.

"Are you talking about how Rosaleen got the bruises and the cut on her head?"

"All she wanted to do was register her name to vote."

August squinted like she was trying to understand. "All right,
15 now, you start at the beginning. Okay? Just take your time and tell me what happened."

The best I could, I told her the miserable details, careful not to leave anything out: Rosaleen practicing writing her name, the three men taunting her, how she poured snuff juice on their shoes.
20 "A policeman took us to jail," I said, and I heard how strange the words sounded to my ears. I could only imagine how they sounded to August.

"Jail?" she said. Her bones seemed to soften a little in her body. "They put you in *jail*? What was the charge?"
25 "The policeman said Rosaleen assaulted the men, but I was there, and she was only protecting herself. That's all."

August's jaw tightened, and her back went ramrod straight. "How long were you in there?"

"Me, I didn't stay long. T. Ray came and got me out, but they
30 wouldn't let Rosaleen go, and then those men came back and beat her up."

---

19 **taunt sb.**: try to annoy sb. by saying unkind things
27 **ramrod straight**: upright and stiff

"Mother of God," said August. The words hovered over us. I thought of Mary's spirit, hidden everywhere. Her heart a red cup of fierceness tucked among ordinary things. Isn't that what August had said? Here, everywhere, but hidden.

"Well, how did she finally get out?"   5

Some things you have to take a deep breath and just say. "I went to the hospital where they'd taken her to get stitches, and I – I sneaked her past the policeman."

"Mother of God," she said for the second time. She stood up and walked one loop around the room.   10

"I never would have done it, except T. Ray said the man who beat Rosaleen was the meanest hater of colored people anywhere, and it would be just like him to come back and kill her. I couldn't leave her in there."

It was scary, my secrets spilled out across the room, like a garbage   15
truck had backed up and dumped its sorry contents across the floor for her to sort through. But that wasn't what frightened me most. It was the way August leaned back in her chair and looked off toward the window with her gaze skimming the top of my head, looking at nothing but the sticky air, her thoughts a nerve-racking mystery.   20

A fever broke along my neck.

"I don't mean to be a bad person," I said, and stared at my hands, how they were folded together like hands in prayer. "I can't seem to help it."

You would think I was totally cried out, but tears beaded again   25
along my lids. "I do all the wrong things. I tell lies, all the time. Not to you. Well, I have – but for good reasons. And I hate people. Not just T. Ray but lots of people. The girls at school, and they haven't done anything to me except ignore me. I hate Willifred Marchant, the poet of Tiburon, and I don't even know her. Sometimes I hate   30
Rosaleen because she embarrasses me. And when I first came here, I hated June."

---

8 **sneak sb. past sb.**: take sb. past sb. else without this person noticing anything

A flood of silence now. It rose like water; I heard a roar in my head, rain in my ears.

Look at me. Put your hand back on mine. Say something.

By now my nose was running along with my eyes. I was sniffling,
5 wiping my cheeks, unable to stop my mouth from spewing out every horrible thing I could drum up about myself, and once I was finished … well, if she could love me then, if she could say, *Lily, you are still a special flower planted on the earth*, then maybe I would be able to look in the mirrors in her parlor and see the river glistening in my eyes,
10 flowing on despite the things that had died in it.

"But all of that, that's nothing," I said. I was on my feet needing to go someplace, but there was no place to go. We were on an island. A floating blue island in a pink house where I spilled out my guts and then hoped I wasn't tossed out to sea to wait for my punishment.
15 "I –"

August was looking at me, waiting. I didn't know if I could say it.

"It was my fault she died. I– I killed her." I sobbed and dropped straight down onto my knees on the rug. It was the first time I'd ever said the words to another person, and the sound of them broke open
20 my heart.

Probably one or two moments in your whole life you will hear a dark whispering spirit, a voice coming from the center of things. It will have blades for lips and will not stop until it speaks the one secret thing at the heart of it all. Kneeling on the floor, unable to stop
25 shuddering, I heard it plainly. It said, *You are unlovable, Lily Owens. Unlovable. Who could love you? Who in this world could ever love you?*

I sank farther down, onto my heels, hardly aware of myself mumbling the words out loud. "I am unlovable." When I looked up, I saw dust particles floating in the lamplight, August standing,
30 looking down at me. I thought she might try to pull me to my feet, but instead she knelt beside me and brushed the hair back from my face.

---

6 **drum sth. up**: (here) think of sth.   13 **spill out your guts** (AE): tell sb. all your secrets   23 **blade**: *Messerklinge*

"Oh, Lily," she said. "Child."

"I accidentally killed her," I said, staring straight into her eyes.

"Listen to me now," said August, tilting my chin to her face. "That's a terrible, terrible thing for you to live with. But you're *not* unlovable. Even if you did accidentally kill her, you are still the most ⁵ dear, most lovable girl I know. Why, Rosaleen loves you. May loved you. It doesn't take a wizard to see Zach loves you. And every one of the Daughters loves you. And June, despite her ways, loves you, too. It just took her a while longer because she resented your mother so much." ¹⁰

"She resented my mother? But why?" I said, realizing that June must have known who I was all along, too.

"Oh, it's complicated, just like June. She couldn't get over me working as a maid in your mother's house." August gave her head a shake. "I know it wasn't fair, but she took it out on Deborah, and ¹⁵ then on you. But even June came around to loving you, didn't she?"

"I guess," I said.

"Mostly, though, I want you to know, *I* love you. Just like I loved your mother."

August stood up, but I stayed where I was, holding her words ²⁰ inside me. "Give me your hand," she said, reaching down. Getting to my feet, I felt dizzy around the edges, that feeling like you've stood up too fast.

All this love coming to me. I didn't know what to do with it. I wanted to say, *I love you, too. I love you all.* The feeling rose up in me ²⁵ like a column of wind, but when it got to my mouth, it had no voice, no words. Just a lot of air and longing.

"We both need a little breather," August said, and she plodded toward the kitchen.

7 **wizard** ['wɪzəd]: magic man   15 **take sth. out on sb.**: treat sb. badly because of sth.   16 **come around to doing sth.**: eventually manage to do sth.
22 **feel dizzy around the edges**: feel unstable   28 **breather** ['briːðər]: short break
plod: walk with heavy steps

August poured us glasses of ice water from the refrigerator. We took them to the back porch, where we sat in the porch swing, taking little gulps of coolness and listening to the chains creak. It's surprising how soothing that sound can be. We hadn't bothered to turn on the
5 overhead light, and that was soothing, too – just sitting in the dark.

After a few minutes August said, "Here's what I can't figure out, Lily – how you knew to come here."

I pulled the wooden picture of black Mary from my pocket and handed it to her. "It belonged to my mother," I said. "I found it in the
10 attic, the same time I found her photograph."

"Oh, my Lord," she said, her hand going up to the side of her mouth. "I gave this to your mother not long before she died."

She set her water glass on the floor and walked across the porch. I didn't know whether to keep talking, so I waited for her to say
15 something, and when she didn't, I went and stood beside her. She had her lips tight together and her eyes scanning the night. The picture was clutched in her hand, but her hand dangled by her side.

It took a full minute for her to pull it up so we could both stare at it.

20 "It has 'Tiburon, S.C.' written on the back of it," I said.

August turned it over. "Deborah must have written that." Something close to a smile passed over her face. "That would've been just like her. She had an album full of pictures, and she'd write on the back of every single one of them the place it was taken, even
25 if it was her own house." She handed me the picture. I stared at it, letting my finger move across the word "Tiburon."

"Who would've thought?" August said.

We went and sat in the swing, where we rocked back and forth, making little pushes on the floor with our feet. She stared straight
30 ahead. Her slip strap had fallen down to her elbow, and she didn't even notice.

4 **soothing**: comforting

June always said that most people bit off more than they could chew, but August chewed more than she bit off. June loved to tease August about the way she pondered things, how one minute she was talking to you and the next she had slipped into a private world where she turned her thoughts over and over, digesting stuff most people would choke on. I wanted to say, *Teach me how to do that. Teach me how to take all this in.* 5

Thunder rumbled over the trees. I thought of my mother's tea parties, tiny sandwiches for a doll's mouth, and it washed me in sadness. Maybe because I would've loved so much to have attended something like that. Maybe because all the sandwiches would've been peanut butter, my mother's favorite, and I wasn't even that crazy about it. I wondered at the poem August had made her learn, whether it had stuck with her after she got married. Had she lain in her bed listening to T. Ray snore, reciting it while she fell asleep, wishing to God she could run away with Robert Frost? 10 15

I gave a sideways glance at August. I forced my mind back to that moment in her bedroom when I'd confessed the worst of human things. Upon hearing it, she'd said, *I love you. Just like I loved your mother.* 20

"All right then," said August, like we'd never stopped talking. "The picture explains how you came to Tiburon, but how in the world did you find *me*?"

"That was easy," I said. "We hadn't been here any time before I spotted your Black Madonna Honey, and there was the same picture on it as my mother had. The Black Madonna of Breznichar of Bohemia." 25

"You said that real nice," August told me.

"I've been practicing."

"Where did you see the honey?" 30

---

6 **choke on sth.**: be unable to breathe because sth. is stuck in your throat

"I was in that Frogmore Stew General Store out on the edge of town. I asked this man in a bow tie where he got it. He's the one who told me where you lived."

"That would be Mr. Grady." She shook her head. "I swear, it
5 makes me think you were *meant* to find us."

I *was* meant to, I didn't have a doubt about it. I just wish I knew where I was meant to end up. I looked down at our laps, how both of us had our hands laying palm side up on top of our thighs, like we were both waiting for something to drop in.

10 "So why don't we talk some more about your mother?" she said.

I nodded. Every bone in my body was cracking with the need to talk about her.

"Anytime you need to stop and take another break, you just tell me."

15 "All right," I said. What was coming, I couldn't imagine. Something that required *breaks*. Breaks for what? So I could dance for joy? So she could revive me after I fainted dead away? Or was the idea of breaks so I could let the bad news sink all the way in?

A dog started barking way off in the distance. August waited for it
20 to stop, then said, "I started working for Deborah's mother in 1931. Deborah was four years old. The cutest child, but always into something. I mean, a real handful. For one thing, she used to walk in her sleep. One night she walked outside and climbed a ladder the roofers had left leaning against the house. Her sleepwalking nearly
25 drove her mother crazy." She laughed.

"And your mother had an imaginary friend. You ever had one?" I shook my head. "She called hers Tica Tee. She would talk to her out loud like she was standing right there in front of us, and if I forgot to set a place for Tica Tee at the table, Deborah would throw a fit. Once
30 in a while, though, I'd set a place and she'd say, 'What are you doing? Tica Tee's not here. She's off starring in the movies.' Your mother loved Shirley Temple."

21–22 **be into sth.**: (here) be in trouble.   24 **roofer**: person who builds roofs
29 **throw a fit**: *einen Anfall bekommen*   32 **Shirley Temple**: American actress

"Tica Tee," I said, wanting to feel that on my tongue.

"That Tica Tee was something," August said. "Whatever Deborah struggled with, Tica Tee could do it perfectly. Tica Tee made hundreds on her school papers, got gold stars in Sunday school, made her bed, cleaned her plate. People told your grandmother – 5 Sarah was her name – that she ought to take Deborah to this doctor in Richmond who specialized in children with problems. But I told her, 'Don't worry about it. She's just working things out in her own way. She'll grow out of Tica Tee in time.' And she did."

Where had I been that I didn't know about imaginary friends? I 10 could see the point of it. How a lost part of yourself steps out and reminds you who you could be with a little work.

"It doesn't sound like me and my mother were anything alike," I said.

"Oh, but you were. She had a streak in her like you do. Suddenly 15 she would up and do something other girls wouldn't dream of."

"Like what?"

August stared over my shoulder and smiled. "One time she ran away from home. I can't even remember what she was upset about. We looked for her long past dark. Found her curled up in a drainage 20 ditch, sound asleep."

The dog had started barking again, and August grew quiet. We listened like it was some kind of serenade, while I sat with my eyes closed, trying to picture my mother asleep in a ditch.

After a while I said, "How long did you work for – my 25 grandmother?"

"A good long time. Over nine years. Until I got that teaching job I told you about. We still kept up after I left, though."

"I bet they hated it when you moved down here to South Carolina." 30

---

15 **streak** [striːk]: character trait   16 **up and do sth.**: suddenly do sth. unexpected
20–21 **drainage ditch**: *Entwässerungsgraben*   28 **keep up**: (here) stay in contact

"Poor Deborah cried and cried. She was nineteen by then, but she cried like she was six."

The swing had slowed to a stop, and neither one of us thought to rev it back up.

5 "How did my mother get down here?"

"I'd been here two years," August said. "Had started my honey business and June was teaching school, when I got a long-distance phone call from her. She was crying her eyes out, saying her mother had died. 'I don't have anybody left but you,' she kept saying."

10 "What about her father? Where was he?"

"Oh, Mr. Fontanel died when she was a baby. I never even met him."

"So she moved down here to be with you?"

"Deborah had a friend from high school who'd just moved to 15 Sylvan. She was the one who convinced Deborah it was a good place to be. Told her there were jobs and men back from the war. So Deborah moved. I think it was a lot because of me, though. I think she wanted me nearby."

The dots were all starting to connect. "My mother came to 20 Sylvan," I said, "met T. Ray, and got married."

"That's right," August said.

When we'd first come out onto the porch, the sky had been clotted with stars, the Milky Way shining like an actual road you could walk down and find your mother standing at the end of with 25 her hands on her hips. But now a damp fog rolled into the yard and settled over the porch. A minute later a light rain fell out of it.

I said, "The part I will never figure out is why she married *him*."

"I don't think your father was always like he is now. Deborah told me about him. She loved the fact he was decorated in the war. He 30 was so brave, she thought. Said he treated her like a princess."

I could have laughed in her face. "This isn't the same Terrence Ray, I can tell you that right now."

4 **rev sth. up**: start sth. moving

"You know, Lily, people can start out one way, and by the time life gets through with them they end up completely different. I don't doubt he started off loving your mother. In fact, I think he worshiped her. And your mother soaked it up. Like a lot of young women, she could get carried away with romance. But after six months or so it started wearing off. One of her letters talked about Terrence Ray having dirt under his fingernails, I remember that. Next thing I knew she was writing me how she didn't know if she could live way out on a farm, that kind of thing. When he proposed, she said no."

"But she married him," I said, genuinely confused.

"Later on she changed her mind and said yes."

"Why?" I said. "If the love had worn off, why did she marry him?"

August cupped her hand on the back of my head and smoothed my hair with her fingers. "I've thought hard about whether I should tell you, but maybe it'll help you understand everything that happened a lot better. Honey, Deborah was pregnant, that's why."

The instant before she said it, I knew what was coming, but still her words fell like a hammer.

"She was pregnant with *me*?" My voice sounded tired saying the words. My mother's life was too heavy for me.

"That's right, pregnant with you. She and Terrence Ray got married around Christmastime. She called long distance to tell me."

Unwanted, I thought. *I was an unwanted baby*.

Not only that, my mother had gotten stuck with T. Ray because of *me*. I was glad it was dark, so August couldn't see my face, how bent in it was. You think you want to know something, and then once you do, all you can think about is erasing it from your mind. From now on when people asked me what I wanted to be when I grew up, I planned to say, *Amnesiac*.

I listened to the hiss of rain. The spray floated over and misted my cheeks while I counted on my fingers. "I was born seven months after they got married."

29 **amnesiac** [æm'niːziæk]: person unable to remember anything

"She called me right after you were born. She said you were so pretty it hurt her eyes to look at you."

Something about this caused my own eyes to sting like sand had flown into them. Maybe my mother had cooed over me after all.
5 Made embarrassing baby talk. Twirled my newborn hair like the top of an ice cream cone. Done it up with pink bows. Just because she didn't plan on having me didn't mean she hadn't loved me.

August went on talking while I leaned back into the familiar story I'd always told myself, the one about my mother loving me beyond
10 reason. I'd lived inside it the way a goldfish lives in its bowl, as if that was the only world there was. Leaving it would be the death of me.

I sat there with my shoulders slumped, staring at the floor. I would not think the word "unwanted."

"Are you all right?" August said. "You want to go to bed now and
15 sleep on all this, talk about the rest in the morning?"

"No" burst out of my lips. I took a breath. "I'm fine, really," I said, trying to sound unruffled. "I just need some more water."

She took my empty glass and went to the kitchen, looking back twice at me. When she returned with the water, she had a red
20 umbrella hooked over her wrist. "In a little while I'll walk you over to the honey house," she said.

As I drank, the glass shook in my hand and the water would hardly go down. The sound of swallowing in my throat grew so loud it blotted out the rain for several seconds.

25 "Are you sure you don't want to go to bed now?" August asked.

"I'm sure. I need to know –"

"You need to know what, Lily?"

"Everything," I said.

August settled herself beside me on the swing, resigned. "All right
30 then," she said. "All right."

"I know she only married him because of me, but do you think she was just a little bit happy?" I asked.

---

4 **coo over sb.**: make soft, loving sounds to sb. 17 **unruffled**: calm

"I think for a while she was. She tried, I know that. I got a dozen or so letters and at least that many phone calls from her, spread out over the first couple of years, and I could see she was making an effort. Mostly she wrote about you, how you were sitting up, taking your first steps, playing patty-cake. But then her letters came less 5 and less often, and when they did come, I could tell she was unhappy. One day she called me up. It was the end of August or first of September − I remember because we'd had Mary Day not long before that.

"She said she was leaving T. Ray, that she had to leave home. She 10 wanted to know if she could stay with us here for a few months till she figured out where to go. Of course, I said, that would be fine. When I picked her up at the bus station, she didn't even look like herself. She had gotten so thin and had these dark circles under her eyes." 15

My stomach did a slow roll. I knew we'd come to the place in the story I feared the most. I began to breathe very fast. "I was with her when you picked her up at the bus station. She brought me along, didn't she?"

August leaned over and whispered against my hair. "No, honey, 20 she came by herself."

I realized I'd bitten the skin inside my cheek. The taste of blood made me want to spit, but I swallowed it instead. "Why?" I said. "Why didn't she bring me?"

"All I know, Lily, is that she was depressed, kind of falling apart. 25 The day she left home, nothing unusual happened. She just woke up and decided she couldn't be there anymore. She called a lady from the next farm to baby-sit, and she drove Terrence Ray's truck to the bus station. Up until she got here, I thought she'd be bringing you with her." 30

The swing groaned while we sat there smelling warm rain, wet wood, rotted grass. *My mother had left me.*

---

5 **patty-cake**: game played with babies

"I hate her," I said. I meant to shout it, but it came out unnaturally calm, low and raspy like the sound of cars crunching slowly over gravel.

"Now, hold on, Lily."

5 "I do, I hate her. She wasn't anything like I thought she was." I'd spent my life imagining all the ways she'd loved me, what a perfect specimen of a mother she was. And all of it was lies. I had completely made her up.

"It was easy for her to leave me, because she never wanted me in 10 the first place," I said.

August reached for me, but I got to my feet and pushed open the screen door leading to the porch steps. I let it slam behind me, then sat on the rain-sopped steps, hunched up under the eave.

I heard August move across the porch, felt the air thicken as she 15 stood behind me on the other side of the screen. "I'm not going to make excuses for her, Lily," she said. "Your mother did what she did."

"Some mother," I said. I felt hard inside. Hard and angry.

"Will you listen to me for a minute? When your mother got here 20 to Tiburon, she was practically skin and bone. May couldn't get her to eat a thing. All she did was cry for a week. Later on we called it a nervous breakdown, but while it was happening we didn't know what to call it. I took her to the doctor here, and he gave her some cod liver oil and asked where her white family was. He said maybe 25 she needed to spend some time on Bull Street. So I didn't take her back to him again."

"Bull Street. The mental institution?" The story was getting worse by the minute. "But that's for crazy people," I said.

"I guess he didn't know what else to do for her, but she wasn't 30 crazy. She was depressed, but not crazy."

---

2 **raspy**: sounding rough   13 **eave**: protruding part of the roof
24 **cod liver oil**: *Lebertran*

"You should've let him put her in there. I wish she'd rotted in there."

"Lily!"

I'd shocked her, and I was glad.

My mother had been looking for love, and instead she'd found T. Ray and the farm, and then me, and I had not been enough for her. She'd left me with T. Ray Owens.

The sky was split by a zigzagged path of lightning, but even then I didn't move. My hair blew like smoke in every direction. I felt my eyes harden, grow flat and narrow as pennies. I stared at a dollop of bird shit on the bottom step, the way the rain was smearing it into the crevices of the wood.

"Are you listening now?" August said. Her voice sifted through the screen, little barbed-wire tips on every word. "Are you?"

"I hear you."

"Depressed people do things they wouldn't ordinarily do."

"Like what?" I said. "Abandon their children?" I couldn't stop. The rain spattered my sandals, dripped between my toes.

Letting out a loud breath, August walked back to the swing and sat down. It seemed like maybe I'd hurt her, disappointed her, and something about that punched a hole in me. Some of my pridefulness drained out.

I eased off the steps and went back inside, onto the screened porch. As I sat down beside her on the swing, she laid her hand on mine, and the heat flowed out from her palm into my skin. I shuddered.

"Come here," she said, pulling me over to her. It was like being swept under a bird's wing, and that's how we stayed for a while, rocking back and forth with me tucked under there.

"What made her so depressed like that?" I said.

---

10 **dollop**: small amount of soft substance   13 **sift through sth.**: move through sth.

"I don't know the whole answer, but part of it was her being out on the farm, isolated from things, married to a man she really didn't want to be married to."

The rain picked up, coming down in large, silver-black sheets. I
5 tried, but I couldn't make heads or tails of my heart. One minute I hated my mother, the next I felt sorry for her.

"Okay, she was having a nervous breakdown, but how could she leave me behind like that?" I said.

"After she'd been here three months and was feeling a little better,
10 she started talking about how much she missed you. Finally she went back to Sylvan to get you."

I sat up and looked at August, hearing the quick suck of air through my lips. "She came back to get me?"

"She planned to bring you here to Tiburon to live. She even
15 talked to Clayton about filing divorce papers. The last time I saw her, she was on a bus waving at me through the window."

I leaned my head on August's shoulder and knew exactly what had happened next. I closed my eyes, and there it was. The longgone day that would never leave – the suitcase on the floor, how she'd
20 tossed clothes into it without folding them. *Hurry*, she'd kept saying.

T. Ray had told me she came back for her things. But she'd come back for me, too. She'd wanted to bring me here, to Tiburon, to August's.

If only we'd made it. I remembered the sound of T. Ray's boots on
25 the stairs. I wanted to pound my fists against something, to scream at my mother for getting caught, for not packing faster, for not coming sooner.

At last I looked up at August. When I spoke, my mouth tasted bitter. "I remember it. I remember her coming back for me."
30 "I wondered about that," she said.

"T. Ray found her packing. They were yelling and fighting. She –" I stopped, hearing their voices in my head.

"Go on," August said.

---

4 **pick up**: (here) become stronger   5 **make heads or tails of sth.**: understand sth.

I looked down at my hands. They were trembling. "She grabbed a gun from inside the closet, but he took it away from her. It happened so fast it gets mixed up in my brain. I saw the gun on the floor, and I picked it up. I don't know why I did that. I – I wanted to help. To give it back to her. Why did I do that? Why did I pick it 5 up?"

August slid out to the edge of the swing and turned to face me. Her eyes were determined-looking. "Do you remember what happened next, after you picked it up?"

I shook my head. "Only the noise. The explosion. So loud." The 10 chains on the swing twitched. I looked over and saw August frowning.

"How did you find out about – my mother dying?" I said.

"When Deborah didn't come back like she said … well, I had to know what happened, so I called your house. A woman answered, 15 said she was a neighbor."

"A neighbor of ours told you?" I asked.

"She said Deborah had been killed in an accident with a gun. That's all she would say."

I turned and looked out at the night, at dripping tree limbs, at 20 shadows moving on the half-lit porch. "You didn't know that I was the one who – who did it?"

"No, I never imagined such a thing," she said. "I'm not sure I can imagine it now." She laced her fingers together, then laid them in her lap. "I tried to find out more. I called back again, and Terrence Ray 25 answered, but he wouldn't talk about it. He kept wanting to know who I was. I even called the police station in Sylvan, but they wouldn't give out any information either, just said it was an accidental death. So I've had to live with not knowing. All these years." 30

We sat in the stillness. The rain had nearly stopped, leaving us with all this quiet and a sky with no moon.

---

11 **twitch**: move suddenly and quickly   24 **lace your fingers together**: connect the fingers of your two hands

"Come on," August said. "Let's get you in bed."

We walked into the night, into the blurring song of katydids, the thud-splat of raindrops on the umbrella, all those terrible rhythms that take up inside when you let your guard down. *Left you*, they drummed. *Left you. Left you.*

Knowing can be a curse on a person's life. I'd traded in a pack of lies for a pack of truth, and I didn't know which one was heavier. Which one took the most strength to carry around? It was a ridiculous question, though, because once you know the truth, you can't ever go back and pick up your suitcase of lies. Heavier or not, the truth is yours now.

In the honey house, August waited till I crawled under the sheets, then bent over and kissed my forehead.

"Every person on the face of the earth makes mistakes, Lily. Every last one. We're all so human. Your mother made a terrible mistake, but she tried to fix it."

"Good night," I said, and rolled onto my side.

"There is nothing perfect," August said from the doorway. "There is only life."

---

2 **katydid** (AE): large grasshopper   3 **thud-splat** (n): dull, wet noise

A worker [bee] is just over a centimeter long and weighs only about sixty milligrams; nevertheless, she can fly with a load heavier than herself.
The Honey Bee

Chapter Thirteen

Heat collected in the creases of my elbows, in the soft places behind my knees. Lying on top of the sheets, I touched my eyelids. I'd cried so much they were puffed out and half shut. If it hadn't been for my eyelids, I might not have believed any of the things that had passed between me and August.

I hadn't moved since August left, only lay there staring at the flat surface of the wall, at the array of night bugs that wander out and crawl around for fun after they think you're asleep. When I grew tired of watching them, I placed my arm across my eyes and told myself, *Sleep, Lily. Please, just go to sleep.* But of course, I couldn't.

I sat up, feeling like my body weighed two hundred pounds. Like somebody had backed the cement truck up to the honey house, swung the pipe over to my chest, and started pouring. I hated feeling like a concrete block in the middle of the night.

More than once, while staring at the wall, I'd thought of Our Lady. I wanted to talk to her, to say, *Where do I go from here?* But when I'd seen her earlier, when August and I had first come in, she didn't look like she could be of service to anybody, bound up with

7 **array**: group

all that chain around her. You want the one you're praying to at least to *look* capable.

I dragged myself out of bed and went to see her anyway. I decided that even Mary did not need to be one hundred percent capable all
5 the time. The only thing I wanted was for her to understand. Somebody to let out a big sigh and say, *You poor thing, I know how you feel.* Given a choice, I preferred someone to understand my situation, even though she was helpless to fix it, rather than the other way around. But that's just me.

10 Right off I smelled the chain, its thick, rusty odor. I had the urge to unwrap her, but of course that would have ruined the whole reenactment August and the Daughters had going.

The red candle flickered at Mary's feet. I plopped onto the floor and sat cross-legged in front of her. Outside, I heard wind high in
15 the trees, a singsong voice that carried me back to longago times when I would wake in the night to the same sound and, muddled with sleep and wanting, would imagine it was my mother out there among the trees, singing her bottomless love. Once I flew into T. Ray's room, yelling she was outside my window. He said three
20 words: "Holy crap, Lily."

I hated when he was right. There had never been any voice in the wind. No mother out there singing. No bottomless love.

The terrible thing, the really terrible thing, was the anger in me. It had started on the back porch when the story of my mother had
25 collapsed, like the ground under my feet giving way. I didn't want to be angry. I told myself, You're not angry. *You don't have any right to be angry. What you did to your mother is a lot worse than what she did to you.* But you can't talk yourself out of anger. Either you are angry or you're not.

30 The room was hot and still. In another minute I would not be able to breathe for the anger filling me up. My lungs went out only so far before they struck against it and closed back in.

20 **holy crap**: swear word

I got to my feet and paced in the darkness. Behind me on the worktable a half dozen jars of Black Madonna Honey waited for Zach to deliver them somewhere in town – to Clayton's maybe, to the Frogmore Stew General Store, the Amen Dollar, or Divine Do's, the colored beauty parlor.   5

How dare she? How dare she leave me? I was her child.

I looked toward the window, wanting to smash the panes out of it. I wanted to throw something all the way to heaven and knock God clean off his throne. I picked up one of the honey jars and hurled it as hard as I could. It missed black Mary's head by inches   10
and smashed against the back wall. I picked up another one and threw it, too. It crashed on the floor beside a stack of supers. I threw every last jar on the table, until honey was spattered everywhere, flung like cake batter from electric beaters. I stood in a gooey room full of broken glass, and I didn't care. My mother had left me. Who   15
cared about honey on the walls?

I grabbed a tin bucket next and, letting out a grunt, threw it with so much force it left a dent in the wall. My throwing arm was nearly worn out, but I picked up a tray of candle molds and flung that, too.

Then I stood still, watching the honey slide along the wall toward   20
the floor. A trickle of bright blood wound down my left arm. I had no idea how it'd gotten there. My heart beat wildly. I felt like I'd unzipped my skin and momentarily stepped out of it, leaving a crazy person in charge.

The room turned like a carousel, with my stomach gliding up   25
and down. I felt a need to touch the wall with both hands to make it still again. I walked back toward the table where the honey jars had been and braced my hands against it. I couldn't think what to do. I felt a powerful sadness, not because of what I'd done, as bad as that was, but because everything seemed emptied out – the feelings I'd   30
had for her, the things I'd believed, all those stories about her I'd

---

5 **beauty parlor**: beauty salon   14 **beater**: *Rührbesen, Quirl*   18 **dent**: hole
25 **carousel** [ˌkærəˈsel]: merry-go-round

lived off of like they were food and water and air. Because I was the girl she'd left behind. That's what it came down to.

Looking around at the wreck I'd made, I wondered if someone in the pink house might have heard the honey jars hit the wall. I went
5 to the window and stared across the gloom in the yard. The panes in August's bedroom window were dark. I felt my heart in my chest. It hurt so badly. Like it had been stepped on.

"How come you left me?" I whispered, watching my breath make a circle of fog on the glass.

10 I stayed pressed against the window for a while, then went and cleared off a few pieces of glass from the floor in front of Our Lady. I lay down on my side, drawing my knees toward my chin. Above me, black Mary was flecked with honey and seemed not at all surprised. I lay in the emptiness, in the tiredness, with everything – even the
15 hating – drained out. There was nothing left to do. No place to go. Just right here, right now, where the truth was.

I told myself not to get up in the night and walk across the floor unless I wanted to cut my feet to smithereens. Then I closed my eyes and began to piece together the dream I wanted myself to have. How
20 a little door in the black Mary statue would open up, just over her abdomen, and I would crawl inside to a hidden room. This was not all my imagination, as I had glimpsed an actual picture of this in August's book – a statue of Mary with a wide-open door and, inside, all these people tucked away in the secret world of consolation.

25 I woke to Rosaleen's big hands shaking me and opened my eyes to a terrible brightness. Her face was bent over mine, the scent of coffee and grape jelly coming from her mouth. "Lily!" she yelled. "What in the Sam Hill happened in here?"

I'd forgotten there would be dried blood caked across my arm. I
30 looked at it, at a piece of glass, small as a stub of diamond, burrowed

---

5 **gloom**: darkness   18 **cut sth. to smithereens**: cut sth. into very small pieces
28 **what in the Sam Hill** (infml, AE): mild swear word   30 **burrow**: dig

in a puckered setting of skin. Around me, jagged pieces of jars and puddles of honey. Blood dotted the floor.

Rosaleen stared at me, waiting, bewildered-looking. I stared back, trying to make her face come into focus. Sunlight slanted across Our Lady and fell down around us. 5

"Answer me," Rosaleen said.

I squinted in the light. My mouth couldn't seem to open up and speak.

"Look at you. You've been bleeding."

My head nodded, bobbed around on my neck. I looked at the 10 wrecked room. I felt embarrassed, ridiculous, stupid.

"I – I threw some jars of honey."

"*You* made this mess?" she said, like she couldn't quite believe it, like what she'd expected me to say was that a roving band of house wreckers had come through during the night. She blew a puff of air 15 over her face, so forceful it lifted her hair, which was not easy to do considering the amount of lacquer she kept smeared on it. "Lord God in heaven," she said.

I got to my feet, waiting for her to bawl me out, but she took her thick fingers and struggled to pluck the piece of glass from my arm. 20 "You need some Mercurochrome on this before you get infected," she told me. "Come on." She sounded exasperated, like she wanted to take me by the shoulders and shake me till my teeth fell out.

I sat on the side of the tub while Rosaleen dabbed my arm with a stinging icy swab. She plastered a Band-Aid across it and said, 25 "There, you won't die from blood poisoning at least."

She closed the medicine cabinet over the sink, then shut the bathroom door. I watched her take a seat on the commode, how her belly dropped down between her legs. When Rosaleen sat on a toilet, the whole thing disappeared under her. I perched on the side of the 30

1 **puckered**: folded up   14 **rove**: travel from place to place
17 **lacquer** (old fashioned): hairspray   19 **bawl sb. out**: speak angrily to sb.
21 **Mercurochrome**: medicine to heal wounds

tub and thought how glad I was August and June were still in their rooms.

"All right," she said, "why did you throw all that honey?"

I looked at the row of seashells on the window ledge, knowing
5 how truly they belonged here even though we were a hundred miles from the ocean. August had said everybody needed a seashell in her bathroom to remind her the ocean was her home. Seashells, she'd said, are Our Lady's favorite items, next to the moon.

I went over and picked up one of the shells, a pretty white one,
10 flat with yellow around the edges.

Rosaleen sat there watching me. "Any time now," she said.

"T. Ray was right about my mother," I said, hearing myself say the words, feeling sickened by them. "She left me. It was just like he said it was. She left me." For a second the anger I'd felt the night before
15 flared up, and it crossed my mind to slam the shell against the tub, but I took a breath instead. Throwing fits wasn't that satisfying, I'd found out.

Rosaleen shifted her weight, and the toilet lid squeaked and slid around on top of the seat. She raked her fingers over the top of her
20 head. I looked away, at the pipe under the sink, at a smudge of rust on the linoleum.

"So your mother did leave after all," she said. "Lord, I was afraid of that."

I lifted my head. I remembered that first night after we ran away,
25 down by the creek, when I'd told Rosaleen what T. Ray had said. I'd wanted her to laugh at the very idea of my mother leaving me, but she'd hesitated.

"You knew already, didn't you?" I said.

"I didn't know for sure," she said. "I just heard things."
30 "What things?"

She let out a sigh, really something more than a sigh. "After your mama died," she said, "I heard T. Ray on the phone talking to that

---

15 **flare up**: start to burn

neighbor lady, Mrs. Watson. He was telling her he didn't need her to watch after you, that he'd gotten one of the pickers out of the orchard. He was talking about me, so I listened." Outside the window a crow flew past, filling the bathroom with a frantic *caw-caw,* and Rosaleen stopped, waiting for it to die down. 5

I knew Mrs. Watson from church, from all the times she stopped to buy peaches from me. She was kind as she could be, but she'd always looked at me like there was something indescribably sad written across my forehead, like she wanted to come over and scrub it off. 10

I clutched the side of the tub as Rosaleen went on, not sure I wanted her to. "I heard your daddy tell Mrs. Watson, 'Janie, you've done more than your share, looking after Lily these past months. I don't know what we would've done without you.' " Rosaleen looked at me and shook her head. "I always wondered what he meant by 15 that. When you told me what T. Ray said about your mother leaving you, I guess I knew then."

"I can't believe you didn't tell me," I said and folded my arms across my chest.

"So how did you find out?" Rosaleen asked. 20

"August told me," I said. I thought of all that crying I'd done in her bedroom. Holding fistfuls of her dress in my hand. The monogram on her handkerchief, scratchy against my cheek.

"August?" Rosaleen repeated. You don't see Rosaleen looking dumbfounded that often, but that's the look she had now. 25

"She knew my mother back when she was a little girl in Virginia," I explained. "August helped raise her."

I waited a few seconds, letting it soak it.

"This is where my mother came when she left. When … Mrs. Watson took care of me," I said. "She came right here to this house." 30

Rosaleen's eyes grew even narrower, if such a thing was possible. "Your mother –" she said, then stopped. I could see that her brain

---

4 **caw**: unpleasant sound a crow makes   23 **scratchy**: rough
25 **dumbfounded**: unable to speak because of a shock

was struggling to fit it all together. My mother leaving. Mrs. Watson watching me. My mother returning, only to get killed. "My mother stayed here three months before she went back to Sylvan," I said. "I guess one day it finally dawned on her: *Oh, yeah, that's right, I've got*
5 *a little girl at home. Gee, maybe I'll go back and get her now."*

I heard the bitter tone in my voice, and it came to me how I could lock that tone into my voice forever. From now on, every time I thought of my mother, I could, so easy, slip off into a cold place where meanness took over. I squeezed the shell and felt it dig into
10 the pad of skin on my palm.

Rosaleen got to her feet. I looked at her, how large she was in the little bathroom. I stood up, too, and for a second we were sandwiched together between the tub and the toilet, staring at each other.

"I wish you'd told me what you knew about my mother," I said.
15 "How come you didn't?"

"Oh, Lily," she said, and there was gentleness in her words, like they'd been rocked in a little hammock of tenderness down in her throat. "Why would I go and hurt you with something like that?"

Rosaleen walked beside me to the honey house with a mop flung
20 over her shoulder and a spatula in her hand. I carried a bucket of rags and the Spic and Span. We used the spatula to scrape honey off places you wouldn't believe. Some of it had gotten all the way over onto August's adding machine.

We wiped off the floors and the walls, then went to work on Our
25 Lady. We picked the place up and turned it back the way it was, and the entire time we didn't speak a word.

I worked with heaviness inside, with my spirit emptied out. There was my breath curling in hard puffs from my nostrils. There was Rosaleen's heart so full toward me it broke through into her
30 sweating face. There was Our Lady talking with her eyes, saying things I could not make out. And there was nothing else.

---

4 **it dawns on you**: you begin to realize   19 **mop**: *Wischlappen*
21 **Spic and Span**: brand name of cleaning liquid or powder
25 **pick the place up**: clean a place thoroughly

꙳

The Daughters and Otis arrived at noon, lugging in all manner of potluck dishes, as if we hadn't eaten ourselves sick the night before. They tucked them into the oven to keep warm and stood around in the kitchen sneaking bites of Rosaleen's corn fritters, saying they were the finest fritters they'd ever had the pleasure of eating, which   5
caused Rosaleen to swell up with pride.

"Y'all stop eating up all Rosaleen's fritters," June said. "They're for our lunch."

"Oh, let 'em eat," said Rosaleen, which floored me, since she'd been known to smack my hand sideways for pinching a single   10
crumb off her fritters before dinner. By the time Neil and Zach arrived, the fritters were nearly gone, and Rosaleen was in danger of floating off into the atmosphere.

I stood numb and plaster stiff in the corner of the kitchen. I wanted to crawl on my knees back to the honey house and ball up   15
in the bed. I wanted everybody to shut up and go home.

Zach started toward me, but I turned away and stared down the sink drain. From the corner of my eye I grew aware of August watching me. Her mouth was bright and shiny, like she'd rubbed on Vaseline, so I knew she'd been dipping into the fritters, too. She   20
walked over and touched her hand to my cheek. I didn't think August knew about me turning the honey house into a disaster zone, but she had a way of figuring things out. Maybe she was letting me know it was okay.

"I want you to tell Zach," I said. "About me running away, about   25
my mother, about everything."

"Don't you want to tell him yourself?"

My eyes started to fill up. "I can't. Please, you do it."

She glanced in his direction. "All right then. I'll tell him the first chance I get."   30

2 **potluck** (AE): meal where everybody brings a surprise dish
4 **fritter**: fruit, meat or vegetable covered with batter (p. 105) and fried
14 **plaster**: substance used to make sculptures

She led the group outside for the last of the Mary Day ceremony. We paraded into the backyard, all the Daughters with tiny smudges of grease clinging to their lips. June was out there waiting for us, sitting in an armless kitchen chair, playing her cello. We gathered
5 around her while the lights of noontime bore down. The music she played was the kind that sawed through you, cutting into the secret chambers of your heart and setting the sadness free. Listening to it, I could see my mother sitting on a Trailways bus, riding out of Sylvan, while my four-year-old self napped on the bed, not yet knowing
10 what I would wake to.

June's music turned into air, and the air into aching. I swayed on my feet and tried not to breathe it in.

It was a relief when Neil and Zach stepped out of the honey house carrying Our Lady; it got my mind off the Trailways bus. They
15 carried her under their arms like a tube of carpet, with the chains slapping back and forth against her body. You'd think they would use the wagon again, something a little more dignified than this. And if that wasn't bad enough, when they set her down, they deposited her in the middle of an anthill, which started an ant
20 stampede. We had to jump around, shaking them off our feet.

Sugar-Girl's wig, which for some reason she insisted on calling a "wig hat," had slid down toward her eyebrows from the jumping around, so we had to have time out for her to go inside and adjust it. Otis yelled after her, "I told you not to wear that thing, it's too hot for
25 a wig. It's sliding around on your head from the perspiration."

"If I wanna wear my wig hat, I'm gonna wear it," she said over her shoulder.

"Don't we know it," he snapped back, looking at us like we were all on his side, when really we were backing Sugar-Girl one hundred
30 percent. Not because we *liked* her wig – it was the worst-looking thing you ever saw – we just didn't like Otis giving her orders.

8 **Trailways**: big US bus company   20 **stampede**: lots of animals running together

When all that finally settled down, August said, "Well, here we are, and here's Our Lady."

I looked her over, proud of how clean she was.

August read Mary's words from the Bible: " 'For behold from henceforth all generations shall call me blessed –' "   5

"Blessed Mary," Violet interrupted. "Blessed, blessed Mary." She stared at the sky, and we all looked up, wondering if she'd caught a glimpse of Mary climbing through the clouds. "Blessed Mary," she said one more time.

"Today we're celebrating the Assumption of Mary," August said.   10 "We're celebrating how she woke from her sleep and rose into heaven. And we're here to remember the story of Our Lady of Chains, to remind ourselves that those chains could never keep her down. Our Lady broke free of them every time."

August grabbed hold of the chain around black Mary and   15 unwrapped a loop before handing it off to Sugar-Girl, who unwrapped it a little further. Every one of us got to join in taking off a loop of chain. What I remember is the clinking noise it made as it uncoiled in a pile at Mary's feet, the sounds seeming to pick up where Violet left off. *Blessed, blessed, blessed, blessed.*   20

"Mary is rising," said August, her voice concentrated into a whisper. "She is rising to her heights." The Daughters lifted their arms. Even Otis had his arms shot straight up in the air.

"Our Mother Mary will not be cast down and bound up," said August. "And neither will her daughters. We will rise, Daughters. We   25 … will … rise."

June sliced her bow across the cello strings. I wanted to lift my arms with the rest of them, to hear a voice coming to me out of the sky, saying, *You will rise*, to feel that it was possible, but they hung limp by my sides. Inside, I felt small and contemptible, abandoned.   30 Every time I closed my eyes, I still saw the Trailways bus.

The Daughters stayed with their arms reaching into the air, giving off the feeling they were rising with Mary. Then August picked up a jar of Black Madonna Honey from behind June's chair, and what she did with it brought everybody back to earth. She opened the lid and
5 turned it upside down over Our Lady's head.

Honey oozed down Mary's face, across her shoulders, sliding down the folds of her dress. A wedge of honeycomb stuck in the crook of Our Lady's elbow.

I looked at Rosaleen as if to say, *Well, great, we spent all that time*
10 *cleaning honey off her, and here they go putting it back on.*

I decided nothing these women did would ever surprise me again, but that lasted about one second, because next the Daughters swarmed around Our Lady like a circle of bee attendants and rubbed the honey into the wood, working it into the top of her head, into
15 her cheeks, her neck and shoulders and arms, across her breasts, her belly.

"Come on, Lily, and help us," said Mabelee. Rosaleen had already dived in and was coating honey all over Our Lady's thighs. I hung back, but Cressie took my hands and dragged me over to Mary,
20 slapped them down in the muck of sun-warmed honey, right on top of Our Lady's red heart.

I remembered how I'd visited Our Lady in the middle of the night, how I'd placed my hand on that same spot. *You are my mother,* I'd told her then. *You are the mother of thousands.*

25 "I don't get why we're doing this," I said.

"We always bathe her in honey," said Cressie. "Every year."

"But how come?"

August was working the honey into Our Lady's face. "The churches used to bathe their special statues in holy water as a way to
30 honor them," she said. "Especially statues of Our Lady. Sometimes they bathed her in wine. We settled on honey." August moved down to Our Lady's neck. "See, Lily, honey is a preservative. It seals over

---

13 **swarm around sb.**: gather around sb.   18 **coat sth.**: cover sth. with a substance
20 **in the muck of sth.**: (here) right into sth.   32 **preservative**: *Konservierungsstoff*

the comb in the hives to keep it safe and pure so the bees can survive the winter. When we bathe Our Lady in it, I guess you'd say we're preserving her for another year, at least inside our hearts we're doing that."

"I didn't know honey was a preservative," I said, starting to like   5 the feel of it under my fingers, how they glided as if oiled.

"Well, people don't think about honey like that, but it's so strong-acting people used to smear it on dead bodies to embalm them. Mothers buried their dead babies in it, and it would keep them fresh."   10

This was a use for honey I hadn't considered. I could just see funeral homes selling big jars of honey for dead people, instead of coffins. I tried to picture *that* in the drive-through window at the funeral home.

I began to work my hands into the wood, almost embarrassed at   15 the intimacy of what we were doing.

Once Mabelee leaned her head over too far and got honey all in her hair, but it was Lunelle who took the cake with honey dripping off the ends of her elbows. She kept trying to lick it off, but of course her tongue couldn't reach that far.   20

The ants started a single-file parade up the side of Our Lady, drawn by the honey, and not to be outdone, a handful of scout bees showed up and landed on Our Lady's head. Let somebody bring out the honey and the insect kingdom will be there in no time.

Queenie said, "Next I guess the honey bears will be joining us." I   25 actually laughed and, spotting a honey-free place near the base of the statue, worked to get it covered up.

Our Lady was covered with hands, every shade of brown and black, going in their own directions, but then the strangest thing started happening. Gradually all our hands fell into the same   30 movement, sliding up and down the statue in long, slow strokes, then changing to a sideways motion, like a flock of birds that shifts

18 **take the cake** (infml): *den Vogel abschießen*

direction in the sky at the same moment, and you're left wondering who gave the order.

This went on for I don't know how long, and we didn't ruin it by talking. We were preserving Our Lady, and I was content – for the
5 first time since I'd learned about my mother – to be doing what I was doing.

Finally we all stepped back. Our Lady stood there with her chains spilled around her on the grass, absolutely golden with honey.

One by one the Daughters dipped their hands into a bucket of
10 water and washed off the honey. I waited till the very last, wanting to keep the coating of honey on my skin as long as I could. It was like I was wearing a pair of gloves with magic properties. Like I could preserve whatever I touched.

We left Our Lady in the yard while we ate, then returned and washed
15 her with water the same slow way we'd washed her with honey. After Neil and Zach carried her back to her place in the parlor, everyone left. August, June, and Rosaleen started doing the dishes, but I slipped off to the honey house. I lay down on my cot, trying not to think.

20 Have you noticed the more you try not to think, the more elaborate your thinking episodes get? While trying not to think, I spent twenty minutes on this fascinating question: if you could have one miracle from the Bible happen to you, what would it be? I eliminated the one about multiplying loaves and fishes, as I never
25 wanted to see food again. I thought walking on water would be interesting, but what good was that? I mean, you walk on water, what's the point? I settled on getting raised from the dead, since a big part of me still felt dead as a doornail.

---

21 **elaborate**: detailed   28 **dead as a doornail** (infml): completely dead

All this took place before I even realized I was thinking. I had just gone back to trying again not to think when August tapped on the door.

"Lily, can I come in?"

"Sure," I said, but I didn't bother to get up. *So much for not thinking.* Try to be five seconds around August and not think.

She breezed in holding a gold-and-white-striped hatbox. She stood a moment looking down at me, seeming unusually tall. The fan on the little wall shelf rotated around and blew her collar, making it flap around her neck.

She has brought me a hat, I thought. Maybe she had gone down to the Amen Dollar and bought me a straw hat to cheer me up.

But that didn't make a bit of sense, really. Why would a straw hat cheer me up? Then I thought for one second it might be the hat Lunelle had promised to make for me, but that didn't fit either. Lunelle wouldn't have had time to sew up a hat this soon.

August sat on Rosaleen's old cot and placed the box on her lap. "I've brought you some of your mother's belongings."

I stared at the perfect roundness of the box. When I took a deep breath, it stuttered strangely as it came out. *My mother's belongings.*

I didn't move. I smelled the air coming through the window, churned up by the fan. I could tell it had turned thick with afternoon rain, but the sky was holding back.

"Don't you want to see?" she said.

"Just *tell* me what's in it."

She placed her hand on the lid and patted. "I'm not sure I can remember. I didn't even remember the box till this morning. I thought we'd open it together. But you don't have to look if you don't want to. It's just a handful of things your mother left here the day she went back to Sylvan to get you. I finally gave her clothes away to the Salvation Army, but I kept the rest of her stuff, what little there was. It's been in this box ten years, I guess."

I sat up. I could hear my heart thudding. I wondered if August could hear it over there across the room. *Boom-boom. Boom-boom.* In spite of the panic that goes along with it, there's something familiar and strangely comforting about hearing your heart beat like that.

5   August set the box on the bed and removed the lid. I stretched up a little to see inside the box, unable to glimpse anything, though, but white tissue paper, turning yellow around the edges.

She lifted out a small bundle and peeled away the tissue. "Your mother's pocket mirror," she said, holding it up. It was ovalshaped 10   and surrounded by a tortoise frame, no bigger than the palm of my hand.

I eased off the bed and slid down onto the floor, where I rested my back against the bed. A little closer than before. August acted like she was waiting for me to reach out and take the mirror. 15   I practically had to sit on my hands. Finally August lifted it up and peered inside it herself. Circles of light bounced around on the wall behind her. "If *you* look in here, you're gonna see your mother's face looking back at you," she said.

I will never look in that mirror, I thought.

20   Laying it on the bed, August reached into the hatbox and unwrapped a hairbrush with a wooden handle and offered it to me. Before I thought, I took it. The handle felt funny in my hand, cool and smooth-edged, like it had been worn down by excessive holding. I wondered if she'd brushed her hair a hundred strokes every day.

25   As I was about to hand the brush back to August, I saw a long, black, wavy hair threaded through the bristles. I brought the brush close to my face and stared at it, my mother's hair, a genuine part of her body.

"Well, I'll be," August said.

30   I could not take my eyes off it. It had grown out of her head and now perched there like a thought she had left behind on the brush. I knew then that no matter how hard you tried, no matter how many

---

10 **tortoise** ['tɔːrtəs]: *Schildpatt*   12 **ease off sth.**: move off sth.

jars of honey you threw, no matter how much you thought you could leave your mother behind, she would never disappear from the tender places in you. I pressed my back against the bed and felt tears coming. The brush and the hair belonging to Deborah Fontanel Owens swam in my vision. 5

I handed the brush back to August, who dropped a piece of jewelry into my hand. A gold pin shaped like a whale with a tiny black eye and a spout of rhinestone water coming from its blowhole.

"She was wearing that pin on her sweater the day she got here," August said. 10

I closed my fingers around it, then walked on my knees over to Rosaleen's bed and placed it alongside the pocket mirror and the brush, moving them around like I was working on a collage.

I used to lay out my Christmas presents on the bed the same way. There would usually be four whole things that T. Ray had gotten the 15 lady at the Sylvan Mercantile to pick out for me – sweater, socks, pajamas, sack of oranges. Merry Christmas. You could bet your life on the gift list. I would arrange them for display in a vertical line, a square, a diagonal line, any kind of configuration to help me feel like they were a picture of love. 20

When I looked up at August, she was pulling a black book from the box. "I gave your mother this while she was here. English poetry."

I took the book in my hand, leafing through the pages, noticing pencil marks in the margins, not words, but strange little doodles, spiraling tornadoes, a flock of Vs, squiggles with eyes, pots with lids, 25 pots with faces, pots with curly things boiling out, little puddles that would suddenly give rise to a terrible wave. I was staring at my mother's private miseries, and it made me want to go outside and bury the book in the dirt.

Page forty-two. That's where I came to eight lines by William 30 Blake that she'd underlined, some words twice.

8 **spout**: fountain   25 **squiggle**: a twisted, curly line

O Rose, thou art sick!
The invisible worm,
That flies in the night,
In the howling storm,
5 *Has found out thy bed*
Of crimson joy,
And his dark secret love
Does thy life destroy.

I closed the book. I wanted the words to flow off me, but they
10 had stuck. My mother was William Blake's rose. I wanted nothing so
much as to tell her how sorry I was for being one of the invisible
worms that flew in the night.

I placed the book on the bed with the other things, then turned
back to August, while she reached down into the box again, causing
15 the tissue paper to whisper. "One last thing," she said, and she drew
out a small oval picture frame of tarnished silver.

When she passed it to me, she held on to my hands for a second.
The frame contained a picture of a woman in profile, her head bent
toward a little girl who sat in a high chair with a smudge of baby
20 food on the side of her mouth. The woman's hair curled in forty
directions, beautiful, like it had just had its hundred strokes. She
held a baby spoon in her right hand. Light glazed her face. The little
girl wore a bib with a teddy bear on it. A sprig of hair on top of her
head was tied with a bow. She lifted one hand toward the woman.
25 Me and my mother.

I didn't care about anything on this earth except the way her face
was tipped toward mine, our noses just touching, how wide and
gorgeous her smile was, like sparklers going off. She had fed me with
a tiny spoon. She had rubbed her nose against mine and poured her
30 light on my face.

---

16 **tarnished**: something shiny gone dull   23 **bib**: *Lätzchen*

Through the open window the air smelled like Carolina jasmine, which is the true smell of South Carolina. I walked over and propped my elbows on the sill and breathed as deeply as I could. Behind me I heard August shift on the cot, the legs squeak, then relax.

I looked down at the picture, then closed my eyes. I figured May 5 must've made it to heaven and explained to my mother about the sign I wanted. The one that would let me know I was loved.

A queenless colony is a pitiful and melancholy community; there may be a mournful wail or lament from within. … Without intervention, the colony will die. But introduce a new queen and the most extravagant change takes place.

The Queen Must Die: And Other Affairs of Bees and Men

Chapter Fourteen

After August and I went through the hatbox, I drew into myself and stayed there for a while. August and Zach tended to the bees and the honey, but I spent most of my time down by the river, alone. I just wanted to keep to myself.

5   The month of August had turned into a griddle where the days just lay there and sizzled. I plucked leaves off the elephant ear plants and fanned my face, sat with my bare feet submerged in the trickling water, felt breezes lift off the river surface and sweep over me, and still everything about me was stunned and stupefied by the heat,

10 everything except my heart. It sat like an ice sculpture in the center of my chest. Nothing could touch it.

People, in general, would rather die than forgive. It's *that* hard. If God said in plain language, "I'm giving you a choice, forgive or die," a lot of people would go ahead and order their coffin.

15 I wrapped my mother's things in the falling-apart paper, tucked them back in the hatbox, and put the lid on it. Lying on my stomach on the floor, pushing the box under my cot, I found a tiny pile of mouse bones. I scooped them up and washed them in the sink.

Every day I carried them around in my pocket and could not imagine why I was doing it.

When I woke up in the mornings, my first thought was the hatbox. It was almost like my mother herself was hiding under the bed. One night I had to get up and move it to the other side of the 5 room. Then I had to strip off my pillowcase and stuff the box down inside it and tie it closed with one of my hair ribbons. All this just so I could sleep.

I would walk to the pink house to use the bathroom and think, *My mother sat on this same toilet*, and then I would hate myself for 10 thinking it. Who cared where she sat to pee? She hadn't cared a whole lot about *my* bathroom habits when she abandoned me to Mrs. Watson and T. Ray.

I gave myself pep talks. *Don't think about her. It is over and done.* The next minute, I swear to God, I would be picturing her in the 15 pink house, or out by the wailing wall, stuffing her burdens among the stones. I would've bet twenty dollars T. Ray's name was squashed into the cracks and crevices out there. Maybe the name Lily was out there, too. I wished she'd been smart enough, or loving enough, to realize everybody has burdens that crush them, only they don't give 20 up their children.

In a weird way I must have loved my little collection of hurts and wounds. They provided me with some real nice sympathy, with the feeling I was exceptional. I was the girl abandoned by her mother. I was the girl who kneeled on grits. What a special case I was. 25

We were deep into mosquito season, so a lot of what I did by the river was swat at them. Sitting in the purple shadows, I pulled out the mouse bones and worked them between my fingers. I stared at things until I seemed to melt right into them. Sometimes I would forget lunch, and Rosaleen would come find me, bearing a tomato 30 sandwich. After she left, I would throw it in the river.

17 **squash sth**.: press sth. flat

At times I could not prevent myself from lying flat on the ground, pretending I was inside one of those beehive tombs. I felt the same way I did right after May died, only multiplied by a hundred.

August had said, "I guess you need to grieve a little while. So go ahead and do it." But now that I was doing it, I couldn't seem to stop.

I knew that August must have explained everything to Zach, and June, too, because they tiptoed around me like I was a psychiatric case. Maybe I was. Maybe I was the one who belonged on Bull Street, not my mother. At least no one prodded, or asked questions, or said, "For Pete's sake, snap out of it."

I wondered how much longer it would be before August had to act on the things I'd told her – me running away, helping Rosaleen escape. Rosaleen, a fugitive. August was giving me time for now, time to be by the river and do what I had to do, the same way she gave herself time there after May died. But it wouldn't last forever.

It is the peculiar nature of the world to go on spinning no matter what sort of heartbreak is happening. June set a wedding date, Saturday, October 10. Neil's brother, an African Methodist–Episcopal reverend from Albany, Georgia, was going to marry them in the backyard under the myrtle trees. June laid out all their plans one night at dinner. She would come walking down an aisle of rose petals, wearing a white rayon suit with frog closings that Mabelee was sewing for her. I could not picture frog closings. June drew a picture of one on a tablet, and afterward I still could not picture them. Lunelle had been commissioned to make her a wedding hat, which I thought was very courageous of June. There was no telling what she would end up with on her head.

---

11 f**or Pete's sake**: *um Himmels willen*   **snap out of it** (infml): stop being depressed   23 **rayon**: smooth artificial material for making clothes
frog closing: highly ornamental sewed button

Rosaleen offered to bake the wedding cake layers, and Violet and Queenie were going to decorate it with a "rainbow theme." Again, all I can say is how brave June was.

One afternoon I went to the kitchen in the middle of the afternoon, nearly dying of thirst, wanting to fill a jug with water and take it back to the river, and found June and August clinging to each other in the middle of the floor.

I stood outside the door and watched, even though it was a private moment. June gripped August's back, and her hands trembled. "May would've loved this wedding," she said. "She must've told me a hundred times I was being stubborn about Neil. Oh, God, August, why didn't I do it sooner, while she was still alive?"

August turned slightly and caught sight of me in the doorway. She held June, who was starting to cry, but she kept her eyes on mine. She said, "Regrets don't help anything, you know that."

The next day I actually felt like eating. I wandered in for lunch to find Rosaleen wearing a new dress and her hair freshly plaited. She was poking tissues into her bosom for safekeeping.

"Where did you get that dress?" I said.

She turned a circle, modeling it, and when I smiled, she turned another one. It was what you would call a tent dress – yards of material falling from her shoulders without benefit of waistband and darts. It had a bright red background with giant white flowers all over it. I could see she was in love with it.

"August took me into town yesterday, and I bought it," she said. I felt startled suddenly by the things that had been going on without me.

"Your dress is pretty," I lied, noticing for the first time there were no lunch fixings anywhere.

---

23 **dart**: pointed fold sewn in a piece of clothing to make it fit better

She smoothed her hands down the front of it, looked at the clock on the stove, and reached for an old white vinyl purse of May's that she'd inherited.

"You going somewhere?" I said.

5 "She sure is," said August, stepping into the room, smiling at Rosaleen.

"I'm gonna finish what I started," Rosaleen said, lifting her chin. "I'm gonna register to vote."

My arms dropped by my sides, and my mouth came open. "But 10 what about – what about you being … you know?"

Rosaleen squinted at me. *"What?"*

"A fugitive from justice," I said. "What if they recognize your name? What if you get caught?"

I cut my eyes over at August.

15 "Oh, I don't think there'll be a problem," August said, taking the truck keys off the brass nail by the door. "We're going to the voter drive at the Negro high school."

"But –"

"For heaven's sake, all I'm doing is getting my voter's card," said 20 Rosaleen.

"That's what you said last time," I told her.

She ignored that. She strapped May's purse on her arm. A split ran from the handle around onto the side.

"You wanna come, Lily?" said August.

25 I did and I didn't. I looked down at my feet, tanned and bare. "I'll just stay here and make some lunch."

August lifted her eyebrows. "It's nice to see you're hungry for a change."

They went onto the back porch, down the steps. I followed them 30 to the truck. As Rosaleen got in, I said, "Don't spit on anybody's shoes, okay?"

She let out a laugh that made her whole body shake. It looked like all the flowers on her dress were bobbing in a gust of wind.

I went back inside, boiled two hot dogs, and ate them without buns. Then I headed back to the woods, where I picked a few bachelor buttons that grew wild in the plots of sunshine before   5
getting bored and tossing them away.

I sat on the ground, expecting to sink down into my dark mood and think about my mother, but the only thoughts I had were for Rosaleen. I pictured her standing in a line of people. I could almost see her practicing writing her name. Getting it just right. Her big   10
moment. Suddenly I wished I'd gone with them. I wished it more than anything. I wanted to see her face when they handed her her card. I wanted to say, *Rosaleen, you know what? I'm proud of you.*

What was I doing sitting out here in the woods?

I got up and went inside. Passing the telephone in the hallway, I had   15
an urge to call Zach. To become part of the world again. I dialed his number.

When he answered, I said, "So what's new?"

"Who's this?" he said.

"Very funny," I told him.   20

"I'm sorry about … everything," he said. "August told me what happened." Silence floated between us a moment, and then he said, "Will you have to go back?"

"You mean back to my father?"

He hesitated. "Yeah."   25

The minute he said it, I had the feeling that's exactly what would happen. Everything in my body felt it. "I suppose so," I said. I coiled the phone cord around my finger and stared down the hall at the front door. For a few seconds I was unable to look away, imagining myself leaving through it and not coming back.   30

5 **bachelor button:** *Kornblume*

"I'll come see you," he said, and I wanted to cry.

Zach knocking on the door of T. Ray Owens's house. It could never happen.

"I asked you what was new, remember?" I didn't expect anything
5 was, but I needed to change the subject.

"Well, for starters, I'll be going to the white high school this year."

I was speechless. I squeezed the phone in my hand. "Are you sure you wanna do that?" I said. I knew what those places were like.

"Somebody's got to," he said. "Might as well be me."

10 Both of us, it seemed like, were doomed to misery.

Rosaleen came home, a bona fide registered voter in the United States of America. We all sat around that evening, waiting to eat dinner, while she personally called every one of the Daughters on the telephone.

15 "I just wanted to tell you I'm a registered voter," she said each time, and there would be a pause, and then she'd say, "President Johnson and Mr. Hubert Humphrey, that's who. I'm not voting for Mr. Pisswater." She laughed every time, like this was the joke of jokes. She would say, "Goldwater, Pisswater, get it?"

20 This went on even after dinner. Just when we'd think she had it out of her system, out of the complete blue, she'd say, "I'll be casting my vote for Mr. Johnson."

When she finally wound down and said good night, I watched her climb the stairs wearing her red-and-white voter-registration
25 dress, and I wished again that I'd been there.

Regrets don't help anything, August had told June, you know that. I ran up the stairs and grabbed Rosaleen from behind, stopping her with one foot poised in the air, searching for the next step. I wrapped my arms around her middle. "I love you," I blurted out, not even
30 knowing I was going to say this.

---

21 **out of the complete blue**: for no reason

❀

That night when the katydids and tree frogs and every other musical creature were wound up and going strong, I walked around the honey house, feeling like I had spring fever. It was ten o'clock at night, and I honestly felt like I could've scrubbed the floors and washed the windows.   5

I went over to the shelves and straightened all the mason jars, then took the broom and swept the floor, up under the holding tank and the generator, where nobody had swept for fifty years, it looked like. I still wasn't tired, so I stripped the sheets off my bed and went over to the pink house and got a set of clean ones, careful to tiptoe   10 around and not wake anybody up. I got dust rags and Comet cleanser in case I needed them.

I came back, and before I knew it I was involved in a fullblown cleaning frenzy. By midnight I had the place shining.

I even went through my stuff and got rid of some things. Old   15 pencils, a couple of stories I'd written that were too embarrassing for anybody to read, a torn pair of shorts, a comb with most of its teeth missing.

Next I gathered up the mouse bones that I'd kept in my pockets, realizing I didn't need to carry them around anymore. But I knew   20 I couldn't throw them away either, so I tied them together with a red hair ribbon and set them on the shelf by the fan. I stared at them a minute, wondering how a person got attached to *mouse bones*. I decided sometimes you just need to nurse something, that's all.

By now I was starting to get tired, but I took my mother's things   25 out of the hatbox – her tortoiseshell mirror, her brush, the poetry book, her whale pin, the picture of us with our faces together – and set them up on the shelf with the mouse bones. I have to say, it made the whole room look different.

---

7 **holding tank**: tank with a honey gate on the side   11–12 **Comet cleanser**
['klenzər]: disinfectant cleaning powder   13 **fullblown**: complete

Drifting off to sleep, I thought about her. How nobody is perfect. How you just have to close your eyes and breathe out and let the puzzle of the human heart be what it is.

The next morning I showed up in the kitchen with the whale pin
5 fastened to my favorite blue top. A Nat King Cole record was going. "Unforgettable, that's what you are." I think it was on to drown out all the commotion the pink Lady Kenmore washer was making on the porch. It was a wondrous invention, but it sounded like a cement mixer. August sat with her elbows on the tabletop, drinking the last
10 of her coffee and reading another book from the bookmobile.

When she lifted her eyes, they took in my face, then went straight to the whale pin. I saw her smile before she went back to her book.

I fixed my standard Rice Krispies with raisins. After I finished eating, August said, "Come on out to the hives. I need to show you
15 something."

We got all decked out in our bee outfits – at least I did. August hardly ever wore anything but the hat and veil.

Walking out there, August widened her step to miss squashing an ant. It reminded me of May. I said, "It was May who got my mother
20 started saving roaches, wasn't it?"

"Who else?" she said, and smiled. "It happened when your mother was a teenager. May caught her killing a roach with a flyswatter. She said, 'Deborah Fontanel, every living creature on the earth is special. You want to be the one that puts an end to one of
25 them?' Then she showed her how to make a trail of marshmallows and graham crackers."

I fingered the whale pin on my shoulder, picturing the whole thing. Then I looked around and noticed the world. It was such a pretty day you couldn't imagine anything coming along to spoil it.

6–7 **drown sth. out**: be louder than sth.   7 **commotion**: (here) noise
10 **bookmobile** (AE): mobile library   16 **deck out**: (here) dress

According to August, if you've never seen a cluster of beehives first thing in the morning, you've missed the eighth wonder of the world. Picture these white boxes tucked under pine trees. The sun will slant through the branches, shining in the sprinkles of dew drying on the lids. There will be a few hundred bees doing laps 5 around the hive boxes, just warming up, but mostly taking their bathroom break, as bees are so clean they will not soil the inside of their hives. From a distance it will look like a big painting you might see in a museum, but museums can't capture the sound. Fifty feet away you will hear it, a humming that sounds like it came from 10 another planet. At thirty feet your skin will start to vibrate. The hair will lift on your neck. Your head will say, *Don't go any farther*, but your heart will send you straight into the hum, where you will be swallowed by it. You will stand there and think, *I am in the center of the universe, where everything is sung to life*. 15

August lifted the lid off a hive. "This one is missing its queen," she said.

I'd learned enough beekeeping to know that a hive without a queen was a death sentence for the bees. They would stop work and go around completely demoralized. 20

"What happened?" I said.

"I discovered it yesterday. The bees were sitting out here on the landing board looking melancholy. If you see bees loafing and lamenting, you can bet their queen is dead. So I searched through the combs, and sure enough she was gone. I don't know what caused 25 it. Maybe it was just her time."

"What do you do now?"

"I called the County Extension, and they put me in touch with a man in Goose Creek who said he'd drive over with a new queen sometime today. I want to get the hive requeened before one of the 30 workers starts laying. If we get laying workers, we've got ourselves a mess."

---

5 **do laps**: (here) fly in circles   23 **loaf**: waste time
28 **County Extension**: administrative centre of a county

"I didn't know a worker bee could lay eggs," I said.

"All they can do, really, is lay unfertilized drone eggs. They'll fill up the combs with them, and as the workers naturally die off, there are none to replace them."

5   As she lowered the lid, she said, "I just wanted to show you what a queenless colony looked like."

She lifted back the veils from her hat, then lifted mine back, too. She held my gaze while I studied the gold flecks in her eyes.

"Remember when I told you the story of Beatrix," she said, "the 10 nun who ran away from her convent? Remember how the Virgin Mary stood in for her?"

"I remember," I said. "I figured you knew I'd run away like Beatrix did. You were trying to tell me that Mary was standing in for me at home, taking care of things till I went back."

15   "Oh, that's not what I was trying to tell you at all," she said. "You weren't the runaway I was thinking about. I was thinking about your *mother* running away. I was just trying to plant a little idea in your head."

"What idea?"

20   "That maybe Our Lady could act for *Deborah* and be like a stand-in mother for you."

The light was making patterns on the grass. I stared at them, feeling shy about what I was going to say. "I told Our Lady one night in the pink house that she was my mother. I put my hand on her 25 heart the way you and the Daughters always do at your meetings. I know I tried it that one time before and fainted, but this time I stayed on my feet, and for a while after that I really did feel stronger. Then I seemed to lose it. I think what I need is to go back and touch her heart again."

30   August said, "Listen to me now, Lily. I'm going to tell you something I want you always to remember, all right?"

Her face had grown serious, intent. Her eyes did not blink.

---

32 **intent**: attentive and determined

"All right," I said, and I felt something electric slide down my spine.

"Our Lady is not some magical being out there somewhere, like a fairy godmother. She's not the statue in the parlor. She's something *inside* of you. Do you understand what I'm telling you?"

"Our Lady is inside me," I repeated, not sure I did.

"You have to find a mother inside yourself. We all do. Even if we already have a mother, we still have to find this part of ourselves inside." She held out her hand to me. "Give me your hand." I lifted my left hand and placed it in hers. She took it and pressed the flat of my palm up against my chest, over my beating heart. "You don't have to put your hand on Mary's heart to get strength and consolation and rescue, and all the other things we need to get through life," she said. "You can place it right here on your own heart. *Your own heart.*"

August stepped closer. She kept the pressure steady against my hand. "All those times your father treated you mean, Our Lady was the voice in you that said, 'No, I will not bow down to this. I am Lily Melissa Owens, I will not bow down.' Whether you could hear this voice or not, she was in there saying it."

I took my other hand and placed it on top of hers, and she moved her free hand on top of it, so we had this black-and-white stack of hands resting upon my chest.

"When you're unsure of yourself," she said, "when you start pulling back into doubt and small living, she's the one inside saying, 'Get up from there and live like the glorious girl you are.' She's the power inside you, you understand?"

Her hands stayed where they were but released their pressure. "And whatever it is that keeps widening your heart, that's Mary, too, not only the power inside you but the love. And when you get down to it, Lily, that's the only purpose grand enough for a human life. Not just to love – but to *persist* in love."

She paused. Bees drummed their sound into the air. August retrieved her hands from the pile on my chest, but I left mine there.

"This Mary I'm talking about sits in your heart all day long, saying, 'Lily, you are my everlasting home. Don't you ever be afraid. I am enough. We are enough.' "

I closed my eyes, and in the coolness of morning, there among the bees, I felt for one clear instant what she was talking about.

When I opened my eyes, August was nowhere around. I looked back toward the house and saw her crossing the yard, her white dress catching the light.

The knock on the door came at 2:00 p.m. I was sitting in the parlor writing in the new notebook Zach had left at my door, setting down everything that had happened to me since Mary Day. Words streamed out of me so fast I couldn't keep up with them, and that's all I was thinking about. I didn't pay attention to the knock. Later I would remember it didn't sound like an ordinary knock. More like a fist pounding.

I kept writing, waiting for August to answer it. I was sure it was the man from Goose Creek with the new queen bee.

The pounding came again. June had gone off with Neil. Rosaleen was in the honey house washing a new shipment of mason jars, a job that belonged to me, but she'd volunteered for it, seeing how badly I needed to write everything out. I didn't know where August was. Probably in the honey house, helping Rosaleen.

I look back and wonder: how did I not guess who was there? The third time the knocking came, I got up and opened the door.

T. Ray stared at me, clean-shaven, wearing a white shortsleeved shirt with chest hair curling through the neck opening. He was smiling. Not a smile of sweet adoring, I hasten to say, but the fat grin of a man who has been rabbit hunting all day long and has just now found his prey backed up in a hollow log with no way out. He said, "Well, well, well. Look who's here."

I had a sudden, terror-stricken thought he might that second drag me out to his truck and hightail it straight back to the peach farm, where I would never be heard from again. I stepped backward 5 into the hallway, and with a forced politeness that surprised me and seemed to throw him off stride, I said, "Won't you come in?"

What else was I going to do? I turned and forced myself to walk calmly into the parlor.

His boots clomped after me. "All right, goddamn it," he said, 10 speaking to the back of my head. "If you want to pretend I'm making a social visit, we'll pretend, but this ain't a social visit, you hear me? I spent half my summer looking for you, and I'm gonna take you out of here nice and quiet or kicking and screaming – don't matter which to me." 15

I motioned to a rocking chair. "Have a seat if you want to."

I was trying to look ho-hum, when inside I was close to fullblown panic. *Where was August?* My breath had turned into short, shallow puffs, a dog pant.

He flopped into the rocker and pushed back and forth, that got- 20 you-now grin glued on his face. "So you've been here the whole time, staying with colored women. *Jesus Christ.*"

Without realizing it, I'd backed over to the statue of Our Lady. I stood, immobilized, while he looked her over. "What the hell is that?" 25

"A statue of Mary," I said. "You know, Jesus' mother." My voice sounded skittish in my throat. Inside, I was racking my brain for something to do.

"Well, it looks like something from the junkyard," he said.

"How did you find me?" 30

Sliding up on the edge of the cane seat, he dug in his pants pocket until he brought up his knife, the one he used to clean his nails with.

---

7 **throw sb. off stride** (AE): make sb. confused and unable to follow their plan
17 **ho-hum** (infml): very ordinary   27 **rack your brain**: think hard

"It was *you* who led me here," he said, puffed up and pleased as punch to share the news.

"I did no such thing."

He tugged the blade out of the knife bed, pushed the point into
5 the arm of the rocker, and carved out little chunks of wood, taking his sweet time to explain. "Oh, you led me here, all right. Yesterday the phone bill came, and guess what I found on there? One collect call from a lawyer's office in Tiburon. Mr. Clayton Forrest. Big mistake, Lily, calling me collect."

10 "You went to Mr. Clayton's and he told you where I was?"

"No, but he has an old-lady secretary who was more than happy to fill me in. She said I would find you right here."

Stupid Miss Lacy.

"Where's Rosaleen?" he said.

15 "She took off a long time ago," I lied. He might kidnap *me* back to Sylvan, but there was no need for him to know where Rosaleen was. I could spare her that much at least.

He didn't comment on Rosaleen, though. He seemed happy to carve up the arm of the rocking chair like he was all of eleven years
20 old, putting his initials in a tree. I think he was glad he didn't have to fool with her. I wondered how I would survive back in Sylvan. Without Rosaleen.

Suddenly he stopped rocking, and the nauseating smile faded off his mouth. He was staring at my shoulder with his eyes squinted
25 almost to the closed position. I looked down to see what had grabbed his attention and realized he was staring at the whale pin on my shirt.

He got to his feet and walked over to me, deliberately stopping four or five feet away, like the pin had some kind of voodoo curse on
30 it. "Where did you get that?" he said.

My hand went up involuntarily and touched the little rhinestone spout. "August gave it to me. The woman who lives here."

5–6 **take your sweet time to do sth.**: enjoy doing sth. slowly
15 **take off**: (here) leave

"Don't lie to me."

"I'm not lying. She gave it to me. She said it belonged to –" I was afraid to say it. He didn't know anything about August and my mother.

His upper lip had gone white, the way it did when he was badly 5 upset. "I gave that pin to your mother on her twenty-second birthday," he said. "You tell me right now, how did this August woman get it?"

"You gave this pin to my mother? *You* did?"

"Answer me, damn it." 10

"This is where my mother came when she ran away from us. August said she was wearing it the day she got here."

He walked back to the rocker, shaken-looking, and eased down onto the seat. "I'll be goddamned," he said, so low I could hardly hear him. 15

"August used to take care of her back when she was a little girl in Virginia," I said, trying to explain.

He stared into the air, into nothing. Through the window, out there in the Carolina summer, I could see the sun beating down on the roof of his truck, lighting up the tips of the picket fence that had 20 all but disappeared under the jasmine. The truck was spattered with mud, like he'd been trolling the swamps looking for me.

"I should have known." He was shaking his head, talking like I wasn't in the room. "I looked for her everywhere I could think. And she was right here. Jesus Christ, she was right here." 25

The thought seemed to awe him. He shook his head and looked around, as if thinking, *I bet she sat in this chair. I bet she walked on this rug.* His chin quivered slightly, and for the first time it hit me how much he must've loved her, how it had split him open when she left.

Before coming here, my whole life had been nothing but a hole 30 where my mother should have been, and this hole had made me

26 **awe sb.**: astonish sb. and fill them with respect

different, left me always aching for something, but never once did I
think what he'd lost or how it might've changed him.

I thought about August's words. *People can start out one way, and
by the time life gets through with them they end up completely different. I*
5 *don't doubt he started off loving your mother. In fact, I think he worshiped
her.*

I had never known T. Ray to worship anyone except Snout, the
dog love of his life, but seeing him now, I knew he'd loved Deborah
Fontanel, and when she'd left him, he'd sunk into bitterness.

10 He jabbed the knife into the wood and got to his feet. I looked at
the handle sticking in the air, then at T. Ray as he walked around the
room touching things, the piano, the hatrack, a *Look* magazine on
the drop-leaf table.

"Looks like you're here by yourself?" he said. I could feel it
15 coming. The end of everything.

He walked straight toward me and reached for my arm. When I
jerked away, he brought his hand across my face. T. Ray had slapped
me lots of times before, clean, sharp smacks on the cheek, the kind
that cause you to draw a quick, stunned breath, but this was
20 something else, not a slap at all. This time he'd hit me full force. I'd
heard the grunt of exertion escape his lips as the blow landed, seen
the momentary bulge of his eyes. And I'd smelled the farm on his
hand, smelled peaches.

The impact threw me backward into Our Lady. She crashed onto
25 the floor a second before I did. I didn't feel the pain at first, but
sitting up, gathering my feet under me, it slashed from my ear down
to my chin. It caused me to drop back again onto the floor. I stared
up at him with my hands clutched at my chest, wondering if he
would pull me by my feet outside to his truck.

30 He was shouting. "How dare you leave me! You need a lesson, is
what you need!"

---

12 **Look magazine**: bi-weekly general-interest magazine (1937 to 1971)

I filled my lungs with air, tried to steady myself. Black Mary lay beside me on the floor, giving off the overpowering smell of honey. I remembered how we'd smoothed it into her, every little crack and grain till she was honey-logged and satisfied. I lay there afraid to move, aware of the knife stuck in the arm of the chair across the   5
room. He kicked at me, his boot landing in my calf, like I was a tin can in the road that he might as well kick because it was there in front of him.

He stood over me. "Deborah," I heard him mumble. "You're not leaving me again." His eyes looked frantic, scared. I wondered if I'd   10
heard him right.

I noticed my hands still cupped over my chest. I pressed them down, hard into my flesh.

"Get up!" he yelled. "I'm taking you home."

He had me by the arm in one swoop, lifting me up. Once on my   15
feet, I wrenched away and ran for the door. He came after me and caught me by the hair. Twisting to face him, I saw he had the knife. He waved it in front of my face.

"You're going back with me!" he yelled. "You never should have left me."   20

It crossed my mind that he was no longer talking to me but to Deborah. Like his mind had snapped back ten years. "T. Ray," I said. "It's me – Lily."

He didn't hear me. He had a fistful of my hair and wouldn't let go. "Deborah," he said.   25

"Goddamn bitch," he said.

He seemed crazy with anguish, reliving a pain he'd kept locked up all this time, and now that it was loose, it had overwhelmed him. I wondered how far he'd go to try and take Deborah back. For all I knew, he might kill her.   30

I am your everlasting home. I am enough. We are enough.

4 **grain**: *Maserung*   **honey-logged**: full of honey

I looked into his eyes. They were full of a strange fogginess. "Daddy," I said.

I shouted it. "*Daddy!*"

He looked startled, then stared at me, breathing hard. He turned
5   loose my hair and dropped the knife on the rug.

I stumbled backward and caught myself. I heard myself panting. The sound filled up the room. I didn't want him to see me look down at the knife, but I couldn't help myself. I glanced over to where it was. When I looked back at him, he was still staring at me.

10   For a moment neither of us moved. I couldn't read his expression. My whole body was shaking, but I felt I had to keep talking. "I'm – I'm sorry I left like I did," I said, taking small steps backward.

The skin over his eyes sagged down onto his eyelids. He looked away, toward the window, like he was contemplating the road that
15   had brought her here.

I heard a creaking floorboard in the hallway outside. Turning, I saw August and Rosaleen at the door. I gave them a quiet signal with my hand, waving them away. I think I just needed to see it through by myself, to be with him while he came back to his senses. He
20   seemed so harmless, standing there now.

For a moment I thought they were going to ignore me and come in anyway, but then August put her hand on Rosaleen's arm and they eased out of sight.

When T. Ray turned back, he fastened his eyes on me, and there
25   was nothing in them but an ocean of hurt. He looked at the pin on my shirt. "You look like her," he said, and him saying that, I knew he'd said everything.

I leaned over and picked up his knife, bent the blade closed, and handed it to him. "It's all right," I said.

30   But it wasn't. I had seen into the dark doorway that he kept hidden inside, the terrible place he would seal up now and never return to if he could help it. He seemed suddenly ashamed. I

4–5 **turn loose sth.**: let go of sth.   13 **sag**: (cf. p. 32)

watched him pushing out his lips, trying to gather back his pride, his anger, all that thunderclap he'd first come striding in here with. His hands were moving in and out of his pockets.

"We're going home," he said.

I didn't answer him, but walked over to Our Lady where she lay   5
on the floor and lifted her upright. I could feel August and Rosaleen outside the door, could almost hear their breathing. I touched my cheek. It was swelling where he'd hit me.

"I'm staying here," I said. "I'm not leaving." The words hung there, hard and gleaming. Like pearls I'd been fashioning down   10
inside my belly for weeks.

"What did you say?"

"I said I'm not leaving."

"You think I'm gonna walk out of here and leave you? I don't even know these damn people." He seemed to struggle to make his words   15
forceful enough. The anger had been washed out of him when he'd dropped the knife.

"I know them," I said. "August Boatwright is a good person."

"What makes you think she would even want you here?"

"Lily can have a home here for as long as she wants," August said,   20
stepping into the room, Rosaleen right beside her. I went and stood with them. Outside, I heard Queenie's car pull into the driveway. It had a muffler you couldn't mistake. Apparently August had called the Daughters.

"Lily said you'd run off," T. Ray said to Rosaleen.   25

"Well, I guess I'm back now," she said.

"I don't care where the hell you are or where you end up," he said to her. "But Lily's coming with me."

Even as he said it, I could tell he didn't want me, didn't want me back on the farm, didn't want to be reminded of *her*. Another part of   30
him – the good part, if there was such a thing – might even be thinking that I'd be better off here.

---

2 **thunderclap**: loud noise made by thunder   23 **muffler** (AE): *Schalldämpfer*

It was pride now, all pride. How could he back down?

The front door opened, and Queenie, Violet, Lunelle, and Mabelee stumbled into the house, all wound up and looking like they had their clothes on backward. Queenie stared at my cheek.
5 "Everybody all right?" she said, out of breath.

"We're all right," said August. "This is Mr. Owens, Lily's father. He came for a visit."

"I didn't get an answer at Sugar-Girl's or Cressie's house," Queenie said. The four of them lined up beside us, clutching their
10 pocketbooks up against their bodies like they might have to use them to beat the living hell out of somebody.

I wondered how we must look to him. A bunch of women – Mabelee four foot ten, Lunelle's hair standing straight up on her head begging to be braided, Violet muttering, "Blessed Mary," and
15 Queenie – tough old Queenie – with her hands on her hips and her lip shoved out, every inch of her saying, *I double-dog dare you to take this girl.*

T. Ray sniffed hard and looked at the ceiling. His resolve was crumbling all around him. You could practically see bits of it flaking
20 off.

August saw it, too. She stepped forward. Sometimes I forgot how tall she was. "Mr. Owens, you would be doing Lily and the rest of us a favor by leaving her here. I made her my apprentice beekeeper, and she's learning the whole business and helping us out with all her
25 hard work. We love Lily, and we'll take care of her, I promise you that. We'll start her in school here and keep her straight."

I'd heard August say more than once, "If you need something from somebody, always give that person a way to hand it to you." T. Ray needed a face-saving way to hand me over, and August was
30 giving it to him.

---

1 **back down**: admit defeat   19–20 **flake off**: fall off in small pieces
26 **keep sb. straight**: make sb. lead an honest life

My heart pounded. I watched him. He looked once at me, then let his hand drop to his side.

"Good riddance," he said, and moved toward the door. We had to open up our little wall of women to let him through.

The front door banged against the back wall as he jerked it open 5 and walked out. We all looked at each other and didn't say a word. We seemed to have sucked all the air from the room and were holding it down in our lungs, waiting to be sure we could let it out.

I heard him crank the truck, and before reason could stop me, I broke into a run, racing into the yard after him. 10

Rosaleen called after me, but there was no time to explain.

The truck was backing along the driveway, kicking up dirt. I waved my arms. "Stop, stop!"

He braked, then glared at me through the windshield. Behind me, August, Rosaleen, and the Daughters rushed onto the front 15 porch. I walked to the truck door as he leaned his head out the window.

"I just have to ask you," I said.

"What?"

"That day my mother died, you said when I picked up the gun, it 20 went off." My eyes were on his eyes. "I need to know," I said. "Did I do it?"

The colors in the yard shifted with the clouds, turned from yellow to light green. He ran his hand across his face, stared into his lap, then moved his eyes back to me. 25

When he spoke, the roughness was gone from his voice. "I could tell you I did it. That's what you wanna hear. I could tell you she did it to herself, but both ways I'd be lying. It was you who did it, Lily. You didn't mean it, but it was you."

He looked at me a moment longer, then inched backward out of 30 the driveway, leaving me with the smell of truck oil. The bees were everywhere, hovering over the hydrangea and the myrtle spread

---

3 **good riddance**: unkind way to say you are glad sb. has left
9 **crank**: start the engine with a crank

across the lawn, the jasmine at the wood's edge, the lemon balm clustered at the fence. Maybe he was telling me the truth, but you could never know a hundred percent with T. Ray.

He drove away slowly, not tearing down the road like I expected. I watched till he was gone from sight, then turned and looked at August and Rosaleen and the Daughters on the porch. This is the moment I remember clearest of all – how I stood in the driveway looking back at them. I remember the sight of them standing there waiting. All these women, all this love, waiting.

I looked one last time at the highway. I remember thinking that he probably loved me in his own smallish way. He had forfeited me over, hadn't he?

I still tell myself that when he drove away that day he wasn't saying good riddance; he was saying, *Oh, Lily, you're better off there in that house of colored women. You never would've flowered with me like you will with them.*

I know that is an absurd thought, but I believe in the goodness of imagination. Sometimes I imagine a package will come from him at Christmastime, not the same old sweater-socks-pajama routine but something really inspired, like a fourteen-karat-gold charm bracelet, and in his card he will write, "*Love*, T. Ray." He will use the word "love," and the world will not stop spinning but go right on in its courses, like the river, like the bees, like everything. A person shouldn't look too far down her nose at absurdities. Look at me. I dived into one absurd thing after another, and here I am in the pink house. I wake up to wonder every day.

In the autumn South Carolina changed her color to ruby red and wild shades of orange. I watch them now from my upstairs room, the room June left behind when she got married last month. I could not have dreamed such a room. August bought me a new bed and a dressing table, white French Provincial from the Sears and Roebuck catalog. Violet and Queenie donated a flowered rug that had been

11–12 **forfeit sb. over**: give sb. up   31 **French Provincial**: elegant style of furniture   **Sears and Roebuck**: American mail order company

laying around in their extra room going to waste, and Mabelee sewed blue-and-white polka dot curtains for the windows with fringe balls along the hem. Cressie crocheted four eight-legged octopuses out of various colors of yarn to sit on the bed. One octopus would have been enough for me, but it's the only handicraft Cressie knows how   5
to do, so she just keeps doing it.

Lunelle created me a hat that outdid every other hat she'd ever made, including June's wedding hat. It reminds me a little of the pope's hat. It is tall, just goes up into the air and keeps going. It does have more roundness than the pope's hat, however. I expected blue,   10
but no, she sewed it in golds and browns. I think it's supposed to be an old-fashioned beehive. I only wear it to the Daughters of Mary meetings, since anywhere else it would stop traffic for miles.

Clayton comes over every week to talk to us about how he's working things out for me and Rosaleen back in Sylvan. He says you   15
cannot beat up somebody in jail and expect to get away with it. Even so, he says, they will drop all the charges against me and Rosaleen by Thanksgiving.

Sometimes Clayton brings his daughter Becca over when he comes. She's a year younger than me. I always picture her like she is   20
in the photograph in his office, holding his hand, jumping a wave. I keep my mother's things on a special shelf in my room, and I let Becca look at them but not touch. One day I will let her pick them up, since it seems that's what a girlfriend would do. The feeling that they are holy objects is already starting to wear off. Before long I'll be   25
handing Becca my mother's brush, saying, "Here, you wanna brush your hair with this?" "You wanna wear this whale pin?"

Becca and I watch for Zach in the lunchroom and sit with him every chance we get. We have reputations as "nigger lovers," which is how it is put to us, and when the ignoramuses ball up their   30
notebook paper and throw it at Zach in the hallway, which seems to be a favorite pastime between classes, Becca and I are just as likely to

---

2 **polka dot**: pattern of dots on a one-coloured background   **fringe ball**: decorative ball hanging at the bottom   30 **ignoramus** [ˌɪgnəˈreɪməs]: idiot

get popped in the head as he is. Zach says we should walk on the other side of the hall from him. We say, "Balled-up notebook paper – big deal."

In the photograph by my bed my mother is perpetually smiling
5 on me. I guess I have forgiven us both, although sometimes in the night my dreams will take me back to the sadness, and I have to wake up and forgive us again.

I sit in my new room and write everything down. My heart never stops talking. I am the wall keeper now. I keep it fed with prayers
10 and fresh rocks. I wouldn't be surprised if May's wailing wall outlasted us all. At the end of time, when all the world's buildings have crumbled away, there it will be.

Each day I visit black Mary, who looks at me with her wise face, older than old and ugly in a beautiful way. It seems the crevices run
15 deeper into her body each time I see her, that her wooden skin ages before my eyes. I never get tired of looking at her thick arm jutting out, her fist like a bulb about to explode. She is a muscle of love, this Mary.

. I feel her in unexpected moments, her Assumption into heaven
20 happening in places inside me. She will suddenly rise, and when she does, she does not go up, up into the sky, but further and further inside me. August says she goes into the holes life has gouged out of us.

This is the autumn of wonders, yet every day, every single day, I
25 go back to that burned afternoon in August when T. Ray left. I go back to that one moment when I stood in the driveway with small rocks and clumps of dirt around my feet and looked back at the porch. And there they were. All these mothers. I have more mothers than any eight girls off the street. They are the moons shining over
30 me.

---

4 **perpetually**: always, for ever   22 **gouge**: dig

Credits

I gratefully acknowledge the following sources, not only for the information they offered me about bees, beekeeping, and honey making but also for providing the epigraph at the beginning of each chapter: *The Dancing Bees* by Karl Von Frisch, *The Honey Bee* by James L. Gould and Carol Grant Gould, *The Queen Must Die: And Other Affairs of Bees and Men* by William Longgood, *Man and Insects* by L. H. Newman, *Bees of the World* by Christopher O'Toole and Anthony Raw, and *Exploring the World of Social Insects* by Hilda Simon.

Additional Texts

The Black Vote

Following the end of the Civil War in 1865, the power of the former states of the Confederacy (that had rebelled against the Union) was limited by the federal government (enforced by the US Army in the South). Congress used its position to force the Southern states to accept the radical reforms contained in the new Amendments to the Constitution, which abolished slavery, declared all people born within the USA to be citizens and banned the denial of voting rights due to race or former slave status. As black citizens were actually the majority in many parts of the South, a large number of black representatives were elected to state and federal legislatures. But newly freed slaves (largely illiterate, poor and politically inexperienced) were often exploited by corrupt white politicians who took advantage of their ignorance and handed out bribes to win public office.

In 1877, the last federal troops left the South, and a white backlash began. Between 1889 and 1910, many southern states introduced "poll taxes" (in effect, voting fees). These special taxes were imposed equally on every member of a community and failure to pay meant that you couldn't vote. Given that many African-Americans lived in poverty, poll taxes effectively stopped huge numbers of black citizens from voting. Another practice was the "literacy requirement" for voter registration. This often saw oral and written examinations unfairly applied to African-American applicants. It might require an applicant to write a passage from the Constitution as dictated by their county registrar, who spoke clearly to white applicants and mumbled to black ones. In the novel, the literacy requirement is the reason why Rosaleen repeatedly practices writing her name perfectly.

Where the law failed, intimidation (including beating and lynching) succeeded. Black faces quickly disappeared from the halls of power. The South was ruled by white men alone; even voting districts with a solid black majority sent white Congressmen to Washington.

Segregation

One of the major pillars of white domination in the Southern states after 1877 was segregation, meaning the separation of races in all areas of life. Schools, restaurants, churches and other public facilities were intended for one race only and interracial marriages were made illegal.

Beginning in 1890, the states of the South rewrote their constitutions and passed new laws (the so-called "Jim Crow" laws) to enforce strict separation of races. One law in particular required separate railcars for whites, blacks and "coloreds" of mixed ancestry. In 1896, when Homer Plessy, a man with a white complexion and a black great grandmother, tested the law by buying a ticket for the "whites-only" section, he was arrested and an historic litigation began. The Supreme Court finally confirmed the legality of segregation in 1896 with its ruling in the case of Plessy v. Ferguson, when it stated that "separate but equal" facilities did not stamp "the colored race with a badge of inferiority."

In reality, the separate facilities for black people were anything but equal. Black schoolhouses, for example, were often little more than shacks: underheated, underfunded and staffed with badly qualified teachers. This systematic humiliation of African-Americans continued until 1954, when the Supreme Court overturned its earlier decision and ruled that segregated schools were "inherently unequal". The Court decision made official school segregation illegal, but the actual desegregation of school systems took place slowly and was often accompanied by violent protest.

The Civil Rights Movement

Rigid segregation and the disenfranchisement of African-Americans continued in the southern USA well into the second half of the 20th century. More than a million black soldiers had fought in the Second World War, but those who returned to homes in the South were not allowed to vote, eat a meal in a white restaurant, or sit in the front of a bus.

Since its foundation in 1909, the National Association for the Advancement of Colored People (NAACP) highlighted discrimination both in the South and in the urban North. In 1955, when Rosa Parks, one of its members in Montgomery, Alabama, refused to give her seat to a white passenger, black citizens came together to fight for their rights. Under the charismatic leadership of a young Baptist minister, Dr. Martin Luther King, Jr., black citizens in Montgomery organized a high-profile boycott of the public transportation system. Their efforts were rewarded with success when the Supreme Court declared the segregation of public transportation in Montgomery unconstitutional in November 1956.

Inspired by their success, King and his followers formed the Southern Christian Leadership Conference (SCLC), which continued to organize non-violent protests in the South. King's ideas, based on those of Mahatma Gandhi, involved breaking the law without violence and accepting whatever punishment their actions provoked. Typical forms of protest were sit-ins (black people would enter segregated facilities and peacefully sit until they were evicted) or "freedom rides" on segregated buses and trains. Imprisonment was welcomed as a way to gain public attention. The protesters frequently met with violence, both from white mobs and the police, but they succeeded in calling the nation's attention to the injustice of the "Jim Crow" laws in the South. Attorney General Robert Kennedy responded by sending federal guards to the South to ensure that national laws for the desegregation of interstate transportation were respected.

One of King's greatest triumphs was in Birmingham, Alabama, in 1963, where a boycott of local businesses that operated segregated facilities led to an agreement after only one month. But there were also failures, and the cost of victory in terms of injury and death was high. Black leaders began to realise that a town-by-town struggle for equality would be too slow and costly. So they planned a mass demonstration in Washington. On August 28th 1963, a quarter of a million people, both black and white, went to Washington, where King delivered his famous "I Have a Dream" speech.

The civil rights movement was rewarded when President Johnson pushed the Civil Rights Act of 1964 through Congress against the bitter opposition of Southern Democrats. The law gave Congress the authority to ban segregation in employment, schools and other public facilities.

The next landmark piece of national legislation was the Voting Rights Act of 1965. It prohibited any "prerequisite to voting, or standard, practice, or procedure ... to deny or abridge the right of any citizen of the United States to vote on account of race or color".

Beekeeping and Honey Processing

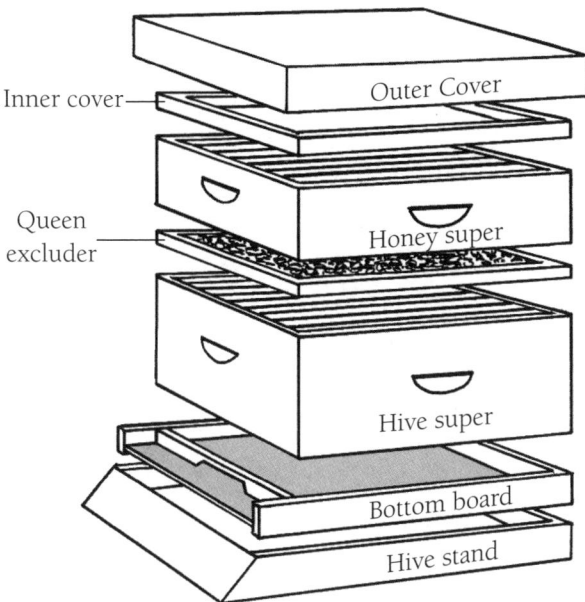

Inner cover — Outer Cover

Queen excluder — Honey super

Hive super

Bottom board

Hive stand

Parts of a Beehive

Outer cover – provides weather protection.

Inner cover – stops bees attaching comb to the outer cover and provides insulation.

Honey super – box filled with frames of comb in which bees store honey that can be harvested.

Queen excluder – placed between the brood super and the honey super. It keeps the queen in the brood nest, so she will not lay eggs in the honey super.

Hive super – holds frames of comb reserved for the bees to rear brood and store honey for their own use.

Bottom board – wooden stand under the hive

The Tools of Beekeeping

Frame – wooden frame with sheets of beeswax that are imprinted with the shapes of hexagonal cells and placed in rows in the supers. Bees use the foundation to build straight combs.

Smoker – The smoke calms bees and reduces stinging.

Feeders – hold sugar syrup that is fed to bees in spring and in autumn.

Veil and gloves – protect head and arms from stings. Most experienced beekeepers prefer to work without gloves.

The Tools of Honey Processing

Uncapping knife – heated knife for cutting cappings off honeycombs. Cappings are made of beeswax, which keeps the honey fresh.

Uncapping tank – container for the cappings. Wet cappings fall onto a screen, and honey drips into the tank.

Extractor or spinner – drum with a rotating wire basket. Uncapped combs are placed in the basket and the basket is turned by hand or by motor. Honey is thrown out of the combs into the tank.

Strainer – mesh of coarse screen or cloth directly under the extractor. It filters out wax and dead bees.

Storage tank – large tank with a tap, or "honey gate", at the bottom.

The Author

© Scott Taylor

Sue Monk Kidd was born in 1948 and raised in the small, rural town of Sylvester, Georgia. She grew up in a traditional Baptist family, went to church regularly and taught Sunday School. At an early age, she dreamt of becoming a fiction writer and was encouraged by her English teachers. But instead she went on to nurse's training, working as a nurse and a nursing instructor during her twenties. In that period she married Sanford Kidd, a Baptist minister and liberal arts college professor, with whom she has two children.

When she was almost thirty, Monk Kidd finally took up writing for a living. Initially, she wrote articles of non-fiction. Her first book, *God's joyful surprise*, was not published until 1988, when she was 40 years old. Over time, Monk Kidd gradually turned her attention to feminist spirituality, alienating herself from traditional Baptist thinking. She was greatly inspired by the 19th century writers Henry David Thoreau and Kate Chopin, whose independent-minded heroines shocked readers of the late nineteenth century.

The Secret Life of Bees, Sue Monk Kidd's first novel, was first published in 2002 and quickly became a hugely successful modern classic. It is set in rural South Carolina and, although Monk Kidd insists the story is pure fiction, she admits it bears traces of her childhood. Her second novel, *The Mermaid Chair* (2005), is also set in South Carolina and explores the relationship between a middle-aged married woman and a monk. Her latest book, *Traveling with Pomegranates* (2009), is a co-production with her daughter Ann Kidd Taylor.